T0247904

The Formation of Affectivity

Other Books of Interest from St. Augustine's Press

Patrick J. Deneen, *Conserving America?: Essays on Present Discontents*

Roger Kimball, *The Fortunes of Permanence:
Culture and Anarchy in an Age of Amnesia*

Pete Fraser, *Twelve Films about Love and Heaven*

Karl Rahner, *Encounters with Silence*

David Ramsay Steele, *Orwell Your Orwell: A Worldview on the Slab*

Zbigniew Janowski, *Homo Americanus:
The Rise of Totalitarian Democracy in America*

Taylor F. Flagg (editor), *The Long Night of the Watchman:
Essays by Václav Benda, 1977–1989*

Daniel J. Mahoney, *Recovering Politics, Civilization, and the Soul:
Essays on Pierre Manent and Roger Scruton*

Rémi Brague, *The Anchors in the Heavens*

Rémi Brague, *Moderately Modern*

Jeremy Black, *The Importance of Being Poirot*

Jeremy Black, *In Fielding's Wake*

Roberto Regoli, *Beyond the Crises in the Church: The Pontificate of Benedict XVI*

Josef Pieper, *Traditional Truth, Poetry, Sacrament:
For My Mother, on her 70th Birthday*

Alexandre Kojève, *The Concept, Time, and Discourse*

Richard Schaefer, *Devotional Activism:
Public Religion, Innovation and Culture in the Nineteenth-Century*

D. C. Schindler, *God and the City: An Essay in Political Metaphysics*

Roger Scruton, *The Meaning of Conservatism: Revised 3rd Edition*

Roger Scruton, *An Intelligent Person's Guide to Modern Culture*

Thomas F. Powers, *American Multiculturalism
and the Anti-Discrimination Regime*

Winston Churchill, *The River War*

The Formation of Affectivity
A Christian Approach
FRANCISCO INSA

ST. AUGUSTINE'S PRESS
South Bend, Indiana

Copyright © 2023 by Francisco Insa

Original title: *Con todo tu corazón, con toda tu alma, con toda tu mente. Formar la afectividad en clave cristiana*, Palabra, Madrid 2021
Translation: Mel Cusi & Dale Parker

All rights reserved. No part of this book may be reproduced, stored in a retrieval system, or transmitted, in any form or by any means, electronic, mechanical, photocopying, recording, or otherwise, without the prior permission of St. Augustine's Press.

Manufactured in the United States of America.

1 2 3 4 5 6   28 27 26 25 24 23

Library of Congress Control Number: 2023934270

Paperback ISBN: 978-1-58731-248-9
Hardback ISBN: 978-1-58731-247-2
Ebook ISBN: 978-1-58731-249-6

∞ The paper used in this publication meets the minimum requirements of the American National Standard for Information Sciences – Permanence of Paper for Printed Materials, ANSI Z39.48-1984.

St. Augustine's Press
www.staugustine.net

To all those who,
by sharing with me their eagerness to improve,
have shown me
the greatness of the human heart

TABLE OF CONTENTS

EPILOGUE

INTRODUCTION

1. Teacher, What Should I Do to Achieve Eternal Life?

"You shall love the Lord your God with all your heart, and with all your soul, and with all your strength, and with all your mind; and your neighbor as yourself" (Lk 10:27). Jesus refers to two texts of the Pentateuch in his dialogue with a doctor of the Law (cf. Deut 6:5; Lev 19:18). The two commandments summarize what we should do to gain eternal life: love God and love our neighbor. Matthew and Mark narrate the story in a way that differs slightly from Luke (cf. Mt 22:37–39; Mk 12:30–31). In their versions, the answer is in response to the question, "What is the first commandment?" In all three gospels, we see Jesus challenging us to live a radical, complete love, because that sort of love not only fulfills all that God asks of us, but opens the door for us to live a happy life and enjoy him for all eternity.

This kind of relationship with God contrasted with some proposals offered by Judaism and especially with those offered by pagan religions, which tended to emphasize adoration, submission, and obedience, attitudes born from consideration of God's absolute transcendence. Before God, man could only prostrate himself and recognize his nothingness.

Jesus Christ opens a new perspective that touches the most intimate aspects of man—but without excluding the previous idea. God calls man to enter a loving relationship that includes several dimensions: heart, soul, strength and mind. Jesus stresses that dealing with God involves all aspects of man: his intellect, his will, his sentiments and his passions. The same should happen in his dealings with his fellow men. Indeed,

> we do not have one heart to love God with and another with
> which to love men. This poor heart of ours, made of flesh, loves

1

with an affection which is human and which, if it is united to Christ's love, is also supernatural.[1]

The twofold precept (loving God and neighbor) is based on a basic tenet: God is a loving Father who cares for us. "He first loved us" (1 Jn 4:19), he *firsted* us, to use the words of Pope Francis. We respond only partially to the love of God, who created us, gave us a family, abilities, talents … and prepared a dwelling in heaven that is waiting for us (cf. Jn 14:2–3). It is the same thought behind the lines we sing at Christmas, "*sic nos amantem, quis non redamaret*" from the hymn *Adeste fideles*: who would not love back one who loves us thus?

The love that all human beings give and receive from God fully satisfies our deepest longings. The first commandment is not forced upon us. It is the proclamation of what makes man happy: "You have made us for yourself, and our hearts are restless until they rest in you."[2] God is not a tyrant who is unhappy with our submission, who *forces* us to love him, but a Father who loves us, cares for us and watches over us, and only he can fulfill an unavoidable need: "What can make us feel happy if not the experience of giving and receiving love?"[3]

2. The Formation of Affectivity

The past few decades have increasingly made clear the need to form others in affectivity. This is especially true for young people. The idea would be to enable them to develop their own interiority in a healthy and serene manner, and so achieve a cheerful, comprehensive, meaningful and apostolically fruitful Christian life. However, those in charge of their formation often state that they have few tools to carry out their task, presumably because the intellectual and spiritual dimensions of formation have been over-emphasized for many centuries. Many excellent works have been written that deal with those areas, but little attention has been given to the formation of affectivity.

1 St. Josemaría Escrivá, *Friends of God*, Scepter, New York (NY) 2002², n. 229.
2 St. Augustine, *Confessions*, I, 1, 1.
3 Francis, *General Audience,* July 14, 2017.

Some dimensions have been stressed to excess at times, to the exclusion of others. The resulting imbalance has created distortions like intellectualism, voluntarism, or sentimentalism. All these dimensions need to be combined within the unity of the person.

Affectivity could initially be defined as the set of emotions, affections, feelings and passions within man that make him feel comfortable or unhappy in his various real-life situations. The result is pleasure or discomfort, which points to what should be sought or avoided. Pleasure or discomfort could be in the sensitive sphere (enjoying a meal) or in the intellectual sphere (a pleasant conversation or a good read).

Having said that, the goods or the evils identified by affectivity are only partial and may contradict each other. For example, short term discomfort (tiredness) pitted against a long-term greater joy (winning a race). We all have a hierarchy of values with which we figure out which goods are worth sacrificing for the sake of greater goods. This hierarchy of values is usually not overt. That is not to say that some affects are bad or mistaken, but that they sometimes claim undeserved priority, and other goods, more important for the whole person, could be jeopardized.

The formation of affectivity seeks to help the intellect and the will achieve a right order: finding out what is good, wanting to reach it, and using the appropriate means to get there. It is not just about controlling or repressing particular human trends, nor rationalizing instincts, but to reach such a deep rapport with the good—in the head and in the heart—as to give all the things that call for our attention the right level of importance almost instinctively (rather, by *connaturality*). This allows us to enjoy both the good achieved and forego those others which need to be sacrificed for the sake of greater ones. The latter point is important because it is less evident. St. Augustine summarized it as follows: "in the case of what is loved, either there is no labor, or the labor also is loved" (*in eo quod amatur, aut non laboratur aut labor amatur*).[4] Thus we return to the gospel quotation from the beginning of this introduction: everything begins with what we genuinely love. Everything else falls into place.

Aspiring to achieve a perfect balance would be wishful thinking. Formation is a process and there is always room for improvement. It will lead

4   St. Augustine, *On the goodness of widowhood,* XXI, 26.

to delving deeper into the meaning of one's vocation, to achieve self-dominion and make it a serene and cheerful reality on a day-to-day basis.

3. Psychology and Formation

St. Paul shows a Hebrew approach in his exhortation to the Thessalonians: "May your spirit (*pneuma*) and soul (*psyche*) and body (*soma*) be kept sound and blameless at the coming of our Lord Jesus Christ" (1 Thess 5:23).[5] This triple distinction is unique in St. Paul's letters. Many early Fathers of the Church, especially in the East, used the same approach.

We are probably more familiar with the twofold distinction of body and soul that arises from Aristotle's hylomorphic theory (matter and form), which became generally accepted in medieval scholasticism. St. Paul also used this distinction several times (cf. 1 Cor 5:3; 7:34; 2 Cor 7:1). Both approaches have their advantages and limitations in explaining human nature, that always remains unfathomable. In any case, both approaches uphold the unity of the person at all times: the unity of the person is not simply about adding two principles that ultimately remain distinct, like water and oil.

In my opinion, however, the three-fold division makes it easier to understand the person's affective dimension. Indeed, the split between body and soul makes it difficult to fit in feelings, passions and emotions. They have a physical foundation (in the brain's activity), but they are also part of the non-material, transcendent reality of man, made in the image of God. Clinical depression would be a good example of this: it is not an illness of the body, but we cannot say that it is a spiritual illness either. The three-fold division better defines the domain of affectivity: it belongs in the *psyche* (soul, mind), and is the subject matter of psychology. When deranged, it is the domain of psychiatry.

If we are to help others as formators, we need to take into account all three dimensions: everybody has a spirit called to enjoy God for all eternity. It is nourished by prayer, sacraments and relationships, especially when charity is their foundation. Everyone has a body that needs sleep, food

---

5   Cf. P. Iovino, *La prima lettera ai Tessalonicesi*, Edizioni Dehoniane Bologna, Bologna 1992, pp. 284–287.

and exercise. And everyone has a psyche subject to mood swings, defined by thinking and feeling in a particular way, conditioned by life experiences, etc. The three dimensions are in constant interplay: no matter how good one's dispositions may be, poor sleep will make it harder to pray, and will make one short tempered, irritable, etc. Likewise, low moods are often associated with physical discomfort (headaches, loss of appetite, tiredness), and it makes it harder to "connect" with God in prayer.

Some knowledge of psychology is very helpful in the task of formation. For example, knowing the main features of the various life stages will help to address matters in the best way for each age range, and to set goals in accordance with the individual's abilities. Similarly, knowing the different types of personalities will help to provide specific advice to each individual person on what traits to improve, or how they can use their strong points in the task of formation.

On the other hand, psychological problems may be confused with a lack of virtue or with sins. For example, narcissism and pride are two different concepts, just as egocentrism and selfishness, shyness and lack of interest in other people, obsession and thinking about oneself, poorly integrated sexuality and impurity, conflict with the authority figure and disobedience, impulsiveness and anger, perfectionism and lack of abandonment, attention deficit and lack of disorganization, inactivity secondary to depression and laziness.[6] The first term of each pair mentioned above may contain a pathological element, a personality disorder, previous traumatic experiences, cognitive errors, poor social skills, etc., and not just poor interior life.

In these cases it would not be enough to provide advice of an ascetical nature (to grow in fortitude, toughness, temperance) or to foster the interior life (prayer, mortification, a sense of divine filiation), because it would not hit the target. It could even be harmful, because it would be a distraction from the real problem, foster guilt or a sense of worthlessness, or encourage an overextension of the will. In the end it would probably be ineffective and exhausting.

Yet, it is not a matter of pretending to be a psychologist in the task of formation. It is rather a matter of realizing that a crucial aspect of this task

---

6   Cf. C. Chiclana Actis, "Formación y evaluación psicológica del candidato a sacerdocio," *Scripta Theologica* 51 (2019) 467–504.

is the human dimension, which remains within the boundaries of psychology and has its own dynamics and laws. We should be familiar with these dynamics and laws to be able to help adequately. Similarly, it is not necessary to be a physician to recommend paracetamol to someone with a headache, some extra rest to someone who is not sleeping well, or to suggest an urgent medical consultation to someone with chest pain. St. Josemaría Escrivá would explain this responsiveness by saying that a formator should have the *psychology of a mother*, who can sense the state of mind of her son, recognize that he had problems at school when he comes home, notice that he had a fight with his girlfriend, etc.

To a certain extent this knowledge comes from intuition, and some people may have it more developed than others. But it also requires specific training, because it is part of the professional skills expected of a formator. This book aims to assist the *formation of formators* in the psychological aspects of the person and how to apply that knowledge in their task.

4. About This Book

Over the past few years I have had the opportunity to teach formators, parents, teachers, priests, seminarians, etc., about the development of affectivity. I was struck by the fact that there was almost no need to adapt the contents to the needs of the different cohorts. They all had the same basic concerns and the feeling that knowledge of psychological dynamics was useful for their task. Many acknowledged that it helped them to know themselves better, and this enhanced the task of formation.

In preparing these classes I have drawn upon my professional background as a psychiatrist, a theologian, and a priest. I have also drawn from my experiences in giving Christian formation to people of all ages, especially the young, which is something I have done both as a layman and as a priest.

The contents of this book are courses I have taught, expanded upon and committed to writing. Therefore, the style is didactic, interrogatory, direct and practical, with many anecdotes drawn from real life to illustrate various points. I refer to several psychological schools without offering systematic descriptions, because they can be found elsewhere.[7] Each chapter

---

7   Cf. among others, M.A. Monge Sánchez (ed). *Medicina pastoral. Cuestiones*

of the book corresponds to a one-hour lecture. For this reason I had to make a selection of the various arguments: I have picked those I consider to be important for a formator and cannot be found elsewhere. On the other hand I have not emphasized other basic and more important topics—though neither have I neglected them—because the reader will probably be familiar with them: the priority of grace, some doctrinal points, the dynamic between human and supernatural virtues, etc. There is an ample bibliography at the end of the book for those interested in further reading on these and other topics.

Since I am a priest, my starting point will be Christian anthropology, which acknowledges man's supernatural end, his tendency towards the good, and the difficulty of recognizing it and putting it into practice, due to man's wounded nature. Man must correspond to God's grace to reach sanctity, and the interaction between these two realities is expressed by St. Thomas Aquinas in two phrases: "grace presupposes nature,"[8] and "grace does not destroy nature but perfects it."[9]

This book offers suggestions to help develop a healthy and focused personality. We can think of plants that need rain to grow strong. In the same way, God's ordinary grace may act as "rain" upon the soul. But if a plant is crooked, a different kind of technique is required to straighten it up. God can certainly do that spontaneously, just as he can cure a physical illness. But it would be something out of the ordinary, even a miracle, and we cannot demand it of God; usually he counts on the person to go to the doctor to return to health.

The book is divided into four sections. The first contains a general description of personality and affectivity, a definition of both concepts and some ideas to foster a mature development. The second describes the various stages of the life cycle, from the cradle to old age. An attempt is made to illustrate how the acquisitions and defects of each stage have an impact

---

de biología, antropología, medicina, sexología, psicología y psiquiatría, Eunsa, Pamplona 2004; J. Cabanyes, M.A. Monge (eds.), *La salud mental y sus cuidados*, Eunsa, Pamplona 2011; W. Vial, *Madurez humana y espiritual*, Palabra, Madrid 2019.

8 St. Thomas Aquinas, *Summa Theologica*, I, q. 2, art. 2, ad. 1.
9 *Ibidem*, I, q. 1, a. 8, ad. 2.

on future development. The third focuses on a specific aspect of affectivity, the sexual dimension. It will propose some strategies to contribute effectively to the holistic good of the person. It will highlight the difficulties of living chastely in 21st century life. The section ends with some thoughts on the vocation to apostolic celibacy and its consequences from a psychological point of view. The fourth and final section covers several psychiatric conditions, and suggests various prevention strategies and ways to support those who have these conditions. A final chapter—in fact an epilogue—has been included in response to the requests of a number of people who attended my courses. It describes the psychological capabilities required for someone involved in formation.

***

At this stage I would like to thank the many people who have helped me in the writing of this book. First, Juan Ignacio Peláez, who was in the very first course I gave. His patient insistence encouraged me to sit down and write this book. Fr. Alfredo Ruiz de Gámiz has reviewed every single chapter and provided excellent suggestions based on his ample priestly experience. I am twice in debt to Dr. Marisol Salcedo, clinical psychologist, who was involved in my initial training in psychiatry many years ago, and who later reminded me of many forgotten concepts, and corrected some inaccuracies that had made their way into the book. Finally, the contributors to the book *Loving and Teaching Others to Love*[10] will find many of their own ideas somewhere in this book: Bishop Jose Maria Yanguas (theological aspects of affectivity), Fr. Paul O'Callaghan (the dynamics of delayed gratification), Fr. Wenceslao Vial (psychopathology), Dr. Carlos Chiclana (comprehensive approach to out-of-control sexual behavior), Fr. Maurizio Faggioni (friendship) and Bishop Massimo Camisasca (the spiritual paternity of celibate people). I strongly recommend reading their work to understand their respective topics better.

Holy Mary, Mother of Fair Love, pray for us!

---

10 F. Insa, D. Parker (eds.), *Loving and Teaching Others to Love. The formation of affectivity in priestly life,* Independently published 2021.

I. Personality and Affectivity

WHAT IS PERSONALITY?

1. The Concept of Personality

It is often difficult to give an adequate definition to concepts that are part of our daily vocabulary. They are usually very rich or complex ideas that resist definitions, because these tend to omit an important element and render the definition invalid. We know what something is, but we cannot define it in a few words.

The concept of personality is one of them. It is part of our daily life, and we use it in a variety of contexts: *he/she has a strong personality, he/she is developing his/her personality, he has no personality at all* ... but, what is personality? It is easy to understand but hard to define.

I have occasionally asked my students for a definition. They have managed to identify many features of personality: it is something specific to each person, it is stable, it covers all aspects of a person (internal and external perceptions, thoughts, behaviors and relationships), it can be seen and assessed from the outside ... but my students were also unable to come up with a definition that everyone was happy with.

Psychologists are specialists in this area and have come up with many definitions, but they have not reached unanimity (nor in many other areas of this particular science). Moreover, the different options proposed are often contradictory.

I have not been able to find a satisfactory definition either. But I find the following to be workable, albeit with some slight changes. It's the one I have adopted for this book: *Personality is a stable way to relate to oneself, to others and to the world.* The idea comes from George Kelly (1905–1967),[1] an American psychologist. It is an incomplete and limited definition, like

---

1   Cf. G. Kelly, *A theory of personality. The psychology of personal constructs,* Norton, New York (NY) 1963.

all others. We could even state that it is not really a definition of personality at all because it simply states how it manifests itself. Having said that, two of its features make it useful for the purposes of this book.

First, it stresses the importance of *relationships*. The word relationship appears almost three hundred times throughout this book. I do not think that it is excessive, and regardless of how we conceptualize it, there are several reasons for insisting so much upon it: personality basically reveals itself in one's dealings with other people, and it would be difficult to identify it in a person who lived in isolation. In addition, a healthy development of one's personality requires mixing with others: friction makes sparks fly, but it also knocks off the edges, shows examples to be emulated and awakens the desire to improve in order to correspond to the affection we receive. A wide range of relationships is crucial for a healthy and harmonious development of one's personality.

Secondly, God is someone we have a relationship with. Each one's personality predetermines how we connect with him, because the idea of God implies paternity, love, care, authority, dependence, forgiveness, reward, punishment ... all these concepts generate an *affective resonance* within the individual. This will determine whether the approach will be based on trust, apprehension, fear, apathy, etc.

Personality reveals itself in three basic ways: emotions, thoughts and behaviors. They usually appear in this order: events awaken emotions. When we become conscious of our emotions they lead us to think about what has happened and possible reactions. Action follows. This process may not be entirely conscious; however, it does not mean that it is purely automatic or instinctive. It is often determined by one's upbringing or by previous experiences. This would be the case of those who were raised with prejudices against people of a different racial background, or who have developed a phobia after a bad experience in the past.

An example can make it easier to understand. I am in a movie theater and someone shouts, "FIRE!" I get a massive, instantaneous adrenaline rush and feel many different things (fear, insecurity); I look for the nearest exit and plan my escape. But I also may realize that other people need help escaping. Lastly I execute my exit strategy, or take a risk trying to save others. But we should not deceive ourselves. Our first reaction may be "every man for himself." But if someone shouts, "women and children first," the individual must have developed an approach to life—regarding his own and other people's—that allows him to make a potentially heroic decision.

We all react differently in given situations. If we are insulted, some of us will react immediately and go on the offensive; others may be cowed and may not know how to respond, or dare not react: they crumble because they are not loved, they think they deserve to be despised, but in their mind they "murder" the offender, and swear everlasting hatred. People react differently (internally and externally) because they have different personalities. I want to mention an idea that will be developed later: we need to *listen to* emotions, because they often account for our thoughts, and in turn our   thoughts account for our behavior. When I *feel* humiliated, upset, despised, *I think* that the other person has been unfair. Or on the contrary, I think I deserve such treatment because I made a big mistake, and therefore *I act* by either facing up to him or by resigning myself to accept the attack more or less peacefully. In the task of formation the emphasis is often to focus on action alone ("do this or do not do it"), without encouraging the learner to look within and discover the emotions and thoughts that have led to his actions.

These examples reveal the two triads we have observed so far: our relationship with ourselves, with other people and with the world; our reaction appears in the shape of affections, thoughts and behaviors. Our idea of personality may fall short (and it may well be beyond reach), but that is a topic for the experts. After all, in our dealings with others we do not assess their personality, but their external behavior and also their internal behavior if we pay greater attention, or if they tell us to.

We will end this section by looking at three more features of personality.

Firstly, it is a *dynamic structure*. We have stated that it is a stable mode of response (we often hear about *behavior patterns*). This does not mean that it is something rigid or stereotyped, like the concrete shell of a building that cannot be altered. It is more like a solid tree that grows and changes its shape between the roots and the branches. It can always change, for better or worse. Moreover, it is *obliged* to change, because new events always demand new strategies, and also because we have our own concerns, a longing for novelty, a desire for new challenges. This leads to the idea of *adjustability*, the ability to adjust to new sets of circumstances (in emotions, thoughts and actions) that life brings with it. For many mental health professionals, *adjustability* is the best gauge of maturity and mental health.

Secondly, personality makes a person *predictable*. An irascible person will jump to a perceived aggression, whereas an introverted person will endure the grievance in silence, but may brood within. Likewise, we are all familiar with people who are responsible, orderly and trustworthy; when given a task we know it will be carried out. But there are others that need constant supervision if we are to avoid disappointment. Being predictable is not contrary to freedom: we are not machines that react the same way every time. It means that our initial impulse is to react in a particular manner, but we are always able—with more or less effort—to resist the initial impulse as long as we have enough self-control. We will look at all this later on.

Finally, personality *evolves* over time. It is whimsical in children, it hardens during the teenage years, and when we enter adulthood it is usually stable, though this stability comes at the cost of the ability to adjust, because changes become increasingly difficult. We will return to this topic when we look at the life cycle.

In summary, personality predetermines behavior (both internal and external). Therefore it will have considerable bearing on our potential to be happy, on our ability to be comfortable with our own thoughts and feelings, with the thoughts and feelings of others, with what happens in our lives. It will also help us to have a good rapport with our friends, with our spouse and with God.

2. Temperament, Character and Personality

The experts usually single out two dimensions of personality: temperament and character.

Temperament is a set of biological, hereditary, genetic, or hormonal features, among others. It consists in our base level of activity (like the idling of a car, which can involve higher or lower engine revolutions), and manifests itself in a greater or lesser degree of anxiety, reactivity, action, intro- or extroversion, etc. It is the least malleable component of personality. We will carry it to the grave, although we can make it smoother with time, effort and patience. We are not born with it in a complete sense: it develops and settles over the first two years of life. During this period, all these factors interact with the environment. This explains why twins are not totally identical in their *modus vivendi.*

On the other hand, *character* encompasses the features acquired through family, education, culture, values assimilated, personal relationships, decisions made, personal struggles, etc. It is a dynamic feedback process. When I face new situations, I discover new strategies, either by chance or by imitating others. Thus I set up mechanisms that become increasingly more refined, more confident, and which lead me to fine tune them to make them more efficient, or mechanisms that fail and make a healthy development problematic. Character is more amenable to change, but this does not mean that it is easy to do so.

3. Personality Traits

Entomologists dissect insects in order to study them. Personality can be studied in a similar fashion. When we do this, we encounter *traits*. These could be defined as *relatively stable dispositions to react in a particular manner*. Just like when we study the organs of a living being, the whole is greater than the sum of the parts. We cannot think of personality as a simple aggregate of traits, but as their orderly interaction.

Some traits tend to go together, as is shown in statistical studies. Others remain independent. For instance, a perfectionist is usually insecure, anxious, and rigid, but could be more or less extroverted. Within this association, some of the traits might be called nuclear or primary, whereas others are derived or secondary. In the above example, insecurity would be a nuclear trait, whereas perfectionism, eagerness to control, order, etc., would be derived traits. Some people feel that when we study personality we should proceed as if we were dealing with the layers of an onion and begin with the more superficial traits until we reach the nuclear traits, which allow us to understand the deepest aspects of the subject (both positive and negative). There are important practical repercussions. If we want to help perfectionists, we need to help them to manage their insecurities.

Many traits emerge as the extremes of a *continuum*: introvert/extrovert, active/passive, intuitive/reflexive, autonomous/dependent, flexible/rigid, conservative/open to novelty, etc. It is normal to feel closer to either of the components of these pairs; however, anyone at the extremes of the spectrum will find it difficult to be comfortable in society. These are the personality disorders, which will be dealt with in the last chapter of the book.

Studying the traits of personality allows for a deeper understanding of people and helps us to figure out how to help them so as to improve their way of being and of relating.

4. OCEAN: The Big Five of Personality

Many authors have carried out statistical studies (experts call them *factorial analysis*). The purpose is to narrow personality to some basic dimensions which they call *orthogonal*, meaning that they are independent of each other. A high score in one trait of these dimensions would not influence the score of a trait in another dimension.

The research of several researchers working in a number of centers independently has identified five groups of mutually independent traits. They are known as the *Big Five*, or OCEAN. The main proponents of the Big Five are the American psychologists Robert McCrae and Paul Costa.[2] The scores in these five groups would determine the personality of a given individual, even at an early age. This would suggest that there is a genetic component (temperament), which is particularly relevant to the traits of extraversion and neuroticism.

Table 1 displays the five traits, the two extreme ranges, and some of the secondary, derived, traits for each one of them.

Openness to experience	Conscientiousness	Extraversion	Agreeableness	Neuroticism
Creative	Conscientious	Extrovert	Compassionate	Sensitive
vs	vs	vs	vs	vs
Cautious	Careless	Introvert	Detached	Equable
Fantasy	Competence	Warmth	Trust	Anxiety
Aesthetics	Order	Gregariousness	Frankness	Angry hostility
Feelings	Dutifulness	Assertiveness	Altruism	Depression
Actions	Achievement striving	Activity	Modesty	Self-consciousness
Ideas	Self-discipline	Excitement-seeking	Conciliatory attitude	Impulsiveness
Values	Deliberation	Positive emotions	Concern for others	Vulnerability

Table 1. The Big Five of personality.

2   Cf. R.R. McCrae, P.T. Costa, *The NEO Personality Inventory Manual*, Psychological Assessment Resources, Odessa (FL) 1985; idem, "Validation of the

We will study the main features of the extremes of each one of the Big Five, and highlight the advantages and drawbacks they have with regard to the three types of relationships (with oneself, with the world, and with others).

a) Openness

The main features of the creative type are an active imagination, creativity, a sense of the aesthetic (often a liking for the arts), and a spirit of initiative. They enjoy variety, adventure, and novelty, to the point of seeking odd novelties that may shock others. Typically, intellectual curiosity of both the internal and external world leads them to become more sensitive to their own feelings as well as the feelings of other people. They are prone to making up their own minds, being idealistic, upholding unconventional values, and being more tolerant of different ways of life. They are not swayed by prejudices, and tend to be less authoritarian and dominant.

They are good at *working with people* and carrying out new projects.

On the other hand, they struggle with monotonous tasks. Given their sensitivity, they are prone to suffering. They are unpredictable, and have greater chances to engage in dangerous practices, including drug use.

A *cautious* individual prefers familiar routine over variety, simple tasks as opposed to complex or subtle issues. They are usually "down to earth," stick to what they know. Conservative in manner and external appearance, they resist change and novelty. As a result their range of interests can be rather limited. They may be suspicious of art and unconventional practices, which they think useless and impractical.

They are ideal for *working with things*, following up on projects already started, and persevering in the same task for long periods.

However, they may show little empathy, especially when others are more whimsical. They can become rigid and dogmatic, adapt poorly, and respond in the same way when facing different scenarios.

five-factor model of personality across instruments and observers," *Journal of Personality and Social Psychology* 52 (1987) 81–90; P.T. Costa, R.R. McCrae, G.G. Kay, "Persons, Places and Personality: Career Assessment using the NEO Personality Inventory," *Journal of Career Assessment* 3 (1995) 123–139; R.R. McCrae, P.T. Costa, T.A. Martin, "The NEO-PI-3: A More Readable Revised NEO Personality Inventory," *Journal of Personality Assessment* 84 (2005) 261–270.

b) Conscientiousness

People high in *conscientiousness* have a heightened sense of duty and doggedly pursue their goals with determination and forethought. They are orderly and possess high levels of self-control and discipline in planning, execution, and completion of tasks and goals.

Therefore, they excel at problem solving and are likely to be successful in school and in their careers and highly valued by others as intelligent and trustworthy. They tend to be stable in their social, professional and family life.

On the other hand, they can become perfectionists, dependent on success, *workaholics*, and run a greater risk of burnout.

At the other end of the spectrum, people low in conscientiousness (*careless*) are more flexible, spontaneous, and informal. They are likely to procrastinate and not stress out. They care more about their own needs and desires than external duties.

Their main asset is that they organize their life in terms of their own aspirations, rather than duties imposed from outside. As things are not rigidly organized, they are better at improvising.

The downside is that they tend to neglect their duties, they can be deemed untrustworthy, and they will find it harder to be socially accepted. They are more prone to having problems at work, and their independent nature can lead them to risk-prone behavior.

c) Extroversion

People high in *extroversion* tend to seek out opportunities for social interaction, where they are often the "life of the party." They have good social skills, which they practice with all kinds of people. They are assertive, talkative and daring in social encounters. They are comfortable with others, gregarious, and are prone to action rather than contemplation. Others see them as full of energy, because they can easily experience—and help others to experience—positive emotions, like happiness, enthusiasm, satisfaction, excitement, etc. They enjoy teamwork and show leadership qualities. They are involved in many activities but are not deep; they avoid loneliness, which makes them feel bored and unmotivated. They are very dependent on external stimuli.

Their main assets are their social skills, their ability to build teams, and their leadership qualities.

They can be superficial because they often need *social reinforcement* to carry out their duties. They are not effective and dislike working on their own.

People low in extroversion (*introverted*) are more likely to be people "of few words": quiet, introspective, reserved, and thoughtful. They enjoy social occasions in small groups of people who are familiar. They are not comfortable in large gatherings and find it difficult to develop new contacts or friendships. They prefer to work on their own and are better at activities such as reading, writing, or thinking. They have fewer interests, but they develop them more deeply. They are self-motivated and persevere in their task independently of others, social recognition, etc.

They are very effective in activities that require thought, determination and perseverance to achieve success in the long term. They have fewer friends, but their friendships tend to be deeper. As they do not rely on the recognition of others, they keep their ideals and values even if they go against the grain. They are more discerning and less dependent on others to carry out their duties.

On the other hand, their poorer social skills can lead them to isolation.

d) Agreeableness

People high in agreeableness are *compassionate*. They tend to be well-liked, respected, sensitive to the needs of others, peacemakers. They have high levels of empathy, and work well with others. It is easy for them to give in to their opinions in order to reach a consensus.

They make friends easily, and are affectionate to their friends and loved ones, as well as sympathetic to the plights of strangers.

It may be difficult for them to contradict others, correct them, or maintain minority opinions. This would be a negative for positions of direction or formation, and makes it difficult for them to uphold their life ideals in adverse environments.

People on the low end of the agreeableness spectrum (*detached*) are less sensitive to the emotional needs of others. They tend to be callous, blunt, rude, ill-tempered, and place their own interests above getting on well with others. Working with others can create hostility and make them as uncomfortable as it makes other people, who think they are selfish and have little empathy.

They are well suited to going against the flow, and maintain their ideals even when they are not considered to be politically correct. As they are autonomous, they can concentrate on their own tasks and be more effective, as long as teamwork is not a requirement.

They run a high risk of falling into narcissism, and of being manipulative and cynical. They may become isolated and socially rejected.

e) Neuroticism

Those high in neuroticism (*sensitive*) are generally prone to anxiety and intense feelings of rejection, anger, sadness, worry, low self-esteem, hatred, jealousy, frustration, envy, and guilt. They are very sensitive to day-to-day events, whether they are positive or negative, and thus they suffer from frequent mood swings. They tend to catastrophize ordinary difficulties. They can find it hard to control their impulses.

When they are calm and composed their emotional wealth gives them great empathy, and they are very easy to get on with.

Interacting with them beyond the short term may repel others, due to their overdramatizing.

Equable individuals score on the low end of neuroticism; they are more likely to be calm and confident, self-assured. They are not likely to feel uptight or nervous, and they remain calm under pressure (although they may not have many positive feelings either).

They are steady, regardless of external factors. This makes them ideally suited to handling crisis situations.

They may not attract many friends because they can give the impression of being cold and unempathetic when dealing with others.

5. The Locus of Control

Early in this chapter we saw that the concept of personality is complex and rich, and therefore it is difficult to identify a system that accounts for it fully. Now I would like to consider a complementary model (though in fact it overlaps with the Big Five to a certain extent), which will add interesting nuances. This is the concept of *locus of control*, developed by the American psychologist Julian B. Rotter.[3]

Locus of control is *the degree to which people believe that they, as opposed to external forces (beyond their influence), have control over the outcome of events in their lives.* The classical example is the student's reaction to exam results: "I passed" (internal locus of control), or "they flunked me" (external locus of control).

For those who have an *internal locus of control*, events are mainly due to one's actions, they control their own lives. Therefore, they value personal effort, ability, and responsibility. It is worthwhile doing one's bit to feel better or be successful.

On the contrary, for those who have an *external locus of control*, events are the result of chance, fate, luck, or other people's decisions. They feel they cannot control events. Their way of relating to the world is that of preventing harm, depending on reward and fearing punishment, all with a good dose of suspicion and hostility. Therefore, it is easy for them to fall prey to *learned helplessness*[4]: "Nothing I can do will change the situation, therefore the best thing is to do nothing." It is best shown with an Asterix comic: the lookout on the pirate ship sees the Gauls from the topmast. As they approach he asks the captain: "why don't we just sink the ship and avoid the beating?"

Clearly, this concept is not really about who or what is responsible for specific events, but *to whom or to what is the responsibility attributed* by the subject. And just like the traits of the Big Five, the locus of control admits of a *continuum*. For any specific individual it will not be entirely internal or external; it will be somewhere between two extremes.

A predominantly internal *locus of control* is preferable, but only to a certain extent: anyone who relies only on the self for success will easily be

---

3   Cf. J.B. Rotter, "Generalized expectancies of internal versus external control of reinforcements," *Psychological Monographs* 80 (1966) 1–28.

4   The concept of learned helplessness was developed by American psychologist Martin Seligman when he was studying the psychological causes of depression. Cf. M.E.P. Seligman, *Helplessness. On Depression, Development, and Death*, W. H. Freeman, San Francisco (CA) 1975; idem, *Learned Optimism. How to Change Your Mind and Your Life*, Nicholas Brealey Publishing, London 2018.

the victim of an exhausting voluntarism. Besides, there is an important external factor in Christian life: God. He respects our freedom, yet leads each one lovingly by his wise providence, and gives his grace to help us behave appropriately on a human and supernatural level. To ignore this fact would lead to a kind of Pelagianism, as Pope Francis has warned.[5]

6. The Defense Mechanisms of the Ego

The *defense mechanisms of the ego* are another approach with which to look at personality. It was first mentioned by Sigmund Freud, the father of psychoanalysis, but was mostly developed by his daughter Anna.[6]

In psychoanalytic theory, defense mechanisms are *unconscious* psychological mechanisms that deal with unacceptable or potentially harmful stimuli. The threat to one's balance and mental wellbeing can come from within the individual (impulses, fears, complexes, trauma) or from without (dangers, offenses, rejection, social sanction). Moreover, external factors trigger internal factors, and these are the true aggressors.

The purpose of defense mechanisms is to minimize the effects of a distressing stimulus so that the individual may continue to operate normally. However, they do not necessarily solve the problem. Moreover, the subject may not be aware of the danger that has been averted, because they act unconsciously. Therefore, the danger remains hidden, and there is a chance that it can silently be the trigger of a psychiatric pathology.

The mechanisms of defense are different from the *coping strategies,* which are conscious activities and behaviors.

The best-known defense mechanisms appear in Table 2.

Acting out	Identification with the aggressor	Rationalization
Condensation	Intellectualization	Reaction formation
Denial	Introjection	Regression
Displacement	Isolation	Repression
Dissociation	Projection	Sublimation
Identification	Projective identification	Etc.

Table 2. The ego's defense mechanisms.

5   Cf. Francis, Apostolic Exhortation *Gaudete et exsultate*, March 19, 2018, nn. 47–62.
6   Cf. A. Freud, *The Ego and the Mechanisms of Defence*, Routledge, London

For the sake of brevity and the fact that they will barely be mentioned in this book, we will not go through them in detail. I will simply make a few practical points.

We perform many of them on a daily basis without even realizing it. Others have become part of daily speech, thus depriving them of some of the original meaning. Repression ("that girl is repressed") or projection ("don't project your problems onto me, you're the one who's upset") are two examples. Defense mechanisms are a readymade true armory for the *ego*. The person who has only a few will be maladapted. They will show the same response to different stimuli, and in Maslow's words "I suppose it is tempting, if the only tool you have is a hammer, to treat everything as if it were a nail."[7]

But they are not all the same in specific cases. Some defenses are better than others at achieving the desired result (protecting the *ego*); others show more maturity than others, and so on. For example, *denial*, or burying one's head in the sand, is a very immature mechanism.

A final warning: defense mechanisms can become pathological when their persistent use results in maladapted behavior, and place the individual's physical or mental health and relationships at risk.

7. Implications for One's Personal Life and for the Task of Formation

The traits help us to get to know a person, but they are not everything. The example of the entomologist illustrates the point. Looking at the wings of a butterfly under a microscope will help us to understand it, but the butterfly is more than its wings. To understand someone, we need to look at the whole. We need to see the person, and not the perfectionist, the timid, the impressionable, etc. Personality is a mystery, and so far we have simply outlined *theoretical constructs* to explain it. These constructs are a sort of methodological reductionism, pointers to study the person from different perspectives.

1992; J. Laplanche, J.B. Pontalis, *The Language of Psychoanalysis*, The Hogarth Press—The Institute of Psycho-Analysis, London 1973, pp. 109–111.

7   A.H. Maslow, *The Psychology of Science: A Reconnaissance*, Harper & Row, New York (NY) 1966, pp. 15–16.

When reading about the *Big Five* the reader will probably relate to all of them, and will feel identified (and identify others) somewhere along the spectrum. We may also have judged whether our *locus of control* is more internal or external, and whether we use *mechanisms of defense*. It is normal to do so, and it is also healthy. But if we identified ourselves only with the extremes, or realized that we only use one or two mechanisms of defense, we should be concerned.

These traits are common to us all, to a greater or lesser degree. A rich personality is the result of their mutual interaction. The more developed these traits are and correct their use is in each case, the better we will adapt to various situations. We can compare them to the clothes we wear for different activities (a work interview, a social gathering, going for a run) or for changing weather conditions (cold, heat, rain). Each trait has limited usefulness, because only the whole is operational. In themselves they are neither good nor bad. What matters is that there be variety, and that they be used in a timely manner. Here we can paraphrase Ecclesiastes: There is a time to reflect and a time to act, a time to be flexible and a time to be rigid, a time to speak and a time to keep silent.

Ultimately, a well-balanced personality knows itself and has enough self-control to tell itself "My first reaction is to do X, but I will do Y instead." The reason is that regardless of our genes and life experience we always possess the freedom of the children of God (cf. Rom 8:21). We are free to resist and react more charitably, according to our upbringing, social customs, work practices, etc. Or at least we can realize *a posteriori* that a specific reaction has not been appropriate, and acknowledge in all humility that we have made a mistake and make the resolution to do better next time. St. Francis de Sales is known as the *saint of kindness*, yet he had a lifelong struggle with his impulsive, irascible temper.

This is the way to improve one's personality. It can be done at any stage in life. There is no need to seek radical changes or to jettison the *pros* of our own way of being in order to avoid the *cons*, and be more flexible, adapt to the various people and circumstance we will face in the course of our life.

Studying personality traits and mechanisms of defense can help us to work out our limitations. For those who are involved in education and formation it can also help to identify the limitations of our students or mentees. Generalizations—seldom useful—should be avoided. Instead of saying, "You have a bad temper, your way of being makes you unfit for this task," a different way of expressing it could be, "This personality trait makes it harder for you to carry out this task, or makes it hard to relate to others." Above all, they help us to *focus*, to set concrete goals that are ambitious and realistic and can be assessed. In other words, setting a specific and personalized program for improvement. Rather than making big changes (they are usually not required, and may well be impossible to achieve), it is a matter of making *adjustments* in one's way of being and one's behavior.

Finally, what we have seen so far can help us organize teams and individuals. We are now aware that different types of personality make individuals more suited for some tasks than others. Indeed, this influences people's choices of study, professional work, and preferences for leisure activities and may determine their ability to engage in tasks of formation. Therefore, it is important to be aware of an individual's way of being and the talents that best fit them for specific tasks. It will facilitate better outcomes, and those involved will be happier, because they have been given a task that fits with their personality.

8. Conditioned but Not Determined

One more consideration is in order before we move on to the next chapter. Many factors are involved in the development of one's personality: genes, educational background, life experience, etc. There is little doubt that they have an important bearing on the way we are, feel, relate to others and to ourselves. But it is also true that these factors do not condemn anyone to be unhappy or maladapted.

The life of St. Josephine Bakhita[8] is an example. She was abducted as a little child, sold as a slave on several occasions, even given as a present, and mistreated by all her owners, freed by an Italian diplomat ... until she finally found God's love and joined the Canossian sisters. Her superiors were aware that her life would be edifying for many people, and encouraged her to tell her story. She obeyed, but she could not talk about it without shed-

---

8   Cf. R.I. Zanini, *Bakhita: From Slave to Saint,* Ignatius Press, San Francisco (CA) 2013.

ding copious tears. However, she was happy for the last fifty years of her life, a time that involved many years of service to God and to the many people who affectionately called her "Madre" (mother).

We are not determined by our genes nor by our past life. We can always change our future by changing ourselves. We also have the love of God, who can heal our deepest wounds.

HOW CAN WE ASSESS MATURITY?

1. When Will You Grow Up?

How many times have we heard—or said—these words, frustrated by children and youngsters acting up? How many times have we heard the same words applied to us? And how many times have we given the standard responses: What do you mean? Where? How? Indeed, it is easier to make progress when we are given specific targets that we—and others—can assess.

Ideally this chapter would begin with a definition of maturity, but we face the same problem we had when we tried to define personality: no definition is entirely satisfactory, because it is hard to encompass the wealth of meaning of the word.

We could begin with the following statement: a mature person *masters his environment*, and *is able to perceive the world and himself correctly, without any fuss*. It is not really a definition, but a description of how maturity reveals itself in a person's behavior: a well-tuned instrument that plays in harmony with the rest of the orchestra, at the right time. Table 3 contains some of the traits of a mature person.

Reason, will and feelings are well balanced.

He shows empathy with the people in his environment.

He has healthy relationships with his peers, does not fall into dependence on others, and does not try to make others dependent on him.

He holds his views and interests firmly but respectfully.

He adapts to whatever scenarios he is presented with.

He does not rush when matters are urgent, and does not procrastinate on those that can wait.

He does not "freeze" no matter how serious a situation may be.

He is responsible and he works proactively to solve his own difficulties.

He gives all matters their proper importance: he does not exaggerate or belittle them.

Table 3. The traits of a mature person.

More importantly, in the tasks of formation maturity is always a process that develops over a lifetime. For this reason it will be hard to find in the flesh *the paragon of maturity*: we will have to make do with people who are *sufficiently mature* for the tasks they have been entrusted: a high-pressure job, marriage, giving one's life within a particular vocation, etc.

Psychological maturity depends initially on biological growth, particularly development of the brain. Therefore it will manifest itself in different ways through the various stages of one's life; a person whose development lags behind or develops too quickly may manifest some level of immaturity. For example, a 70-year-old man who dresses, talks, or behaves like a teenager would be absurd (he would fail to understand the meaning of *being young at heart*). At the other end of the spectrum we find the *hyper mature* child, who is comfortable in the company of adults, but cannot relate to his peers. Ultimately, maturity is a relative term, and the best way to assess it is to compare the subject with what is expected of someone his/her age. We will consider these ideas in greater depth in a subsequent chapter when we cover the life cycle.

Rather than making theories about the concept, in this chapter I would like to talk about the signs of maturity: what makes us say "this guy is very mature" or "that one is immature"? The idea is to be able to work out the extent of the problem, and to grow—and help others to grow—in an appropriate way.

We will follow the approach of American psychologist Gordon W. Allport (1897–1967), who taught at Harvard and is considered one of the fathers of the psychology of personality. It is interesting to note that he does not venture to propose a precise definition because, he says, to do so would have too many repercussions, even of an ethical nature. In his book *Pattern and Growth in Personality*[1] he proposes six criteria (Table 4), which we can use as a guide to assess ourselves and those who depend on us. I will describe

1   G.W. Allport, *Pattern and Growth in Personality*, Holt, Rinehart and Winston, New York (NY) 1961, pp. 275–325. The following paragraphs are edits from an article I wrote: "Accompagnare i candidate al sacerdozio sulla strada della maturità. Una proposta dalla psicologia di Gordon Allport," *Tredimensioni* 14 (2017) 176–187.

them in turn, together with a few practical guidelines for the task of formation of young people, but equally applicable to older persons.

1. Extension of the sense of self.

2. Warm relating of self to others.

3. Emotional Security (Self-acceptance).

4. Realistic Perception, Skills and Assignments.

5. Self-objectification: Insight and Humor.

6. The Unifying Philosophy of Life.

Table 4. The Criteria of Maturity by Gordon W. Allport.

2. Criterion Zero: Identity

I have taken the liberty to include a criterion not included in Allport's list. He—and many others—repeatedly mentions *identity*, and in my opinion identity precedes the other six.

The first and most basic trait of a mature personality is to know *who I am*, a set of X-Y-Z coordinates where I can position myself. A newborn does not know who he is, and is not self-conscious; he will develop this ability little by little: he recognizes himself in the mirror (it is funny to see a baby fighting his own image in the mirror), in a set of name and surnames, as the child of his father and mother, as a boy or a girl, as a member of a family, a culture, a country. All these make up a core around which we can construct a stable personality.

If his identity is missing, the child begins life at a disadvantage. He can still achieve a fulfilled and happy life, but he will have to make up for his handicap. Children of broken families or those who are adopted are known to have difficulties. It is not simply a problem of being left out or of a lack of affection; often the problem is deeper: knowing *who I am*. Part of knowing who I am is to know who my parents are, my own history, a history that began before my own birth (we could call it a personal "prehistory"). The formator is in a good position to help these individuals to reconcile with their own biography, to know that they have not been born by chance or by their parents' "mistake," to discover (with the help of faith) that a Someone has loved them before they were born. This will give them the confidence to commit to a lifestyle that will lead them to be what they aspire to be.

People with gender identity disorders often experience emotional difficulties that go far beyond eventual social rejection. The core issue here is not knowing clearly *what am I* (man or woman), or feeling a disconnect between one's body, the gender one identifies with, their role in society, etc. It is a complex and socially sensitive problem, that needs to be dealt with in depth. I refer the reader to some bibliography where the topic is well covered from a scientific perspective and compatible with Christian anthropology.[2]

3. First Criterion: Extension of the Sense of Self

Children are typically *egocentric*, which is not the same as being selfish: this is one of many overlaps between psychology and morals. Children tend to think only of themselves, and they are focused on meeting their own needs and wants: taking the biggest piece of cake, the best piece of fruit, and as many sweets as they feel like, not thinking that others may go without, not giving thanks because they think of everything as their due, etc. With time, upbringing, and patience the child will come to realize that there are other people in the world who too have rights, needs and wants, and gradually the child will open to them. This process takes place above all in the home, which highlights the formative influence that large families can have.

2   Cf., among others, A. Cencini, "Omosessualità strutturale e non strutturale. Contributo per un'analisi differenziale (I)," *Tredimensioni* 6 (2009) 31-42; idem, "Omosessualità strutturale e non strutturale. Contributo per un'analisi differenziale (II)," *Tredimensioni* 6 (2009) 131–142; J. de Irala Estévez, *Comprendiendo la homosexualidad*, EUNSA, Pamplona 2006; J. Nicolosi, *A Parent's Guide to Preventing Homosexuality*, Liberal Mind Publishers, 2017; J. Harvey, *Same Sex Attraction: Catholic Teaching and Pastoral Practice*, Knights of Columbus Supreme Council, New Haven (CT) 2007 (available at: http://www.kofc.org/un/en/resources/cis/cis385.pdf; access September 8, 2021).

When children become adolescents,

> this intimate surge attaches itself to another person. The bound-
> aries of self are rapidly extended. The welfare of another is as
> important as one's own; better said, the welfare of another is
> identical with one's own.[3]

Consequently, their relationships, friendships, ambitions, ideas, and hobbies take a different tack, because they realize that these things don't re- volve around them but are part of their own identity.

Team sports are a clear example of this process. As the child grows, he realizes that the victory of the team is more important than him having a good time; sometimes it means that every player makes a sacrifice (someone has to play goalie). Play is unquestionably a very good educational and so- cializing tool.

The above ideas are valid not only for children: adults too should ex- pand their *sense of self* in diverse environments: in the workplace, in a cause they have committed themselves to, marriage, and other vocational paths. Tolstoy reveals his genius in a passage of the classic novel *Anna Karenina*. Levin, a character in the novel, ponders how the bond with his wife is much deeper than he had ever thought.

> He felt now that he was not simply close to her, but that he did
> not know where he ended and she began. He felt this from the
> agonizing sensation of division that he experienced at that in-
> stant. He was offended for the first instant, but the very same
> second he felt that he could not be offended by her, that she
> was himself. He felt for the first moment as a man feels when,
> having suddenly received a violent blow from behind, he turns
> round, angry and eager to avenge himself, to look for the of-
> fender, and finds that it is he himself who has accidentally struck
> himself, that there is no one to be angry with.[4]

3   Allport, *Pattern and Growth in Personality*, p. 283.
4   L. Tolstoy, *Anna Karenina*, V, 13.

How many marital problems could be solved if both spouses saw each other like Levin came to think of his beloved Kitty.

How can we foster this criterion of maturity in the task of formation? The ultimate goal is vague: that the person comes out of herself and looks around. The first step is to discover and then put into practice the Golden Rule: *do unto others what you would want them to do unto you*. This rule is much deeper than a functional *do ut des* (I give so that you give). The child ought to be involved in a group from an early age. Or better, several groups of various types: school friends, sporting teams, outdoor activities, the parish. The feeling of being a member of a community will help the child to become interested in the interests of the others, and enjoy their successes.

A further step would be to develop an appreciation for the spiritual and material needs of others; sometimes they may need a more obvious indication, delivered in a refined way: "Have you noticed that today So-and-So looks unwell?" Often he will be able to help in some way.

Another way of helping others is to offer corrections as often as may be necessary. The formator should do this in a calm, fraternal way, and not to fall into *holy anger* before the defects of others (it is often not that holy, because it lacks charity or good manners). The manner of the correction will be an example for the corrected party to temper his criticism of the people or of the groups that he is involved with (sporting, cultural, religious, etc.), no matter how deserving of criticism they are in his opinion. It is fair to point out deficiencies in an organization, or in how it is run, but it should be done *from within*. If the criticism is about people and undertakings that one is more closely related to, it should be done as a son pointing out defects to his father, or the other way round, not like a self-appointed "expert" criticizing the opposite team while watching a game on television.

It is very useful for young people to have contact with the underprivileged, especially in today's welfare society. It will help them to appreciate what they have and spontaneously feel that they should help others, even at their own cost, whether in time or money. They will thus learn to do good without seeking personal gain, whether material or psychological—the latter often unconsciously—such as self-affirmation, mastery, recognition, "feeling good about it," etc.

Within Christian formation, the sense of self includes being part of the Church: it is part and parcel of one's identity, the family one belongs to. It will therefore help one to get to know the gospel and the lives of the saints, the growth and the difficulties that Christianity faces in various parts of the world, the wealth of the various charisms and vocations in the Church, etc.

Finally, the one being formed should apply this same criterion to the people responsible for his formation. Seeing them as someone who sets demanding goals that call for a defensive attitude would be a mistake. On the contrary, when a learner acknowledges that he is the person most responsible for his own formation, the defensive attitude fades away: he accepts that the mentor is "on his side" and learns to appreciate his care, to share his problems in a trusting manner, and be thankful for the corrections and the help they receive to reach their own goal, which is to improve both as a human person and as a Christian.

4. Second Criterion: Warm Relating of Self to Others

The mature person

> is capable of great intimacy in his capacity for love—whether the attachment is in family life or in deep friendship. On the other hand, he avoids gossipy, intrusive, and possessive involvements with people (even his own family). He has a certain detachment which makes him respectful and appreciative of the human condition of all men. This type of warmth may be called *compassion.*[5]

We go from relationships with an institution, or with other people in general, to relationships with specific persons. It is not as easy a step as it may seem at first: in Dostoyevsky's masterpiece *The Brothers Karamazov, starets* Zosimus, one of the characters, tells what someone said to him in confidence.

> I love humanity, but I wonder at myself. The more I love humanity in general, the less I love man in particular. In my

5   Allport, *Pattern and Growth in Personality,* p. 285.

dreams, I have often come to making enthusiastic schemes for the service of humanity, and perhaps I might actually have faced crucifixion if it had been suddenly necessary; and yet I am incapable of living in the same room with any one for two days together, as I know by experience.[6]

A mature person thinks differently: he is close and accessible, he takes an interest in everything around him, shows empathy and understanding, bears other people's defects and listens to those who think differently or who have other interests. He may share hobbies, tastes and ways of being with some people, and makes unselfish relationships of true friendship with them that result in more intense contact, but that does not exclude others.

Having said that, Allport warns of emotionally dependent relationships: ultimately these relationships eliminate the person, because they do not respect otherness. A mature person does not seek to impose or to control, does not need a retinue of uncritically obedient admirers. On the other hand, he does not surrender to the dictates of anyone who tries to override his personality, and is able to break a harmful relationship without becoming anxious about becoming lonely or neglected. We will return to this matter in the chapter that deals with the dependent personality.

Allport highlights a trait of the balanced personality that makes social interaction easier: "avoiding constant complaining and criticizing, jealousy and sarcasm [that] are toxic in social relationships."[7] Reading these words one cannot but think of how often Pope Francis has criticized these attitudes.[8]

---

6   F. Dostoyevsky, *The Brothers Karamazov*, I, II, 4.

7   Allport, *Pattern and Growth in Personality*, p. 285.

8   Some of these occasions: *General Audience*, November 25, 2013; October 9, 2013; February 12, 2014; August 27, 2014; *Christmas Address to the Roman Curia*, December 21, 2013; *Angelus*, February 16, 2014; *Address to Rectors and students of the Pontifical Colleges and Residences of Rome*, May 12, 2014; *Meeting with the Clergy of Caserta*, July 26, 2014; *Address to the Participants in the General Chapter of the Congregation of the Daughters of Mary Help of Christians*, November 8, 2014; and above all the homilies of the daily Masses in *Domus Sanctae Marthae*: April 13, 2013; May 18, 2013; November 2, 2013; September 13, 2013; January 23, 2014; April 11, 2014; September 12, 2014, etc.

If we apply all this to formation, it makes a lot of sense to keep an eye on the relationships the learner may develop with his peers. Any pattern of control, dependence or detachment, friendships closed to other parties, difficulty establishing interpersonal relationships, or a tendency to harsh criticism or backbiting, are all danger signals. They point to possible difficulties the learner may have before reaching full human and Christian maturity. Indeed, "the higher the level of personal maturity, the greater the ability to relate to others will be open to true self-giving, inspired and driven by a theocentric self-transcendence."[9]

5. Third Criterion: Emotional Security (Self-acceptance)

"This feature of maturity includes the ability to avoid overreaction to matters pertaining to segmental drives"[10]: anger, sex, fear of death, etc.

The person does not need to be calm, serene, and cheerful at all times: it is neither desirable nor a sign of maturity, because he would have no *emotional reactivity*. But these states of mind should be proportionate to the circumstances that prompted them, both in quality and quantity.

A mature person expresses his convictions and feelings with respect for the convictions and feelings of others; and he does not feel threatened by his own emotional expressions or by theirs. His emotional experiences—no matter how intense—are not the only deciding factor when it comes to discharging one's duties or living in harmony with others.

Allport highlights *frustration tolerance* as an especially important quality[11]: knowing how to handle other people's mistakes or one's own. When things go wrong, a mature person does not fall into fits of anger and self-pity, or blame others. A healthy dose of self-criticism leads him to look for solutions and adapt to the circumstances. He *sees challenges rather than*

---

9   A.M. Ravaglioli, "Educare alla relazione interpersonale i futuri presbiteri (I). Maturità personale, processi simbolici e relazione," *Tredimensioni* 10 (2013), pp. 121–133).

10 Allport, *Pattern and Growth in Personality*, p. 287.

11 Frustration tolerance has been studied extensively by Albert Ellis (1913–2007) within the context of his rational emotive behavior therapy. Cf. *The Road to Tolerance. The Philosophy of Rational Emotive Behavior Therapy.* Prometeus, Amherst (NY) 2004.

problems, the well-known motto of all MBA Courses. Ultimately, he acknowledges not being perfect, but tries to get better all the time.

The ability to accept *deferred rewards* is closely related to Self-Acceptance: to persevere in one's endeavor with a view to a greater long-term reward. As nothing is achieved without effort, making the effort brings with it increased self-esteem and autonomy (a healthy detachment of more or less material rewards, from a medal to recognition).

I venture to add a social skill that Allport does not mention, possibly because it is a more recent concept: *assertiveness*. It is the ability of being true to oneself, to do what one considers appropriate regardless of whether others disagree, to express negative emotions, to uphold one's rights, to set boundaries to a relationship, to express negative emotions, to say that something has bothered me, to say *no* in a polite way overcoming both being rude or fearing rejection or causing grief. Rebellion and submission are, in a way, two sides of the same coin.

In the tasks of formation it is important to be aware of how people manage their moods. They need help to avoid excessive reserve that gives the impression of being cold and lacking in empathy, or on the contrary, emotional outbursts caused by strong feelings. Another aspect to be borne in mind is whether they remain serene in the face of obstacles and their readiness to overcome them with a positive yet realistic approach. It is also worthwhile to assess how they guard their intimacy in their dealings with others, and do not open up to those who are not in a position to help. This attitude often leads to mutual grievances, and psychological harm.

Naturally, they will need to be encouraged to pray, not as a desperate measure, but as a natural resource, the best way to confide one's difficulties to whom is always listening and helps to endure them with the same attitude as Christ's on the Cross.

Finally, we need to assess their ability to listen and understand other people's failures. This is a fundamental attitude for all those preparing to carry out tasks of formation; therefore, they will need to learn to be welcoming to the weak and sinful.

We will return to emotional security in the section on the life cycle, specifically in relation to the *theory of attachment*, because its roots are found in early childhood.

6. Fourth Criterion: Realistic Perception, Skills and Assignments

This trait refers to how one relates to the world (what refers to oneself will be covered in the next criterion). Allport's description reads,

> The sound person has "sets" that lead to veridicality to a greater degree than do persons not so sound. Maturity does not bend reality to fit one's needs and fantasies.[12]

Basically, it means a way of thinking based on "the real world.' It is not about logical reasoning or intellectual ability, but about having overcome what is now called the *magical thinking* typical of a child, or the adult *emotional reasoning* (we will talk about both later). A mature person reaches the truth (acknowledges and understands it) more easily than immature persons, who tend to bend reality to fit one's needs and fancies.

Allport sees *aptitude* as a necessary adjunct for this view of the world: the ability to interact effectively within one's milieu. Aptitude includes *flexibility* and *adaptability* to the different environments and ways of being of those who live around him.

He finally mentions "the capacity of lose oneself in one's work."[13] It includes problem solving, forgetting about egoistic impulses of drive-satisfaction and self-defense mechanisms. This ability relates to *responsibility*. It brings forth a person who works efficiently, solves the problems that he faces, plans out his work, perseveres and fulfils it, etc.

In summary,

> a mature person will be in close touch with what we call "the real world." He will see objects, people, and situations for what they are. And he will have important work to do.[14]

---

12 Allport, *Pattern and Growth in Personality*, p. 289.
13 *Ibidem*, p. 290.
14 *Ibidem*.

In the field of education, we will need to assess whether the young person perceives reality as it really is, or allows himself to be led by subjective criteria that stem from personal interest, defense mechanisms or moods. A good way to assess it is to observe how he deals with obstacles: whether he is carried away by daydreaming, by a naïve confidence that things will get better on their own, by indefinite delays while waiting for the ideal situation which is very unlikely to occur. Admitting one's failures without excuses is another marker of being realistic, and an essential first step in deciding to improve.

In positive terms, we will need to help him to approach problems realistically and to look for solutions according to his possibilities, by helping him set ambitious but achievable goals, with the help of others and working as a team; by helping him work hard, especially when sacrifice is required, and not losing heart when he finds obstacles along the way.

7. Fifth Criterion: Insight and Humor

The term *insight* comes from the field of psychiatry, according to the awareness that mental patients (particularly psychotic patients) have of their illness. For Allport the term has a wider meaning. He defines it as the relationship between how he believes himself to be and how he really is—the latter is difficult to define, so Allport brings in a third criterion: what others think of him. In the case of a mature person, self-understanding would be similar to that of others who know and love him.

The difference between one's own assessment and that of others may go in opposite directions: one would be low self-esteem, an excessively poor concept of self. The opposite extreme would be to think that others, even those who are closer to the subject, do not really know him, or appreciate him, or do not treat him as he deserves. We are reminded of the adage "the best business in the world is to buy a man for what he is worth, and sell him for what he thinks he is worth."

On the other hand, Allport and many psychologists have noticed that those persons who are aware of their defects or shortcomings are much less likely to attribute them to other people, they are less prone to *project them* (we have already commented on this defense mechanism). They are also better judges of other people, and are more likely to be accepted. St.

Augustine said the same thing many centuries ago: "Try to acquire the virtues you believe lacking in others. Then you will no longer see their defects, for you will no longer have them yourself."[15] There is no need to stress that those called to mentor others need to have insight for themselves.

According to Allport, a sense of humor strongly correlates with insight, to the point of looking at them as the same phenomenon. For Allport a sense of humor is "the ability to laugh at the things one loves (including, of course, oneself and all that pertains to oneself), and still love them."[16] This is quite different to "being funny"; it helps to overcome defects, limitations and mistakes—one's own and others'—and not stress unduly. However, like in all things, humor needs to be balanced, lest an excess of humor becomes cynicism; a cynical person laughs at what he loves, but the price is loving it no longer.

The direct opposite of self-knowledge and a healthy disrespect for self is affectation: "the tendency of some people to appear outwardly to be something they cannot be."[17] It is the attitude of the teenager who tries to act differently than he is and usually ends up being ridiculous.

Those who mentor people and try to help them mature should be encouraged to ask two questions: "How do others see me?" and "What do I think about it?" A sincere and realistic examination of one's actions and motives would be very useful. Putting together self-knowledge and an accurate perception of reality (the fourth criterion) will lead the subject to take on tasks that are both realistic and ambitious; he will be aware of his talents (without false humility) and his limitations, will admit his mistakes without making excuses, will be able to plan and ask for help, and will run the race to maturity with a sporting spirit, without discouragement, and always at arm's length from himself: he will then be able not to take himself too seriously and laugh at his mistakes.

It is important to note that young people may fall into the *tyranny of expectations*: what they think that others (parents, teachers, mentors, superiors, etc.) expect of them. The weight of expectation—which is not always realistic—may stress them out and lead to a voluntaristic struggle—

15 St. Augustine, *Exposition on Psalm 30*, 2, 7.
16 Allport, *Pattern and Growth in Personality*, p. 292.
17 *Ibidem*, p. 294.

probably with the best of intentions—that would end up being alienating: they would not be seeking their own improvement but the fulfilment of other people's wishes for them, which they may not understand, let alone share. At the risk of making a tongue twister, there should not be much difference between what *I am*, what *I could be*, what *I would like to be*, what *I think I should be*, and what *others tell me I should be*.

How one handles other people's mistakes is another pointer to how the learner lives fraternity, but also his own self-knowledge: anyone who is aware of his own defects will not be surprised when he finds that other people too have defects.

8. Sixth Criterion: The Unifying Philosophy of Life

Allport defines the last criterion of a mature personality as "a clear comprehension of life's purpose in terms of an intelligible theory. Of, in brief, some form of a unifying philosophy of life."[18] Each person has something to live for, a goal (or goals) that directs his actions and provides an integrated purpose for his existence (for example, a Christian, a pacifist, an environmentalist, a Communist); these would be *value-orientations*. A person can have several of them, although usually there is a predominant system, and the rest are subordinates.

Allport groups them into six *ideal types* or *schemata of comprehensibility* according to the main ideologies and currents of thought in society. They allow us to understand what motivates a specific person and assess how this person has organized his life and worked for consistency in the framing of his value-systems. Of course, these types are not found in their pure form, and they do not encompass the whole of reality. Different authors classify them in slightly different ways.

Allport distinguishes six types, and their highest value:

- *The theoretical*: search for truth.
- *The economic*: search for what is useful.
- *The esthetic*: search for form and harmony.
- *The social*: search for love.

18 Cf. *ibidem*, p. 294.

- *The political*: search for power.
- *The religious*: search for unity.

The definition of the religious type is somewhat surprising from a Christian perspective: at first glance the Christian view would appear to be closer to Allport's social type. Given that the other four are more straight-forward, we will develop those two to define them and establish the differences among them.

For the social type, according to Allport, love of people is the highest value, whether one person or many, and whether the love is conjugal, filial, friendly, or philanthropic. The social man values other persons as ends in themselves and is kind, sympathetic and unselfish. Is there a difference with the religious man? Yes, the fact that the social schema is purely horizontal, refers only to men, and does not "look up" toward God.

On the other hand, the religious type seeks to comprehend the cosmos as a whole and relate to its embracing totality. Some who follow this way of life are *immanent mystics*, who seek the religious experience in the affirmation of life and in active participation therein. Others are *transcendental mystics*: they seek to unite themselves with a higher reality by withdrawing from worldly life through asceticism, self-denial, and meditation.

Allport seems to miss a third variety of the religious type: the man who seeks unity with a personal God, and thus seeks some withdrawal from material realities, but only as a means to facilitate the relationship with the divine being through prayer (not pure abstract meditation) and, as a member of the community of the children of God, he concerns himself for his brother men, and takes an active part in the affairs of the world.

Having said that, we should acknowledge that Allport was a psychologist, not a theologian, and this is not the place to study his outlook on religion. However, when he criticizes immature manifestations of religiosity (which most certainly exist), he admits the possibility of a mature religiosity within the traditional and institutional religions.

The *schemata of comprehensibility* (using Allport's term) that fits a Christian attitude would be a combination of the social (horizontal) and religious (vertical) types, with some input from the other four. This person would not be closed in his opinions, and would not despise those who do not share his view of the world: such an attitude would reveal an immature religiosity, which is precisely what Allport criticizes. On the contrary, he would not seek union with the cosmos but with a Triune God with whom he can have a one-on-One loving, personal relationship.

This schema may be proposed, but never imposed. It is up to each individual to discover his path and follow it freely. The task of the formator is to introduce a concept of life and present it as being attractive and achievable. God's grace and personal correspondence will do the rest.

Choosing that philosophy of life is not a straightforward choice, like comparing one garment with another to see which one fits best when we go shopping. It is the active search of something very intimate: asking oneself what type of person I want to be, what ideal appeals to me, fills me, what is the best for me and how can I be most useful to others. It has an element of commitment, because putting it into practice requires a struggle. God will certainly assist anyone who sincerely seeks it.

Unity of life is not only a religious concept, but also a psychological one (known as *consistency*); it needs to be based on the *schema of comprehensibility*. It will lead the person to act in accordance with his values, to internalize what he hears from his educators, to be able to leave things behind and keep his composure and not fall into nostalgia, because he knows he has chosen the better part (cf. *Lk* 10:42).

The *schemata of comprehensibility* can be used as a measure of consistency. Anyone who has freely chosen a lifestyle and has internalized it consciously will easily appreciate that some behavior, environments, etc., are not compatible with it and could lead him to live a double life, which would only make him unhappy.

This search for the ideal must also be realistic. According to Allport, when the mature person experiences the difference between what he aims at and what he really is, he will reason that "I ought to do the best I can to become the sort of person I partly am, and wholly hope to be."[19]

9. From Maturity to the Identification with Christ

The six criteria proposed by Gordon Allport encompass how we relate to ourselves, to other people, and to the world. Therefore, they fit within the

19 *Ibidem*, p. 303.

definition of personality that we saw in the previous chapter; they also include many other factors, both inherited and acquired, conscious and unconscious, that have a bearing in our way of being.

Allport proposes them as a growth process, a path that leads people to go outside themselves and to forget their own ego. Therefore, they harmonize with the Christian ideal, and they are practical and useful for the task of formation. When educators assess them, they will have a solid starting point to set goals for improvement throughout life.

When aiming for maturity we cannot forget that the most important force comes from God's grace, and the primary goal of Christian formation—very different from the purpose of any psychological theory—is much greater than becoming a balanced person: a Christian seeks sanctity, a life of love for God and men; and the model is Jesus Christ.

The balance that results from such maturity will help the young person, and later the adult, to react appropriately to the stressors that they will undoubtedly find, and give things their due importance. Nothing more, nothing less.

LOVING ONESELF TO BE ABLE TO LOVE

1. God, Myself, and Others?

What is the order of charity? For those who have received a Christian formation from childhood, the answer comes without much thought: *God, other people, and myself.* Yet Aquinas appears to say the opposite. The *Summa* deals precisely with this topic in Question 26: *On the order of charity.*[1] There he asks a number of questions. *Is there an order in charity? Should man love God more than his neighbor? Should man love God more than himself?* and *Should man love himself more than his neighbor?*

He answers the first three questions with a resounding Yes, but his last answer is initially surprising: "out of charity, a man ought to love himself more than his neighbor." When I first read this passage, I felt betrayed by all the religion teachers I've ever had, going back to my first Communion. Aquinas stated that the order of charity should be: *God, myself, and other people.* If we investigate further, we can draw some interesting conclusions.

St. Thomas begins with the *first commandment*: "You shall love the Lord your God with all your heart, and with all your soul, and with all your strength, and with all your mind; and your neighbor as yourself" (Lk 10:27). As you can see, Jesus applies a double standard when he speaks about love. We should love God absolutely, in a radical way; "the measure is to love without measure."[2] But when we talk about our neighbor it is no longer an absolute measure, and it is not even related to God (to love others a little less than to God, or almost as much as God, etc.). The yardstick is oneself: as I love myself. It reminds us of the *golden rule*, already mentioned in the previous chapter: "do unto others what you would want them do unto you."

1   St. Thomas Aquinas, *Summa Theologica*, II-II, q. 26, art. 1–4.
2   St. Augustine, *Letter 109*, 2. This is usually quoted as one of his letters, but was in fact a letter he received from Severus, bishop of Milevi and a friend of St. Augustine.

Therefore, we should love ourselves. It's not a tactic to arrive at what matters, namely charity towards others; love for oneself is a natural thing to do, and it is good and healthy. Everyone needs a dose of self-esteem, because it's only just and because we are worth a great deal notwithstanding our defects and shortcomings. In addition—as an aside—it is necessary in order to love others: it helps me to know how much I should love them. In the negative we would say: if I do not love myself, if I do not value myself, it will be very difficult to love and value the others. Similarly, if I am not loved, it will be difficult for me to love. We will return to this idea as we go along.

2. The Origin of Self-love

The positive or negative concept we have of ourselves depends on our self-knowledge. It changes according to how we reach our goals.[3]

Every time we reach a difficult goal, we are pleasantly surprised, and we tell ourselves, perhaps unconsciously: *I am worth much more than I thought.*

But before that, everyone has an *internal image of oneself.* It goes back to early childhood, well before we had developed the ability to know ourselves fully. The messages parents transmit to little children—their words and gestures—about their worth foster or hinder a good self-image. This is best shown by an example.

A boy is building a castle with wooden blocks; when it reaches a certain height, the whole thing collapses, and he starts crying. Mom or dad will try to console him and will encourage him to start again; they can do it in either of two ways. The quick solution, easier in the short term, is to build the castle themselves, and tell the boy: "there it is, now you can play with it." But the child could internalize the following message: "you are useless, whatever you do always breaks down, you need someone else to do everything for you."

3   C. Cavanyes, "El amor a uno mismo," in W. Vial (ed.), *Ser quien eres. Cómo construir una personalidad feliz con el consejo de médicos, filósofos, sacerdotes y educadores*, Rialp, Madrid 2017, p. 32.

Alternatively, the parents can sit down with the boy, show him where he went wrong, and do it again *together*: put the blocks in place, warn him when it can become unstable, or when it is tall enough, and withdraw little by little to let the boy be the main builder. At the end he will be proud of the castle he has built—with the help of others, but *he* carried it out.

I am not suggesting that parents should do this all the time, but the more often we do it the better. We can swap the castle for homework, order in the wardrobe, cooking dinner, sewing a button, sorting out a conflict with a friend from school, making up when he has broken something. Any educator will find lots of chances to help the child, the teenager, and the young person to develop their talents and maintain a good self-image. It requires patience, but it works much better in the long run.

A second way to promote love of self is *appreciation*. The Oxford English Dictionary definition of the verb appreciate is "Recognize as valuable or excellent. Raise in value." To recognize is to increase, and to tell someone *you are worth a lot* is to help him to be worth more. Another example will help here: a boy comes home with a C- on his last school test. Mothers have an intuitive knowledge of appreciation, and may congratulate the boy by acknowledging the work he has put in. But the litmus test is the father's reaction when he comes home. He can do a lot of harm with an "it's not that bad" type of comment: he would virtually wipe out the hours of study the boy has put in, the sacrifice and the things he gave up, etc. It could be worse if the father is only happy when the boy gets A+. If the boy can only bear to hear "I am proud of you" then a perfectionist, insecure personality may be brewing, with poor self-esteem, never happy with his achievements, because he will always be falling short of the Olympic motto "faster, higher, stronger."

Appreciation speaks the language of affections, not the language of things. When we do something well, the reward we expect may be acknowledgement, a smile, applause; but not things, or presents. The best reward would be a combination of both: taking the boy out for dinner, or a football game, or something he enjoys, etc.

The effects of appreciation are not limited to children. I talked with a friend of mine about these ideas when I was writing this chapter. When I reached the idea of appreciation, he turned pale, and said: "my father never appreciated me." My friend was an adult, but the hurt was still present. He also acknowledged that his father had given him many other things that were just as important, and indeed my friend had managed to achieve a good life and was a successful professional, in addition to being the head of a stable family. More importantly, the pain did not stop him from taking good care of his father with Alzheimer's disease for many years, until his death. God will reward him in due course.

Now for the million-dollar question: how can we congratulate the boy for good grades, and at the same time tell him that he can do even better? Education is an art, and there are no fixed rules to strike the right balance. Every child, every student has a sweet spot that we need to identify. To make it even more challenging, the sweet spot changes with age, with moods, after the task is completed, etc.

Blanket statements should be avoided, however often we fall into them: "you are always late," "you leave everything all over the place," "you are lazy and a mess." Using relative terms is usually more refined, more effective, and especially more realistic: "you are often late," "you could be more organized with your things," "you need to work more steadily on your subjects," etc. In other words, it's better to *pinpoint* what needs to be worked on (some of the traits of the *big five* or the criteria of maturity we have seen so far could come in handy), and to swap "*you are*" for "*you do*." When we tell someone "You are like this," we can convey the idea that there is no solution ("That's how you are, there is nothing you can do…"). On the contrary, the general thinking is that it is feasible to change behavior over time. We will seldom hear anyone saying: "I cannot stop doing this, ever." It reminds us how important it is to promote a mainly *internal locus of control* to solve problems effectively.

At the other end of the spectrum, a father who offers excessive appreciation to the achievements of his son will create a laughable narcissist who can only connect with weak individuals. And in the end life will find him out. Such a person will be prone to discouragement, even depression, when he finds out that he is not as clever or as competent as he thought he was, or as daddy always told him.

Children tend to assimilate what people say about them (the technical word is *introjection*). If we keep on saying "you are bad," "you are lazy," "you are out of this world," the child will end up believing it, make it his own and somehow will find a reason to persist in his behavior: "I am expected to fail in the exams at school because I am lazy," "it made sense to be expelled from school, because I am a bad boy." It is also worthwhile to take care of making verbal and non-verbal language coherent when congratulating and correcting: tone and volume of the voice, a look that affirms or rejects, body language, etc.

I like the maxim: *children need the mother's cuddle and teenagers need the father's appreciation.* I think it applies equally to both boys and girls. However, it is more noticeable in boys because boys and girls experience affectivity in different ways.

Boys are more active and are keener to generate; they need to be taught how to do things and to do them well. They are also very competitive. This can be an incentive to improve, but it can also drive them to frustration if their expectations are too high. Mentors can take advantage of these traits by saying things like "you are among the best in the class" (a word of caution: it is not a good idea to push them to be "the best"). Or even better "you have outdone yourself," where oneself is the benchmark, and the chances for growth are unlimited. One final comment: they give greater importance to physical strength and dexterity, so this aspect should be acknowledged: "you are becoming a man," "how strong you are."

Girls are the opposite. They are more affectionate; therefore, it is necessary to be particularly expressive or overt when showing affection. They are more inclined to seduce, so one needs to appear "touched" by their external appearance, admire them: "you are very pretty," "you look good in this dress." Finally, they are more insecure, and their decisions need to be confirmed, while ensuring that they are the ones who make them and who bear the consequences. Comparisons for them are more about acknowledgment than achievement: the others are more admired or loved, have more friends, are more popular with boys, etc.

Both boys and girls need to receive *feedback*, but not excessively, so that they do not become "addicted to external recognition." The goal is that both boys and girls internalize the appreciation, so that they can be happy with what they are doing, even though they have to against the tide, or nobody congratulates them.

Allow me to digress. Parents—and educators generally—make mistakes in their educational task, and some of these mistakes will come up in this book. My intention is not to blame anyone. As a matter of fact, the epilogue of this book, *A Healthy Style of Formation*, contains further ideas on the topic. Everyone raises his children to the best of his knowledge, and he usually does it the way he has been taught himself. Often the mistakes a father makes are the same as his own father's. The danger is perpetuating our errors: the boy will transmit them to his own children, and they will be passed on from generation to generation, not through genetics (though genes have an influence because they condition temperament), but through upbringing. Unfortunately, parents often have no one to teach them how to raise their children, and they work on intuition, which is always a risky business. It highlights the importance of self-training with readings, courses, etc.—just like they do in their professional work—for the most important task in their life, the one that will have the greatest impact. There is no such thing as the perfect father or the ideal educator, but there sure are parents and educators who train themselves so as to bring out the best in their children and their students.

On the part of the children, it is necessary to reconcile with the figure of the father so as to avoid that he cause an open wound. At the beginning of the previous chapter we said that identity includes recognizing oneself as a child of parents and family members. A difficult, traumatic, or even abusive relationship can lead to the complete rejection of that parent, but that rejection usually entails a certain denial of who one is, leaving him or her uprooted. If all resentment is harmful, that directed against one's parents is especially pernicious. Forgiving one's parents—which does not mean ignoring that they have done wrong or necessarily restoring a fluid relationship—is a source of peace and a way to strengthen one's identity and self-esteem. No doubt this healing process takes time, but it is especially pleasing in the eyes of God, who will give his grace abundantly to those who decide to carry this out.

3. Seeing Oneself in the Light of God

Those who lived with St. Josemaría tell us that occasionally he would look at the young people sitting around him during a get-together, and ask them: "my children, do you know why I love you so much? [...] because I see the Blood of Christ coursing in you."[4] Our Lord died for each one of us; not

4   A. Vazquez de Prada, *The Founder of Opus Dei*, Vol. III, Scepter, New York (NY) 2002, p. 273.

for humankind in general but for each person (cf. Gal 2:19). And when he died for us he raised us to a level higher than *the image and likeness* of God when he created us: he has made us his *children*.

Has anyone seen how the son of a great figure—a politician, an artist, a sports star—feels "taller" as he walks past a group of his father's fans? This is what St. Josemaría recommended Christians do all over the world:

> "Father," said that big fellow (I wonder what has become of him), a good student at the Central, "I was thinking of what you told me—that I am a son of God!—and I found myself walking along the street, head up, chin out, and a proud feeling inside… a son of God!" With sure conscience I advised him to encourage that "pride."[5]

Having said that the foundation of love for oneself lies in the fact that we internalize the appreciation of others, how important should our awareness be that no less than God himself loves us with a Father's love? No matter what, even when our parents have not behaved as they should have, God always loves each one of us unconditionally: I am worthy to be loved, I am worthy to exist.

You might ask, though, "what if I misbehave?" I was once in the waiting room of a hospital. There were four nurses at the nursing station, speaking softly. I was minding my own business when I heard this question: "Father, does God love this one here?" They were obviously asking me because I was the only priest in the room. I looked at them, and saw that one of them was looking down; clearly, the question was about her. I answered, "of course he does." Then she raised her head a little and asked me, "even if I misbehave sometimes?" The Holy Spirit must have come to my help because I did not hesitate: "God loves you always, even when you behave badly. Just like you love your own children." If you are familiar with the expression *her face lit up*, this is precisely what happened, believe it or not: she was transformed, and then followed a great five-way conversation until it was my turn to go in to see the doctor.

5   St. Josemaría Escrivá, *The Way*, Scepter, New York, 1992, n. 274. "The Central" University was the name of the University of Madrid at the time.

God always loves us, even when we behave badly. Like the father of the prodigal son, who went out every day to wait for the son who had left home to waste his inheritance (cf. Lk 15:11–32). He loves us and he forgives us. Pope Francis told a personal anecdote during his very first Angelus address in St. Peter's Square. Many years earlier, he had been hearing confessions in a parish, and was about to leave to attend to other pastoral duties, when

> an elderly woman approached me, humble, very humble, and over eighty years old. I looked at her, and I said, "Grandmother"—because in our country that is how we address the elderly—"do you want to make your confession?" "Yes," she said to me. "But if you have not sinned…" And she said to me: "We all have sins…." "But perhaps the Lord does not forgive them." "The Lord forgives all things," she said to me with conviction. "But how do you know, Madam?" "If the Lord did not forgive everything, the world would not exist." […] Let us not forget this word: God never ever tires of forgiving us! "Well, Father, what is the problem?" Well, the problem is that we ourselves tire, we do not want to ask, we grow weary of asking for forgiveness. He never tires of forgiving, but at times we get tired of asking for forgiveness.[6]

We are only human, and it is not easy to live only on *supernatural consolations*—we need to hear from others that they love us. But we may be able to learn to hear this consolation in the prayer and teach it to others. Awareness of the unconditional love of God will give us a mindset steady enough to overcome any difficulty, whether internal or external. It will help us to keep our victories and defeats in perspective, to keep the focus on the life goal we have set out to achieve (our *schema of comprehensibility*, using Allport's expression): to grow in the love of God and enjoy eternal happiness with him in heaven. Everything that happens in our life, whether good or bad, even sin itself, can be redirected to this goal. It is the right balance between *the internal and the external locus of control*. It's a very difficult balance to find; all we can do is settle for getting close to it.

6   Francis, *Angelus*, March 17, 2013.

Looking at ourselves in the light of God will also help us to look at others with the same perspective. We are all partially responsible for the self-esteem of the people around us. Therefore, we should strive to talk with them and to act in a way that is consistent with their being children of God. If we are in a position of authority or guidance (father-son, teacher-student relationship, etc.) the advice and suggestions we give will help them to reaffirm their own self-worth, even on the occasions we need to correct them in no uncertain terms. St. Josemaría used to say to his spiritual children: "I love you and I love seeing you become saints."

If we act this way, we will manage to live in an imperfect world, surrounded by people who are imperfect, we ourselves also being imperfect. But we will be serene and eager to improve, and above all to be happy.

4. Humility and Truth

Is there a risk of loving ourselves too much? How can we prevent overrating ourselves, and falling into pride? The danger is certainly there, but there are also many good people who suffer excessively from their defects, because they ignore their own achievements and virtues. When they are about to feel accomplished and congratulate themselves… they reject it as a bad thought, and end getting caught up in a net of dissatisfaction and guilt. They have not understood the meaning of humility.

C. S. Lewis describes it brilliantly in *The Screwtape Letters*. This old devil writes to his nephew, Wormwood.

> You must therefore conceal from the patient the true end of Humility. Let him think of it, not as self-forgetfulness, but as a certain kind of opinion (namely, a low opinion) of his own talents and character. Some talents, I gather, he really has. Fix in his mind the idea that humility consists in trying to believe those talents to be less valuable than he believes them to be. No doubt they *are* in fact less valuable than he believes, but that is not the point. The great thing is to make him value an opinion for some quality other than truth, thus introducing an element of dishonesty and make-believe into the heart of what otherwise threatens to become a virtue. By this method *thousands of*

*humans have been brought to think that humility means pretty
women trying to believe they are ugly and clever men trying to believe they are fools.*[7]

The last sentence is in italic because I think it is brilliant.

St. Teresa of Avila wrote that "to be humble is to walk in truth."[8] To
see ourselves in the light of God means to look at and to accept ourselves
as we are, with talents and virtues that we have to use and bear fruit until
our Lord comes (cf. Lk 19:11–27).

This will allow us to accept our errors and face them. I once heard that
"we have defects, but we are not our defects." We will acknowledge that
others are more intelligent, more personable, more athletic, without being
discouraged, and we will calmly try to imitate them. Envy is the sadness
caused by the achievements of others, and to wish their failure so as to remain above them. Emulating them is the opposite: acknowledging the mer-
its of others and learning from them in order to better ourselves.

Earlier on we asked the question: what to do to prevent pride? One
way is to be able to laugh at our own mistakes. In the letter we quoted,
Screwtape recommends to his nephew Wormwood "don't try this too long,
for fear you awake his sense of humor and proportion, in which case he
will merely laugh at you and go to bed."[9]

A second way is to allow the people who love us to help and correct us:
first of all, our parents, and also teachers, friends and those to whom we entrust our desire to improve. This is a great tradition in the Church: spiritual
direction. When we entrust ourselves to the objective appraisal of someone
who knows us and sees us from the outside—with affection and understanding—we can go forward, knowing that whenever we lose our way, which
will undoubtedly happen in the course of our life, we will be told.

> Here is a safe doctrine that I want you to know: one's own mind
> is a bad adviser, a poor pilot to steer the soul through the storms

---

7   C.S. Lewis, *The Screwtape Letters*, HarperSanFrancisco, San Francisco (CA)
    2001, pp. 70–71.
8   St. Teresa of Avila, *The Mansions*, VI, 10.
9   C.S. Lewis, *The Screwtape Letters*, pp. 69–70.

and tempests and among the reefs of the interior life. That is why it is the will of God that the command of the ship be entrusted to a Master who, with his light and his knowledge, can guide us to a safe harbor.[10]

5. God, the Others and Myself

We go back to the opening question of this chapter: *What is the order of charity?* Were we really deceived, according to St. Thomas Aquinas? Not really, if we read further in the *Summa Theologica*. We had stopped at Article 4 of question 26: *a man ought to love himself more than his neighbor.*

There is however a fifth article, *Should man love his neighbor more than his own body?* The answer is, of course, yes. I should love the others more than my comfort, my time, my desires....

Yes, we can indeed say that the order of charity is *God, the others and myself.*

10 St. Josemaría Escrivá, *The Way*, n. 59.

WHAT DO WE MEAN BY AFFECTIVITY?

1. A Teenager's Text Messages

Some time ago, a teenager sent me the following text messages (Figure 1), and later gave me permission to use it in this book.

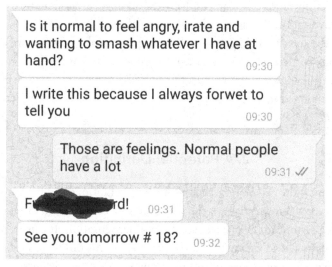

Figure 1. A Teenager's Text Messages.

He was a good guy going through a rough time, stuck on an emotional rollercoaster. He came to me for spiritual direction. I was trying to help him cope with his situation and identify the cause of his problems. He sent these messages shortly after he told me about some issues he was dealing with. Our conversation enabled him to achieve success in confronting these problems, and he experienced a sense of freedom. Yet he had worked himself up just by telling me about them, as these messages give proof. I must admit that my response was a bit flippant—and he sent me a reply that I had to censor for this book. Luckily, he was a good fellow and we had a good relationship, which explains why he immediately asked for an appointment for spiritual direction, as if nothing had happened.

Why do I mention this story? Because many people find it hard to acknowledge their emotions and to call them by name. As a result, they have trouble managing them. They would score poorly on the *Openness to Change* category from the Big Five personality traits (which we discussed in the first chapter). In other words, they are more *cautious*. They are surprised by their moods and by their reactions—whether internal or external—and they ask themselves, somewhat confusedly: "What is happening to me? Why do I feel this way?" I usually recommend that these people take it easy and watch the Pixar movie *Inside Out*: we all have the five basic emotions (joy, sadness, fear, displeasure and anger), permanently engaged in a conversation that is not always peaceful.

In the next two chapters I will attempt to explain the nature of these emotions so that we can *understand affectivity*, which happens to be the title of a book I often recommend.[1] I will also suggest a few ideas to make these reactions more balanced and mature. This is nothing less than to *educate affectivity*.

2. A Potential Definition

Affectivity is the *emotional reaction*—feelings, emotions and passions—that we all have when we relate to the world, to ourselves, and to others. When we face a significant event, we notice an inner sensation. It can be pleasant or unpleasant, and we say that *it has affected me*. Accordingly, we feel comfortable with positive events and unhappy with negative events.

We can appreciate that affectivity has a very important role: *to inform* us that something is pleasant or unpleasant; therefore it *leads us to act*, either to seek or to avoid that something. It would be the psychological equivalent of physical pleasure and pain. On the other hand, affectivity reveals the unity of body, mind, and spirit, because emotions, feelings, and passions often give rise to somatic reactions: rapid heartbeat, sweats, pallor, blushing, abdominal cramps, headache or backpain, etc. These are known as *psychosomatic reactions*.

1   F. Sarráis, *Entender la afectividad*, Teconté, Madrid 2017.

It is worth stopping at this point to make a distinction. In everyday language, "emotions," "feelings," and "passions" are virtually interchangeable, but in fact there is a great difference between them.

Emotions tend to appear suddenly. They can be very intense, and are usually short-lived. For example, an explosion of joy when we receive good news, or anger when we are insulted.

Feelings are similar, but they remain for a longer period of time, and they are usually less intense. Rather than a momentary reaction they are a steadier state, like falling in love.

Passions have features in common with the other two. They are intense and long lasting, and their main trait is to move us to action. The personality of the individual will make them more or less powerful and hard to resist. We can think of the "passionate" football fan who can only think of the next game all week, and nothing would stop him from watching it.

A classical classification of passions appears in Table 5 below. It can help us to understand them better.

Event	Perspective	Inclination	If we do not have it	If we have it
Good	Present	Love: *beginning*	Desire	Joy: *end*
Bad		Hatred	Flight	Sorrow, sadness, anxiety, boredom
Good	Future and arduous	Hope (it is looked upon as possible)	Courage, daring, action	Joy: *end*
Bad		Despair (it is looked upon as impossible)	Fear, freeze	Anger, vengeance

Table 5. Classification of passions.[2]

We can draw several conclusions from this short description. First, affectivity is something we feel or endure (*passion* is a rich term). Therefore, *in principle* we are not responsible for having them; sometimes we would rather not experience them: we endure or suffer them.

---

2   Adapted from: R. Yepes Stork, J. Aranguren Echevarría, *Fundamentos de Antropología. Un ideal de la excelencia humana*, Eunsa, Pamplona 1999[4], p. 48. These authors have summarized St. Thomas Aquinas, *Summa Theologica*, I-II, qq. 22–48.

The words *in principle* are highlighted because passions do not come from outside, which would render us helpless. On the contrary, we can *temper how much attention we pay* to these inner sensations to encourage the positive ones and hold back the negative ones. Most of us know that the more we think about an insult we have received, the angrier we become; on the other hand, if we see things from the other's perspective and forgive them (or at least try to) it is easier to calm down.

We can also *regulate our behavior*. Affections are given to us. But we always have the last word on what we do or do not do. Otherwise, we would be looking at a weak or even sick will. This is what happens in addictions, compulsive behavior, etc.

Finally, we have the task of *educating our own affectivity*, so that the appearance and intensity of emotions, feelings, and affections are more in keeping with how we would like them to be (within our life project or *schema of comprehensibility*, as we saw in the previous chapter). This is the main purpose of this book. Such a self-education will help us to love what is good and reject what is bad, and to make sure pleasure or pain don't lead the will to seek or reject them inappropriately.[3]

3. The Shortcomings of Affectivity

We have learned that affectivity plays a very important role in our lives. It tells us what is pleasant or unpleasant, and moves us to act accordingly. But we need to listen to it critically because it has several shortcomings.

Emotions, affections, and passions are very individualistic: each one goes its own way. They are like a child that tends to get carried away when it comes to food by what he likes or dislikes, and needs mother to tell him that some tastier foods are not healthy, and others that look less appetizing are necessary to become strong and healthy. A coordinator is required to arrange all the many preferences that sometimes oppose each other. This is the role of prudence, rightly called from ancient times *auriga virtutum*,[4]

---

3   For a deepening in the education of the feelings I recommend the book: A. Cencini, *"Dall'aurora io ti cerco": Evangelizzare la sensibilità per imparare a discernere*, San Paolo Edizioni, Cinisello Balsamo (Milano) 2018.

4   Cf. St. Bernard, *Sermons on the Song of Songs*, XL, 5.

the charioteer of the virtues; its role is to ensure that all the horses (often purebreds) pull together in the same direction.

The basic language of the affections is pleasant/unpleasant, not good/bad. Affections are not about moral subtleties; anger can drive to vengeance and pleasure seeking can lead to gluttony or to lust. Reason is a higher court. Its role is to regulate the moral dimension of the passions. In other words, it tells us which tendencies will help us to be better persons and which will make us worse.

Finally, affectivity only looks at the short term. Fear makes us flee as quickly as we can from a possible evil. But at times there is a higher good at stake. At those times we need to confront our fears with courage and daring. Prudence needs a guiding light to direct the horses towards that good. We will say this once more. The goal is the schema of comprehensibility, the life goal each one has freely chosen.

We come to the conclusion that affections are a good thing. It could not be otherwise, because they are part of our nature, and they are part of the satisfaction God experienced when he looked at creation after it was completed: "God saw everything that he had made, and indeed, it was very good" (Gen 1:31). It was not only good, but it was *very good*, as if he were reveling in the work that had come out of his hands. Only God could have done something like it.

Yet on occasion affectivity leads us to make mistakes. Why?

4. Original Sin and Its Consequences

Right after the creation account, Genesis tells us about the sin of Adam and Eve (cf. Gen 3). It is the well-known episode of the serpent and the forbidden fruit. (Incidentally, nowhere does it say that it was an apple.) Adam and Eve become guilty, not only of disobedience to a rather specific precept of God (they could eat from all trees but one), but also of mistrusting God and wanting *to be like gods*, thus denying that they were creatures.

We know that the outcome was a litany of misfortunes. They were expelled from paradise and they lost the harmony of the various dimensions of their being, among other things. The limitations of affectivity became difficult to manage, and each affection, emotion, and passion pulled in a different direction, threatening to tear the subject apart. Christian tradition has coined a word for this state of affairs: *concupiscence* (cf. Jn 2:16). It is defined as inclination to sin.[5] Sometimes concupiscence is misunderstood as a tendency toward evil. This is not so, because the will can only be attracted by good, even if it is only the partial good of anything real. Hence St. Augustine's definition of sin: "a turning away from the creator, who is more excellent, and a turning to created things, which are inferior" (*aversio a Deo et conversio ad creaturas*).[6]

Even the human mind was obscured. Not because it confused good and evil, but because it held a partial good as the absolute good. It became clouded and lost sight of the goal, which was to enjoy God for all eternity.[7] It is possible to do good after original sin, but there are so many obstacles in the path of the intellect and the will that in practice it is impossible to do it all the time.

Everyone notices an inner struggle, brilliantly described by St. Paul: "I can will what is right, but I cannot do it. For I do not do the good I want, but the evil I do not want is what I do" (Rom 7:18–19). Who has not felt the struggle between what one feels and knows he should do, between what one would like to do and what he ends up doing? Someone could answer that this is just what happens when the alarm goes off in the morning and stays in bed for a while, knowing well that it is time to get up right away. The Apostle too felt that tension, to the point of shouting: "Wretched man that I am! Who will rescue me from this body of death?" (Rom 7:24). He had his own struggles, which were probably more substantial than getting up in the morning. But it is also worthwhile listening to our Lord's answer on another occasion: "My grace is sufficient for you, for power is made perfect in weakness" (2 Cor 12:9). Christian life is not about pushing ourselves into making huge efforts. God is more than happy to give us extra help, his grace.

---

5   Cf. *Catechism of the Catholic Church*, nn. 405, 1264, 1426, 2514.
6   St. Augustine, *To Simplicianus, Responses to Miscellaneous Questions*, I, II, 18.
7   I like that what G.K. Popcak proposes in *Broken Gods: Hope, Healing, and the Seven Longings of the Human Heart*, Image Books, New York (NY) 2015. According to this American psychologist, capital sins are the mistaken and ineffective responses to the seven longings of the human heart (abundance, dignity, justice, peace, trust, well-being and communion) that only God can fulfill.

It is easy to appreciate that there is a grey area between psychology and morals. Disordered affectivity impels us to doing things, today and now, that are inappropriate because we are rational creatures made in the image and likeness of God: venting our anger on someone who insulted us, eating too much of what we like, drinking alcohol to excess, seeking a sexual union with someone other than one's spouse, etc. Yet, regardless of the tendency, we only commit a sin when we use our freedom to make the decision and indulge in those actions.

5. Restoring the Image of God

A poor and limited understanding of human nature leads us to be wary of the world of affections, and see it as a source of obstacles towards leading a solid Christian life; affections would just be a threat to fall into sentimentalism. People who think this way take for granted—implicitly most times—that the greater the ability to operate against the demands of sensitivity, or at least resist them, the greater the virtue. Kantian ethics would be an example: actions carried out by voluntary choice are not morally positive, and could indeed be negative. They would be a way to seek one's own advantage. The only ethically meritorious motive would be to act out of duty. This kind of ethics tends to voluntarism, to uptight and insensitive persons; they may be able to reach a high heaven, but they will find it hard to find happiness on earth.

Aristotle's approach can help us to correct this mistake.[8] His definition of virtue as *a good operative habit* has often been misinterpreted as a kind of routine to act in an automated way, always the same, with little effort and almost without realizing it. But this is not what Aristotle said. For him an honest person is not one who does not steal, but one who does not steal because it displeases him; he is attracted to money, and can feel tempted to take what is not his, but realizes that these kinds of things are not for him or not part of the lifestyle he has chosen. There is no elaborate thought process, it is done almost automatically or intuitively. It comes out from inside as a second nature, not as an external law that constrains the conscience.

8   Cf. Aristotle, *Nicomachean Ethics*.

This is the content of the formation of affectivity: that we, and those who come to us to receive formation, progressively and freely acquire that second nature, because we realize that it is best. To be attracted to and enjoy the good, although it may be arduous, although we remain attracted to other things, which are good in themselves, but which are incompatible with the direction we want for our own lives. This is only possible if the reason is educated (not only to know whether something is good or not, but also why), and if the will is also trained to be strong enough to resist undesirable attractions and remain steadfast in the search for goodness. Thus the three pathologies of affectivity can be prevented—namely, sentimentalism, voluntarism, and intellectualism. These pathologies indicate that one of the three dimensions of the person has taken over the other two.

This formation does not eliminate the sense of duty. Those who begin (or restart) their life journey need a clear and objective goal. Even those who are already a long way in can use this guide during times of darkness or uncertainty. However, to operate only out of a sense of duty is not only not enough, but also exhausting. To operate "because I want to"—ultimately out of love—gives meaning to one's life. And a well-educated affectivity ensures that we love the good.

In this way we learn to listen to affectivity and follow it, but not always letting it have the final decision. It acts as a traffic agent in a busy intersection. He lets some cars go, and when he hears an ambulance approaching he stops all traffic; he hails a rogue driver and does not let him drive again, etc. Mind and heart, intelligence and affections are no longer in conflict. They do not go hand in hand, but they act in synergy. And the individual goes forward in life, trying steadfastly to be better each day.

I think that this approach, based on the work of a pagan philosopher, is consistent with Christian anthropology. Anyone can take it up, believers or non-believers; and it *does not alienate* us from God. Pessimistic anthropologies are those where man is a magma of impulses that need to be repressed under the motto "don't trust what comes out of you."

On the contrary, Christianity encourages us to act in accordance with our deepest reality. It repairs the image of God that is wounded—but not destroyed—by original sin and by personals sins committed ever after. Adam and Eve were not angels, but people like us, with body, psyche and souls, with emotions, feelings and passions. The difference is that before the fall there was harmony among them. They saw all the good things in creation and were attracted to them, but they knew when to leave them for later, and they did it easily.

Educating affectivity is helping people to be free and to have deep inside them a foretaste of heaven: to feel and to act as children of God that have come out of his hand and are called to enjoy him for ever and ever.

THE DEVELOPMENT OF AFFECTIVITY BASED ON THE THEOLOGICAL VIRTUES

1. One of Many Approaches

Many books provide *formulas* to develop the world of affections in a healthy and mature way. Many of them do not even mention God, let alone the existence of a "beyond." The starting premise of this book is an openly Christian anthropology, but we recognize that insights from other sources can also be useful.

In this chapter I propose a different perspective for the development of our inner world. We will take as our starting point the three theological virtues—faith, hope, and charity. They are the framework for the entire life of a Christian. At the same time, I will draw out some practical ideas that can be used by anyone, Christians and non-Christians alike.

2. Faith

"Those who are unspiritual do not receive the gifts of God's Spirit, for they are foolishness to them, and they are unable to understand them because they are spiritually discerned" (1 Cor 2:14). St. Paul's style was quite straightforward, and no doubt he was inspirational for those who listened to his letters.

Some people cannot understand Christian life. They find it difficult because their initial assumptions are rather limited. Christianity is difficult to comprehend when pleasure is the rationale for distinguishing good from evil. In other words, it is difficult for those who ignore the fact that the *language* of affections is always limited. We saw this in the previous chapter. On the contrary, being open to concerns beyond the material world *brings order to* our passions and puts the soul *in sync* with the supernatural sphere. It is not only a matter of prayer, or of having *heavenly concerns*, but rather of promoting everything that showcases the non-material dimension of a person. We will start by looking at the corporal dimension of each of the senses to show how we can tune into the supernatural dimension, which is the main trait of a life of faith.

The sense of sight. Some questions are useful to work out someone's affective world: "What kind of movies do you like? Are you able to enjoy a work of art? When did you last go to a museum? What kind of novels do you read?" Is this related to affectivity? Yes, in a way.

Think about anyone who spends many hours every day watching action videos on TV or the computer (and this includes sport). They will find novels with many descriptions and adjectives (I dare not mention poetry) to be boring. Books or movies that are not so striking but help us reflect and contemplate are likely to trigger a yawn. This person is probably *stuck to the ground*, too close to the material world. Concern for higher matters would help him to boost his *inner world*.

Such a person could be introduced to age-appropriate activities that he is interested in, and little by little, widen and deepen his range of interests. Art (particularly good literature like the Russian classics, Tolstoy, Dostoyevsky, etc.) helps us to understand the wealth and complexity of the human psyche, both one's own and that of other people. Thus it helps us live with ourselves, with others, and with the world. The specific way to help someone grow in culture will depend on the individual's starting point. Excessive demands, especially at the beginning, will frustrate him to the point of thinking that *high culture* (art, literature, etc.) is not for him.

The sense of hearing. Video and audio material are so readily available on our smartphones that it is difficult to have time for the silent reflection we so badly need. Many people listen to music or podcasts when they travel by public transport. Others automatically switch on their music or podcasts when they get into the car, go for a run or bike ride, do odd jobs, and even when they study. There is a kind of fear of silence (like the *horror vacui* of rococo art). The problem with music—especially some styles of music like rock, heavy metal, etc.—is that it *fills up the brain*, and makes inner life problematic. How many people complain that they cannot concentrate when they study or pray. It is not surprising, for their brains have been subjected to non-stop stimuli all day long.

Radical changes, such as never or always, are not necessary. It is worth conducting the following experiment: try to make room for some *islands of silence* throughout the day. Jesus Christ did the same many times: "many crowds would gather to hear him and to be cured of their diseases. But he would withdraw to deserted places and pray" (Lk 5:15–16).

It is not just a matter of setting times aside to ponder, but of using the time of going from one place to another, or waiting times, *to let things come to the mind*. I was told by a psychologist that she enjoyed spending a few days each year in one of the cells that a cloistered religious community made available. The only condition was to respect the recollection of the community of monks. People who were looking for a few quiet days went there, whether to make a spiritual retreat, prepare for exams, work on their Ph.D. dissertations or simply to catch up on sleep for a few days. This psychologist explained that she spent her quiet days "contemplating her thoughts": she let her mind wander, to allow memories, thoughts, and images appear before her; she would look at them, interpret them, reflect on them, and get to know herself. It sounds odd, but it shows that she had a great inner life, that she was aware of the wealth she had within, and the desire to dwell on them.

Benedict XVI said in an audience:

> Silence can carve out an inner space in our very depths to enable God to dwell there, so that his word will remain within us and love for him take root in our minds and hearts and inspire our life. Hence, the first direction: relearning silence, openness to listening, which opens us to the other, to the Word of God.[1]

I am not talking about *empty silence* but about having a conversation with oneself, *and* with God. Indeed, the average Christian—not only the cloistered religious—is called to be contemplative in the midst of his daily occupations, and it is hard to do it without a minimum of interior silence. Not surprisingly, Cardinal Sarah has written a 248-page book with the title *The Power of Silence: Against the Dictatorship of Noise*.[2]

1   Benedict XVI, *General Audience,* March 7, 2012.
2   R. Sarah, *The Power of Silence: Against the Dictatorship of Noise*, Ignatius Press, San Francisco (CA) 2017.

The sense of taste. The sense of taste is good for a whole new set of questions: "What is your favorite dish? Where do you like to go when you eat out?" If the answer is, for example, the local takeaway to order a hamburger with chips and lots of ketchup, there is room to increase one's sensitivity and learn to appreciate more subtle flavors.

Of course, virtue is somewhere in the middle, following the classic dictum: *in medio virtus*. Sometimes reading the label of a bottle of wine is fun: it seems impossible that someone could capture the flavor that someone described, with more than a touch of irony, as "intense, complex, with rigor and paucity filled with hues, a touch of vanilla and sandalwood and a powerful tannic ending that reveals long toasted tones."

But here again sensitivity can grow. And again, little by little, a small effort can be made to stick to the dish that has been served today and slowly progress to more delicate cuisine, by eating carefully, savoring what we eat, and enjoying a good meal. As a side benefit, we'll make the person who cooks for us happy.

The sense of smell. We can relate this sense to bodily hygiene: being clean and neat, and perhaps a discreet fragrance, to make our appearance more pleasant. We could also include care for our clothes (clean, ironed, *presentable*). Although it has more to do with the sense of sight, we might include a clean shave, etc. It is not about looking picture perfect nor dressing to the nines at all times, but developing a sense of aesthetics regarding our external appearance. We could say the same thing of so many small pleasures in life that we miss without even realizing it: the scent of a flower, the smell of wet ground after the rain, the blossoming of spring in a garden, or even in the streets of the neighborhood, etc.

The sense of touch. It is the most basic and roughest of all senses. We could talk about refinement, *human tone*, and manners in social life. These are not mere social conventions, but rather a way to show respect in the ways we present ourselves, speak, eat, converse, and disagree.

To ask for things with a "please," to give thanks, to call others by their names instead of their nicknames, to offer polite greetings, avoiding certain four letter words, yawning, stretching in public—these are but a few examples that make our time with others so much more pleasant, and help develop the *inner environment* we have been talking about.

There remain the internal senses: *memory* and *imagination*. We can always switch on the *interior music* in the midst of external silence. However, this would make it just as difficult to achieve the recollection needed to live in the presence of God, to do mental prayer, or even to study for a few hours.

We are called to enjoy heaven, which is basically *to contemplate* God for all eternity. When some people hear this, they cannot help themselves: "How boring! All day seeing the same thing!" Yet, they miss the fact that eternal life is not about remaining still, always looking at the same thing, like watching a movie for the hundredth time. God's capacity is infinitely rich and full of hues, it can fill the intellect, the will, and the sentiments of the person who contemplates him. Hence it never sates, it is impossible to get bored contemplating God, provided we have a modicum of sensitivity. Heaven will be looking at God "without needing rest or feeling tired,"[3] while using our emotions, affections and passions.

I trust you have had a chance to visit (or simply view) the Sistine Chapel in the Vatican museums, one of the world's masterpieces. The scenes of Genesis in the ceiling; on both sides, frescos of the Old and New Testaments; in the front wall, behind the altar, the awesome scene of the Final Judgement. I have encountered two extreme attitudes among the thousands of daily visitors. Some of them, already tired of seeing so many masterpieces—the Sistine Chapel is at the end of the visit itinerary—stop, have a quick glance, and head for the exit after a few minutes. And there are those who spend hours contemplating such a grandiose panorama, both the overall scene and the little details. I know of people who go straight to the chapel to spend their whole Sunday mornings there. They are sensitive to art, to beauty, and I would dare say that they are more able to grasp the immaterial.

Occasionally, when I explain these things to a class, some of the students react with the comment, "I just like different things," or assert, "there is nothing written about taste." The latter is not quite right. There is a lot written about taste. Among other things, that there are people with bad taste. But tastes can be educated, and then help anyone to become attuned to the supernatural.

I am not referring to posh or snobby tastes, available only to those with

3   St. Josemaría Escrivá, *Friends of God*, Scepter, New York 2002[2], n. 296

specialist training and lots of money. We do not all have the same artistic instruction, but we are all capable of admiring beauty. I once heard that *contemplating that which we cannot possess* helps so much to develop a mature affectivity: a sunset, a pretty landscape, a funny building we come across in the street, or a work of art. Anyone can appreciate these things, and experience tells us that many people with only elementary education could teach the great figures of social life a thing or two.

Fascination with beauty is one way to sense God's greatness, and to open oneself to faith. Benedict XVI explains it in this way:

> It may have happened on some occasion that you paused before a sculpture, a picture, a few verses of a poem or a piece of music that you found deeply moving, that gave you a sense of joy, a clear perception, that is, that what you beheld was not only matter, a piece of marble or bronze, a painted canvas, a collection of letters or an accumulation of sounds, but something greater, something that "speaks," that can touch the heart, communicate a message, uplift the mind. [...] Art is able to manifest and make visible the human need to surpass the visible, it expresses the thirst and the quest for the infinite. Indeed it resembles a door open on to the infinite, on to a beauty and a truth that go beyond the daily routine. And a work of art can open the eyes of the mind and of the heart, impelling us upward. However, some artistic expressions are real highways to God, the supreme Beauty; indeed, they help us to grow in our relationship with him, in prayer.[4]

I think that Jesus' statement, "Blessed are the clean of heart, because they shall see God" (Mt 5:8), does not only mean that those who behave badly will be punished in hell. Jesus may have meant to say that those who cannot relate to the immaterial will not be able to enjoy a spiritual God, not even in his presence. "The unspiritual man does not receive the gifts of the Spirit of God, for they are folly to him, and he is not able to understand them because they are spiritually discerned" (1 Cor 2:14).

4   Benedict XVI, *General Audience*, August 31, 2011.

3. Hope

Hope is

> the theological virtue by which we desire the kingdom of heaven
> and eternal life as our happiness, placing our trust in Christ's
> promises and relying not on our own strength, but on the help
> of the grace of the Holy Spirit.[5]

It is the *virtue of the wayfarer*, who looks forward because he hopes to achieve something that is not immediate, but more worthwhile. It calls for a definite hierarchy of values and the courage to be detached from the here and now.

The problem we face today is that the current pace of life reinforces the present moment, especially with access to the internet in our pocket, in the shape of a smartphone, that gives us immediate information, and then we assume that everything *must be* immediate. Who has not been talking with someone, studying, or even praying, and the phone rings or vibrates? We realize that although the content of the message is not really important, and that waiting is the right thing to do, we cannot control our curiosity. Or the other way around, we send a WhatsApp to a friend, and we cannot wait until we see the icon indicating he has received it, or he acknowledges it with a text or an *emoji*. How many times have we looked at the phone after sending a photo or a message on Instagram or Snapchat, etc., to check whether anyone commented on it, or we got a *like*. The internet facilitates immediacy, but the price is that we have not learned to wait.

Yet, we know from experience that those who cannot control their curiosity find it hard to say *no* to the promptings of passions when they ask for something that is inconsistent with the lifestyle we want to lead, for instance, to stop reading something, or looking at a YouTube video or an inappropriate photo.

A useful challenge for us and for anyone: to wait for a few seconds before checking on that message, not to look so often at the news or social media. Even further: to put the phone on airplane mode sometimes (during lectures, when we study or pray) and to operate offline. Usually the result is

5   *Catechism of the Catholic Church*, n. 1817.

also immediate: not only do we listen, study, or pray better, but we also gain self-control. We become ready to grow in hope when we mortify what is before us because we are aware that there are greater things beyond it, and that they are worthwhile. And we are hereby in a position to live a happier life.

The *marshmallow experiment* is well-known in the field of educational psychology. It was first carried out by Professor Walter Mischel at the University of Stanford in 1962. In this study, children aged between 3 and 5 were offered a choice between one small but immediate reward, or two small rewards if they waited for a certain period of time. The researcher left the room for about 15 minutes and watched from an adjacent room where he could see the child without being seen, and then returned. The reward was either a marshmallow or pretzel stick, depending on the child's preference. You can have some fun on YouTube watching "marshmallow experiment" and what the children did to hold out for the period of time. If the experiment were carried out today for the first time, I fear Professor Mischel would be tried for child cruelty.

The result of the experiment was to be expected: only one third of the children managed to wait until they received the double reward. More interestingly, Mischel followed these children for several decades to assess their social adaptability. It turns out that when they reached maturity, the young children who had been able to wait held better jobs, had more stable marriages, more friends and interests, and fewer problems related to *sex, drugs, and rock and roll.*

There is a simple lesson for educators: *teach the children to wait from their early childhood* and they will be happier when they grow up.[6] Some people call this approach the *dynamic of delayed gratification.*

Pope Francis explains this point by relating it to other dimensions we have already looked at.

> In our own day, dominated by stress and rapid technological advances, one of the most important tasks of families is to provide an education in hope. This does not mean preventing children from playing with electronic devices, but rather finding ways to help them develop their critical abilities and not to

6   Cf. W. Mischel, *The Marshmallow Test: Why Self-Control Is the Engine of Success,* Little, Brown and Company, New York (NY) 2015.

think that digital speed can apply to everything in life. Postponing desires does not mean denying them, but simply deferring their fulfilment. When children or adolescents are not helped to realize that some things have to be waited for, they can become obsessed with satisfying their immediate needs, and develop the vice of "wanting it all now." This is a grand illusion which does not favor freedom but weakens it. On the other hand, when we are taught to postpone some things until the right moment, we learn self-mastery and detachment from our impulses. When children realize that they have to be responsible for themselves, their self-esteem is enriched. This in turn teaches them to respect the freedom of others. Obviously, this does not mean expecting children to act like adults, but neither does it mean underestimating their ability to grow in responsible freedom. In a healthy family, this learning process usually takes place through the demands made by life in common.[7]

People who cannot wait behave like puppets moved by their emotions, feelings, and passions that lead them to do what they know they should not, that they would like not to do, but who find themselves powerless to avoid them. They are not free, as St. Peter says, "for whatever overcomes a man, to that he is enslaved" (2 Pet 2:19). They will not get to enjoy those higher goals that can only be reached by renouncing, day in and day out, things which are good in themselves, but an obstacle in the path of higher goals. This will set the foundations to secure the greatest reward possible: heaven.

4. Charity

a) If I Have No Love, It's No Use to Me

This was the chorus of a song I learned in my parish many years ago, that paraphrases St. Paul's *hymn to charity* (cf. 1 Cor 13:1–13). It certainly fits with what we have said so far. Someone could think that the previous

7   Francis, Post-Synodal Exhortation *Amoris Laetitia*, March 19, 2016, n. 275.

sections can be summarized in one word: *self-control.* Not really, because the purpose of this book goes much further. Self-control was already preached by many pagan philosophers, like the Stoics, but what Christianity proposes is something else. The teachers of the Stoa proposed strict control of the passions for two reasons: to acquire absolute dominion over one's moods and to achieve *apatheia,* that de-sensitizes us against affections (both pleasant and unpleasant), because they could make self-control hard to achieve, and lead to frustration when they are not fulfilled. The Stoics motto would be something like this: "It is better not to love so as not to suffer."

Christianity has the occasional point in common with these doctrines, but the differences are greater. We have borrowed the pagan word *ascesis,* often used in both civil and religious spheres to point out the soul's struggle to open itself to wisdom and access it.[8] We have already seen that Christian life seeks to rebuild the order broken by sin. Not to become slave to passions, to recover the state prior to original sin as much as possible, and to live on earth the way we are called to live in heaven.

But the main difference is that Christians should absolutely not eliminate their affections; on the contrary, the idea is to direct them towards God, to love him "with all your heart, and with all your soul, and with all your strength, and with all your mind" (Lk 10:27). The problem is that nobody gives what he does not have: it is necessary to possess oneself entirely in order to put oneself entirely in the service of God and one's fellow men.

The pagan philosophers were not able to discover love, nor what satisfies all the needs of the human heart. The mere continence of the Stoics, an honest life, may resemble a virtuous Christian life, but it lacks its soul, that is love, and therefore it is unable to satisfy. Quite the contrary, God never leaves anyone feeling cheated.

I have digressed toward a more supernatural discourse, but I feel it is important to pause from time to time as we proceed, and remind ourselves that the purpose of this book is not to produce balanced persons, but Christians who can lead a life of self-giving, with definite demands but not losing one's

---

8   Cf. J. Gribomont, "Ascesis," in A. Di Berardino (ed.), *Encyclopedia of Ancient Christianity,* Vol. 1, InterVarsity Press Academic, Downers Grove (IL) 2014, p. 253.

peace of mind. I will leave the *vertical* discourse of the love to God to others because I will now focus on the *horizontal* dimension: love for others.

b) Loving and Feeling Loved

We all need to love and to feel loved. On this point I had to change my line of argument in the last few years. It would seem that the words *loving and being loved* would be more appropriate; however, we do not need *to be* loved as much as *feeling loved*. It matters little to be assured people love us, that they care for us, that we are the object of attention and manifestations of affection. If we do not *feel* loved—subjectively—all the rest may seem like a formality that does not provide for our needs.

It becomes a double challenge for those individuals responsible for the task of formation. On the one hand, the need to foster an environment in families, schools, associations, workplaces, etc. where everyone loves everyone else in such a way that *everyone notices it*. On the other hand, being aware of the affective needs of those who are under our charge, because some individuals need *many* shows of affection to feel that they are loved. These external manifestations may be physical (a kiss, a hug, a tap on the shoulder), verbal (encouragement, congratulations, thankfulness, showing we are interested), or gestures (a look, a deed of service, paying attention, etc.). This often happens when people had an *affection deficit* in childhood (they did not feel loved or appreciated by their parents), and there is an *emotional black hole*. They then unsuccessfully attempt to make it up as a young man or an adult in their dealings with others, but the way they try to draw attention to themselves is inappropriate or immature. The latter is a sensitive area, because it is difficult to balance accepting individuals as they are, and helping them to become better. We leave this matter for later when we look at the diseases of personality. For the time being we will focus on individuals without major problems.

What do we mean when we say that we need to love? In the words of St. Josemaría:

> for Christians (for you and me) our life is a life of Love. This heart of ours was born to love. But when it is not given something pure, clean and noble to love, it takes revenge and fills itself with squalor. True love of God, and consequently purity of

life, is as far removed from sensuality as it is from insensitivity, and as far from sentimentality as it is from heartlessness or hard-heartedness.[9]

This can be applied to the love of God but also to the love of others. We need to love not only because as Christians we should live charity, see God in others, etc., but because *loving is healthy*. And not loving, falling into being insensitive and hard-hearted, is an obstacle for the sound development of personality.

c) Learning to Love

"Learn to do good" (Isa 1:17), said the prophet Isaiah. Good intentions are assumed in all persons, certainly in the readers of this book, but good intentions are not enough. The trick is to do it in such a way that we hit *the target* with everyone before us. We should not worry because we will never achieve it completely. But at least we can try; and when we fail, when we trip, to make sure we get up. Several suggestions along these lines will help us to *love well*.

Being unselfish. Love seeks to give without seeking anything in return. We could object that this is true for charity in general—for instance, giving alms—but that friendship is not quite like that. We choose our friends because we like them, because they have something that meets our needs, and therefore there is an exchange (which in itself is not a bad thing) that is part and parcel of the nature of friendship. We can refine the description: friendship seeks to give without seeking *instant gratification*, a short-term gain for our *investment* of affection. It implies a degree of selflessness: I give something to my friend because he needs it. Even if he does not return the favor now, he will do it later if the occasion arises. But he owes me nothing if the occasion does not arise; even if it does, I do not feel I am entitled to demand it. When I say *give*, I mean not only material things, but also affection, company, time, interest in his tastes or his problems, although I may find them boring. Otherwise, we are not talking about real friendship but about a commercial exchange, or a *trade-off*. The same can be said of other kinds of bonds: family, classmates, workmates, etc.

9   Josemaría Escrivá, *Friends of God*, n. 183.

Respecting the way of being of other people. To love is to accept others as they are, not the way I would like them to be. It is to love them *with* their defects, not *despite* them. Hence charity adapts to the different tastes, rhythms, times, opinions, ways of being, ways of doing things, etc. The technical term is *respect for alterity (otherness)*. Therefore it avoids the urge to dominate, it is not invasive, it respects the silence of others, or the limits that they want to set to our curiosity. Accepting the defects of others means to reject complaints, criticism, and gossip when we encounter them.

Not to make cliques. We come across many people through the day, but we only coincide with a few on tastes, hobbies, ways of being, and therefore we have more contact with them, and that leads to friendship. But this is not the same as being locked in an exclusive circle. This would be an immature kind of friendship, more typical of children and adolescents. Charity is inclusive, respects and accepts everyone, even those we do not get on so well with.

Choosing one's friends. If a friend makes it hard for us to lead the kind of life we want to live, it may be worthwhile letting that friendship cool down a bit (not severing it altogether), and foster instead our friendships with those who will help us to become who we want to be with their example and their word.

Being empathetic. Five years before her baptism in 1917, Edith Stein defended her Ph.D. thesis, *On the problem of empathy*.[10] "Empathy" was originally a technical term, but it has been studied so much that it has become part of everyday speech. It is the ability to be aware of how other people are feeling, and to show emotional closeness to them. It is not just realizing' how the other feels, and it does not necessarily mean sharing their emotional state. It is rather understanding—with the mind and with the heart—what they are going through and helping them accept that it is alright to feel that way. Technically we call this *validating their feelings*.

Valuing. We have dealt with this concept two chapters ago, but I want to bring it up again: To value someone is to improve them; telling someone "You are worth it" helps them to be worth more.

A love "made to measure." Unequal people require unequal treatment. This is not contrary to justice. The classical definition of the virtue of justice,

10   E. Stein, *On the Problem of Empathy*, Springer Netherlands, Dordrecht 2013.

attributed to Ulpian, is "to give each one his due,"[11] and each person needs and deserves something different. The "off the shelf approach" is not right: we need to act with each person as he or she needs, not the way we would like to treat them. "Something is better than nothing," they say, but it may be the wrong thing for a particular person.

Appreciating the gestures of the other. This is the other side of the coin: to accept that each one has their own way to show their affection. Some people are more affectionate and thoughtful, others are more on the dry side. The former can overwhelm us with their affection, the latter could leave us somewhat unfulfilled. Respect for their way of being means that we should neither demand from them more than what they can give comfortably, nor force them to stifle their affection.

Letting others love us. If we all need to feel loved, our happiness is totally dependent on the others. Oddly enough some people put up obstacles—they are prickly, like *sea urchins*. Why is that so? Not so much because they do not need affection, but because they are afraid of suffering, like the Stoics. The reason is that love makes us vulnerable: if I become fond of someone, he might let me down, he might distance himself from me, he might die. Is it better not to love and not suffer? In the best-case scenario this would ensure a *moderately* tranquil life. But there would remain an unfulfilled need deep in one's heart. We need to open up without fear, whether we have had our share of disappointments, or discover that people are not perfect (not much of a discovery, because we are not perfect either). It has already been stated: everyone needs to learn to live in an imperfect world, surrounded by imperfect people like us who are also imperfect, but keen to improve.

Showing we are vulnerable. It is an aspect of the previous point, but worth highlighting. Some people unconsciously always try to appear solid, show no cracks, hide their shortcomings beyond what we would call a healthy modesty. When the shortcomings become evident (it will happen sooner or later) they justify themselves, compare themselves to others, and rationalize. When these attempts fail, they look vain; worse still, if they triumph and convince others that they are really solid, they will be like cold marble statues, which can be admired but not loved. Chances are these people were not valued as children,

11 *Digest*, I, I, 10.

and under a hard, exterior shell lies a good dose of insecurity and fear of rejection; it is as though they need to be perfect to earn affection. However, they forget that normal people like people who are like them: people with shortcomings, but also with good will.

Wasting time with other people. Going with someone for a stroll, or shopping, taking an interest in their ambitions and professional successes, talking about what is on the other's mind even when we think it is trivial. All those things can be manifestations of selflessness for the sake of the others. The film director Frank Capra's account of his first meeting with President Roosevelt is a good example:

> He knew that the overpowering presence of the President of the United States could turn strong men weak, and weak men imbecilic. So with a big friendly smile, and the glint of intense interest in his sparkling eyes, he would encourage you to talk about yourself, your family, your work, anything. "Well, I declare" he'd exclaim after you'd made some inane statement. By little laughs, and goads, and urgings such as "Really? Tell me more!"... "Well, what do you know!"... "Same thing's happened to me dozens of times"... "Oh, that's fascinating"... his warmth would change you from a stuttering milquetoast to an articulate raconteur. And you would remain forever in debt.[12]

Forgiving. St. John Chrysostom said, "Nothing makes us so like God, as being ready to forgive the wicked and wrong-doers."[13] The effort to overcome the shortcomings of others, to avoid resentment, expands man's heart. He becomes able to love in a divine way. This is how God loves us, who forgives us every time we go to confession; hence Jesus asks us to forgive everyone, "not seven times, but, I tell you, seventy-seven times" (Mt 18:22).

Helping others to become better. Our acquaintances are as excited to be good people as we are, and many would like to be good Christians as well. We can help them with our example, with a conversation that opens up

---

12 F. Capra, *The Name Above the Title: An Autobiography*, Macmillan, New York (NY) 1971, p. 346.

13 St. John Chrysostom, *Homilies on the Gospel of St Matthew*, XIX, 7.

new horizons, or making subtle suggestions on areas where they could improve. Always with prayer, praying for our relatives, for our friends, for those who depend on us in one way or another.

Looking at people in the eye. It is not uncommon when sharing a meal, meeting someone in the hallway, or even starting a conversation that the other person—even for a few seconds—focuses on his screen, ignores us or at most gives us his divided attention. When we are with someone it is much nicer to avoid *multitasking* and give them our time and attention: listen, look, smile.

5. A Fertile Ground

Asking for God's grace is paramount. But we also need to make sure that our life is fertile ground, with no rocks or thorns, capable of receiving that grace and make it bear fruit, like Jesus proposed in the parable of the sower (cf. Lk 8:4–15). The seed is always the same (God's grace), but it only blossoms and bears fruit in some places; in others, instead, it only yields sterile promises. It is food for the birds, it withers for lack of soil, or it is choked by the thorns around it.

In this chapter we have covered a few situations that foster the inner environment that facilitates the growth of the divine seed in one's heart. In the task of formation, it cannot be imposed, only proposed.

II. INNER GROWTH THROUGHOUT THE LIFE CYCLE

THE LIFE CYCLE

1. What Is the Life Cycle

This section begins with some general thoughts on what we understand by *life cycle*. Developmental psychology studies the growth of the individual throughout life, from birth to death, and how the individual develops his abilities in various domains:

- Cognitive: how he thinks.
- Affective: how he feels, and how he gets excited.
- Behavioral: how he acts.
- Social: how he relates.

The vital cycle is initially conditioned by biological aspects: the way a child thinks is simpler, because the brain is still not well developed; the main trait of the adolescent is the hormonal explosion that takes place during puberty; old age is determined by the wear and tear of the various organs and systems of the body, etc. However, physical influences are not the only ones: one's environment, upbringing, lifestyle, and efforts to improve one's character will accelerate or delay the progress of aging.

There are several traits in this process, and they are outlined below.

It is *constant*: the child is always evolving from the moment of birth, or rather from the moment of conception (although we will not speak here of the multiple influences the child receives during pregnancy).

It is also *progressive*: we always go forward gaining or losing skills as we get older. We should not confuse progressive with linear. There may be setbacks, such as the ups and downs of a company's profit charts, but the *trend-line* always points in a clear direction. Stagnation is an abnormal situation, like the *Peter Pan syndrome*, or the eternal teenager.

This is an *irreversible* process: going back to the thinking, feeling,

THE FORMATION OF AFFECTIVITY

relating, etc. of a previous stage of the life cycle is not healthy. This situation would be called *regression*. Similarly, the *involution* of an old person is a natural process of physical and mental decline. The elderly do not revert to prior stages (unless medicine manages to change that).

Finally, it is *necessary*: we need to go through each of the stages. A person who "could not be a child"—e.g., because life's difficulties forced him to join the workforce too early — may prematurely develop some of his skills, but it would be at the expense of others he will miss throughout his life. Likewise, each stage involves some *crises*, that must be overcome.[1] In several courses for married couples, when I mentioned this "need to go through each of the crises," some young parents asked me in fear if their young children had to all go through the dreaded crisis of adolescence. I am afraid that it is so. We will cover this in greater detail in the corresponding chapter, but we can offer some basic ideas here.

Crises are moments of change, when the previous way of thinking, feeling, relating, and acting is no longer adaptive, and it becomes necessary to find new ones. We can notice the tension typical of these moments: what was successful so far no longer works, new situations and challenges arise that require new instruments, and contextual expectations are no longer the same. Let us think of a boy who enters adolescence: his parents will expect him to take on responsibility for his studies, and the care of his younger siblings, school demands become greater, and he sees himself differently than he did a few years earlier, as he has new interests and ambitions. He sees himself forced to find new tools.

Another reason for this tension is that the traits of both stages must coexist during the transition period. The individual must forego the security

---

1   R. Guardini made interesting observations in *Die Lebensalter. Ihre ethische und pädagogische Bedeutung*, Matthias-Grünewald, Mainz 1986, pp. 38–43 (unfortunately not yet translated into English). He approaches life stages from a phenomenological and ethical point of view, not from a psychological or theological perspective. However, his outlook is compatible with that of the two authors that we will study. This is apparent in how he distinguishes the various phases and crises: mother's womb [birth], child [crisis of puberty], youth [crisis of experience], legal age [crisis of experiencing limits and of neglect (monotony)], mature person [crisis of separation from things and from people], elderly [crisis of the loss of autonomy] and senile person.

of the well-known in order to enter an unknown stage; sometimes this entails resistance to change; alternatively, he launches into a "flight forward" and rushes too quickly to the next stage.

The intensity and the length of these crises vary for each person, and they may be more or less conscious, more or less apparent, and the solution may be more or less traumatic. But in any case, they need to be resolved: in other words, finding the new instruments, better fitted to relate to oneself, the others, and the world. Otherwise, the individual will be left with shortcomings that will make life difficult, unless he manages to compensate for them. This will require extra effort on his part and on those around him. It is like what happens in a building which has a faulty structure because of some mistake in the construction process. Most of the time there is no need to demolish the building and start from scratch, but it may require a slow and painstaking task to reinforce the foundations and inject cement. It may be that the building can only be used for limited purposes. In the end the construction may be just as strong or even stronger than originally designed, but it has required extra work compared to a building built properly from the beginning. This is a good example, but it has important limitations, because personality is not a rigid block, nor is there a specific paradigm that everyone should aim for.

Different authors and psychological schools have suggested different arrangements of phases and stages of the vital cycle. The results vary, among other reasons because each particular school has its own approach and because there are personal and cultural differences at play. For our purposes we only need a very simple classification, and a relatively flexible age range:

- *Infancy*: from 0 to 11 years, that is from birth to puberty. A distinction is usually made between *early childhood*, from 0 to 6 years, and a *second infancy*, from 6 to 12; the distinction comes with the *use of reason*, which is the ability to be aware, and therefore, to be responsible for one's actions.
- *Adolescence:* from 12 to 18. It covers the period from puberty to the end of high school.
- *Youth*: from 19 to 30. This period involves leaving the family home, beginning one's working life and setting up a home of one's own.

- *Adulthood*: 30 to 65. It includes most of one's working and married life.
- *Third age*: from 65 onward, from the age of retirement.

We should not think of each stage as being a mere preparation for the next. Each has its own characteristics, challenges, and goals to be reached. Together with those already achieved they will facilitate further achievements. According to Guardini,

> Youth includes childhood, whether it was correctly or incorrectly lived; in the adult there is the upward impulse of the young; in the mature person, the fullness of activity and experience of maturity; in the elderly, the inheritance of life as a whole. [...] On the other hand, each stage is a particular form of life, it has its own meaning, it cannot be replaced by any other.[2]

Many authors cover the various life stages at length, or focus on just one of them. My intention is to cover only the aspects that are more directly related to the task of formation. It is very useful for an educator to know the specific traits of each stage: spiritually accompanying a fifteen-year-old boy is different than accompanying a seventy-year-old. The holistic understanding of a person, meaning his resources, challenges, and weaknesses, will allow the guide to help him overcome these crises, and make up for possible deficiencies acquired in the past.

One final thought: one of the main biological factors that impacts the vital cycle is being male or female. Sex has major repercussions at different levels. Girls reach adolescence earlier, have different social roles and expectations (which vary across different cultures), and to a certain extent have a different way of thinking; the experience of motherhood or fatherhood is obviously very different, etc. It is a very extensive topic, one that would require in-depth study, and it would cover each one of the stages. My aim here is more limited. Whenever appropriate, I will only highlight the specific traits for each sex that have greater bearing in each stage, and once

2   *Ibidem*, pp. 77–78.

more I will refer those who want further information to the suggested bibliography.[3]

Before moving on to the stages of the life cycle, I would like to present the thinking of two recent authors in the field of developmental psychology. They happen to be compatible (which is somewhat unusual in psychology) both with each other and with Christian anthropology. They will give us a theoretical foundation for the practical aspects that will be covered in the following chapters.

2. The Psychosocial Stages

The German-born American psychoanalyst Erik Erikson (1902–1994) developed the so-called *psychosocial theory.* He identified eight stages in life, which he called *psychosocial stages* (Table 6).[4] Each one of them represents a crisis or conflict. When the individual faces it, he develops an evolutionary competency, the first term of the dyad that gives name to the crisis. Acquiring this competency will prepare the person to confront the next stage, will enable him to solve it correctly and will give him a sensation of mastery, that Erikson calls *strength of the ego*, which can be partly superimposed on what we now call self-esteem.

On the other hand, there is a radius of significant relationships in each stage. It expands from the maternal figure (infancy) to the entire human species (old age). Finally, progress in each stage is guided by a *virtue*, or *basic*

3 Among many others, cf. J. Gray, *Men Are from Mars, Women Are from Venus. A Practical Guide for Improving Communication and Getting What You Want in Your Relationships*, HarperCollins, New York, New York (NY) 1993; B. Castilla de Cotázar, *Persona femenina, persona masculina*, Rialp, Madrid 1996; N. López Moratalla, *Cerebro de mujer y cerebro de varón*, Rialp, Madrid 2007; S. Feldhahn, J. Feldhahn, *For Men Only. A Straightforward Guide to the Inner Lives of Women*, Multnomah, Sisters (OR) 2013; S. Feldhahn, *For Women Only. What you Need to Know About the Inner Lives of Men*, Multnomah, Sisters (OR) 2013; M. Ceriotti Migliarese, *Erotica & materna. Viaggio nell'universo femminile*, Ares, Milano 2015; idem, *Maschi. Forza, eros, tenerezza*, Ares, Milano 2017.

4 Cf. E. Erikson, *The Life Cycle Completed*, W.W. Norton, New York–London 1998.

strength (also known as the *ego quality*), with an opposing *vice* or *core pathology* that threatens the resolution of the crisis and at the same time serves as an engine, because it forces the basic strength to be put into practice.

Age	Stage	Psychosocial crises	Radius of significant relations	Basic strengths	Core pathology
0–18 months	Infancy	Basic trust vs. mistrust	Maternal person	Hope	Withdrawal
1.5–3 years	Early childhood	Autonomy vs. shame and doubt	Parental persons	Will	Compulsion
3–5 years	Play age	Initiative vs. guilt	Basic family	Purpose	Inhibition
5–13 years	School age	Industry vs. inferiority	"Neighbor-hood," School	Competence	Inertia
13–21 years	Adolescence	Identity vs. identity confusion	Peer groups and outgroups; models of leadership	Fidelity	Repudiation
21–40 years	Young adulthood	Intimacy vs. isolation	Partners in friendship, sex, competition, cooperation	Love	Exclusivity
40–60 years	Adulthood	Generativity vs. stagnation	Divided Labour and shared household	Care	Rejectivity
60 years...	Old age	Integrity vs. despair	"Mankind" "My kind"	Wisdom	Disdain

Table 6. Stages and evolutionary competencies of Erik Erikson.[5]

These stages are not watertight compartments where one moves in a linear fashion; competencies are perfected in subsequent stages. In Erikson's words, "'after' should mean only a later version of a previous item, not a loss of it."[6]

5   Adapted from *ibidem*, p. 39.
6   *Ibidem*, p. 62.

3. The Theory of Attachment[7]

Most psychological schools agree that the personality of the adult person has its origin in the initial experiences of the child, even as early as the breastfeeding period, with the bond the child establishes with the lactating mother. One of the more popular approaches is the *theory of attachment* proposed by the British psychoanalyst John Bowlby (1907–1990).[8]

In summary, *attachment* is the affective bond that the child develops with its mother from the moment of birth, through the interactions between the two. It can also be applied to the relationships between the child and his father and his caregiver, and to a lesser degree to the relationships he will develop with other significant figures.

Experience tells us that the newborn seeks contact with its mother from the first days of life: she provides him with security, protection, and comfort, particularly when the baby feels threatened. Therefore, the child tries to be close to her, who is the *primary attachment figure*. On the other hand, he resists separation, and when it takes place, he feels anxious (precisely called *separation anxiety*) and a feeling of abandonment because it interprets the separation as a loss. When the mother returns the child settles down once more. The baby uses the attachment figure as the *secure base*, a point of reference from which it explores the physical and social world, after which it goes back to her. Finally, it seeks refuge in that figure in moments of sadness, fear or discomfort, in search of support and emotional well-being.

---

7   This section is adapted from F.J. Insa Gómez, "Affective Dependency and Perfectionism: A Proposal Based on Attachment Theory," in F.J. Insa Gómez, D. Parker (eds.), *Loving and Teaching Others to Love. The Formation of Affectivity in Priestly Life*, Independently Published, pp. 85–89.

8   Cf. J. Bowlby, *A Secure Base. Parent-Child Attachment and Healthy Human Development*, Basic Books, New York (NY) 1988. This theory has been widely used for a Christian approach to psychology; cf., among other examples, S. Bruno, "La costruzione dei legami di attaccamento nel rapporto uomo-Dio," *Tredimensioni* 5 (2008) 292–302; J.R. Prada Ramírez, *Psicologia e formazione Principi psicologici utilizzati nella formazione per il Sacerdozio e la Vita consacrata*, Editiones Academiae Alfonsianae, Roma 2009 146–157; P. Ciotti, "Teoria dell'"attaccamento" e maturazione di fede," *Tredimensioni* 7 (2010) 266–278; W. Vial, *Madurez psicológica y espiritual*, Palabra, Madrid 2016, pp. 72–75.

The above account describes a normal mother-son relationship. It would lead to the child's *secure attachment*. The baby *knows*—by instinct more than by conscious knowledge—that the mother is there unconditionally, and this strengthens the communication and affection between them. The psychic apparatus is developed through early childhood. During this period, the foundations of a solid building are laid because the world appears trustworthy and consistent: the child feels he is not alone, that he is valued, because he is worth something in himself. He knows that he is loved and supported.

When the child cannot establish this bond with the biological mother due to her death, broken families, etc., the role can then be taken up by a *substitute attachment figure*, who takes on the mother's function. It can be the father, a grandmother, a caregiver, etc.

What happens when the mother cannot carry on this mission? Then an insecure attachment ensues. Its origin might be caused by:

- An *absent mother*: this is often the case for children raised in orphanages; when parents split when the child is young, or when the mother spends long periods away from the home, and the child has not been able to form that tight bond with her, nor with anyone else that takes on the role of substitute attachment figure.
- An *anxious mother*: she is unable to *absorb* the anxiety of the child (to *sponge* off) because she becomes distressed at the sight of her child's anxiety, and transmits her own anguish to the child, so that both enter a distress cycle.
- An *overprotective mother*: she does not allow the child to become nervous, therefore she prevents him from exploring the unknown, or opening up to the world. As a result, the child does not learn to endure the frustrations caused by suffering or manage his states of anxiety. Since life will provide these situations, the child will end up developing a low frustration tolerance.
- An *inconsistent* mother: this is the most detrimental style. The mother reacts differently to the same stimuli; this is the case of unstable personalities, or when they abuse drugs or alcohol. If the child misbehaves and the mother is calm, she will punish him proportionately; but if she is drunk her response will be uncontrolled. In the end, the simple

fact of hearing mother approaching will result in the child becoming tense. With his poor capacity to reason, he will not know what to do, whether to speak, or tell her about his successes and failures; the child will often withdraw into silence. He sees that the world is inconsistent, unreliable, and he can do little to change it.

The early experiences have a bearing on future development. If the foundations are not strong enough, if an insecure attachment has developed, difficulties will arise in different settings, when the child, the teenager, and the adult attempt to explore the world and interact with others. Then the individual will continue to seek contact or proximity with a secure base, whether this be the mother or a *substitute attachment figure*, but will never reach the autonomy he needs. In other words, he will seek emotional support when he faces any problem because he will be unable to manage it by himself; but if he finds someone to solve it for him it will only make his dependence worse. He will develop an unhealthy *separation anxiety*; this happens every year in the first few days of school. The child cannot adapt to the mother's absence, cries all day long, and must be picked up by a parent.

Such a person develops low self-esteem, because he has been taught that he is not able to fend for himself. He will find it hard to establish two-way equal relationships, and will seek either *dependence* (if he feels incapable) or its opposite, *dominion*. The latter happens when he has been acclaimed by his mother for everything he ever did; this has led him to believe that he is best, and to despise everybody else; he develops a *hypertrophy of the ego*, typical of a narcissistic personality. In either case, when the child leaves the family environment, he will not be able to establish normal relationships on an equal-to-equal basis. The tendency will be either to submit or to impose oneself, and to manipulate others in every case. We will return to these extremes in the section on pathological personalities.

The style of attachment acquired in early childhood influences the personality of the adult. Indeed in the 1980s various authors worked to adapt Bowlby's theory of attachment to couples' relationships and their attitudes toward work.[9] From these studies, Kim Bartholomew and Leonard

9 Cf. M. Main, N. Kaplan, J. Cassidy, "Security in Infancy, Childhood, and Adulthood: A Move to the Level of Representation," in I. Bretherton, E. Wa-

Horowitz[10] identified four styles of attachment in the adult, based on two parameters: self-image (it tends to establish dependence when it is negative) and the image of others (it leads to intimacy avoidance when it is negative) (Figure 2).

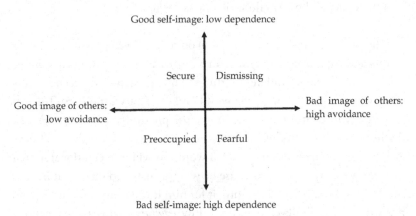

Figure 2: Kim Bartholomew and Leonard M. Horowitz styles of adult attachment.

- *Secure*: they have a more positive outlook on themselves and on their relationships. They are comfortable both in situations of emotional affectivity and of autonomy, and manage to balance them.
- *Preoccupied*: negative self-image combined with positive image of other people. They seek intimacy, approval, and response in their relationships, and become excessively dependent. They can display high levels of emotional expression, worry, and impulsiveness.

ters (eds.), *Growing Points in Attachment Theory and Research*, Wiley-Blackwell, Boston (MA) 1985, pp. 66–106; C. Hazan, P.R. Shaver, "Romantic Love Conceptualized as an Attachment Process," *Journal of Personality and Social Psychology* 52 (1987) 511–524; idem, "Love and Work: An Attachment Theoretical Perspective," *Journal of Personality and Social Psychology* 59 (1990) 270–280; idem, "Attachment as an Organizational Framework for Research on Close Relationships," *Psychological Inquiry* 5 (1994) 1–22.

10 Cf. K. Bartholomew, "Avoidance of Intimacy: An Attachment Perspective," *Journal of Social and Personal Relationships* 7 (1990) 147–178; K. Bartholomew, L. M. Horowitz, "Attachment Styles Among Young Adults: A Test of a Four-Category Model," *Journal of Personality and Social Psychology* 61 (1991) 226–244.

- *Dismissive*: positive self-image and negative image of other people. They display a high level of emotional autonomy. They see themselves as self-sufficient, emotionally invulnerable, and in no need of close relationships. They tend to repress their affections and distance themselves from others.
- *Fearful:* self-image and image of other people are both negative. They have mixed feelings about relationships because they feel the need for contact with other persons, but they are uncomfortable with emotional intimacy for fear of being harmed. Therefore, they either reject close relationships or feel very tense when they have them. They tend to repress their affectivity.

Anyone in the last three categories will be apprehensive when they have to make decisions where there is no guarantee of success, such as choosing a career path or a job, or a vocation such as marriage or dedication to God. On the other hand, insecure attachments have implications on one's relationship with God. Those who have internalized their figure of attachment as not fulfilling their needs for affection and protection, but as intransigent, controlling, demanding, punishing, arbitrary and impervious to other people's needs, will find it difficult to find peace in the Lord.

The same biases can also be projected onto the figure of the educator, who will be in a privileged position to *heal the attachment*, that is, to allow the subject to experience (not only to *know* because he has been told, but to *live* it) that he is valuable, that he can relate to others—his peers, his superiors and his subordinates—confidently, that it is worthwhile to undertake projects without certainty of success, that he can take risks, that a mistake is not a fatal failure. This healing process will help him feel accepted and loved unconditionally, while he is gently and respectfully encouraged to improve. This context will shore him up when he dares to explore the world autonomously, and will prevent him from feeling blocked by the fear of failure, or discouraged by the inevitable setbacks in life. It is a key role in any task of formation. We will therefore return to it on two occasions: when we talk about personality disorders, and in the epilogue, where we will propose a healthy formative style.

We will end this rather theoretical section by repeating what we said at the end of the first chapter: we all have had negative experiences in our early years, and we still have small emotional deficits that we attempt to make up for in our relationships. Ultimately, we are all of us a little insecure. Therefore, we should not worry if we notice—in ourselves or in others— some of the traits that have been described, as long as they do not have a significant impact on our activities or relationships, and we don't lose hope of continuing to improve throughout our whole lives.

CHILDHOOD AND ADOLESCENCE

1. The Child

a) The Developmental Stages of Childhood

This stage extends from birth to puberty, and is usually divided into first and second childhood.[1] We will not cover this section in great detail because it is only partially related to the aim of this book. However, it needs to be addressed so that the review of the vital cycle may be complete. More importantly, we have already pointed out that the achievements and shortcomings of this stage will have a bearing on subsequent stages.

Early childhood extends to the age of 6. The child develops basic motor skills, language skills, etc., over this period. He also builds character, and moral conscience begins to emerge. It is a crucial period, to the point that Erikson identifies in it three of the eight developmental stages.[2]

The first stage is *infancy* (0–18 months). It can be added to what has been said about the theory of attachment can be repeated here: the acceptance, security, frustration tolerance, and emotional satisfaction that the child develops relating to parents and caregivers extends to other relationships.

Table 7 (a summary of Table 6 from the previous chapter) shows that the maternal relationship is most decisive, as we would expect. The crisis to be overcome is the dissonance between the *basic trust* shown toward the

1   The work of the Swiss biologist Jean Piaget on the psychological development of the child is crucial. Cf., among other works, J. Piaget, *The Moral Judgment of the Child*, Free Press, New York (NY) 1965[19]; J. Piaget, B. Inhelder, *The Early Growth of Logic in the Child. A Classification and Seriation*, Routledge and Kegan Paul, London 1964.

2   Cf. E. Erikson, *The Life Cycle Completed*, W.W. Norton, New York-London 1998, pp. 77–82.

mother and the *basic mistrust* that may occur when she cannot satisfy his needs. The basic strength is *hope*, the expectant desire to begin to relate to the world,[3] and the core pathology is *withdrawal*: not daring to explore the world because it feels dangerous.

Age	Stage	Psychosocial crisis	Radius of significant relations	Basic strength	Core pathology
0-18 months	Infancy	Basic trust vs. basic mistrust	Maternal person	Hope	Withdrawal
1.5-3 years	Early childhood	Autonomy vs. shame, doubt	Parental persons	Will	Compulsion
3-5 years	Play age	Initiative vs guilt	Basic family	Purpose	Inhibition
5-13 years	School age	Industry vs. inferiority	"Neighborhood," school	Competence	Inertia

Table 7. Stages and developmental competencies in childhood according to Erikson.[4]

Early childhood (1.5–3 years) follows. The radius of significant relations expands to both *parents*. Erikson links it to two factors: cognitive development that provides the child with sufficient self-awareness, and muscular development/sphincter control. The latter gives the child great *autonomy* because he is no longer dependent on his parents for self-care. He only achieves it gradually, with breakthroughs and setbacks that imply occasions of *shame and doubt*. These are the two components of the crisis.

Achievement helps the child to feel bodily independent, and this gives him the chance to consolidate his own self, that is, to assert his own *will* on the others. It is the core strength of this stage. It sets the foundation for the process of emancipation, which will be completed at a much later date. Sometimes the child asserts himself *in opposition* to the others, which results in episodes of negativity and stubbornness. Here *compulsion* is the core pathology.

The third stage is the *play age* (3–5 years). The radius of significant

3   Cf. *ibidem*, p. 59.
4   Adapted from *ibidem*, pp. 32–33.

relations expands to the *basic family*. During this period there is rapid physical and intellectual growth, and the child is more energetic and talkative. He becomes curious (the age of asking questions non-stop), and his games and fantasies may have sexual connotations (it coincides with Freud's *phallic stage*; in other words, the Oedipus complex).

On the other hand, he comes into contact with other children, particularly through play. This tests his imagination, creativity, capacities and personal abilities. The motor development that takes place at this time enables him to act with greater *initiative*. This is the main skill of this stage and the first component of the crisis he will have to overcome. The second component is *guilt*, described below.

In this stage the child makes many discoveries and develops many new skills. *Purpose* is the basic strength. The parents' role is to provide support, encouragement and guidance in the child's journey of discovery, and to answer his multiple questions. On the other hand, reprimands and/or lack of support can cause the child to lose his initiative (*inhibition* is the core pathology), and bring on fear and *guilt*. We need to remember that *initiative* and *guilt* are the dual components that characterizes the crisis of this particular stage.

The main feature of the *second childhood* (5–13 years, according to Erikson) is that the child arrives at the *age of reason*. He acquires an awareness that he is master of his actions, and therefore responsible for them. This stage lasts till the advent of puberty, which varies a lot. It happens around the age of 10 for girls and 13 for boys. Erikson calls it the *school age*, meaning elementary school.[5]

The radius of significant relations widens to include *neighborhood* and *school*. The child displays a tremendous interest in learning and doing things. He asks, explores, plans and tries out a variety of activities, either by himself or with others. This forces him to bring into play his skills and determination. The basic skill he needs to acquire is *industry*. According to the results, he will feel that he is capable (the basic strength is *competence*), and his self-image will improve. Otherwise, when he compares himself to his peers he will be frustrated and feel insecure and less able. The second component of the crisis is *inferiority*, and the core pathology is *inertia*. Support and

5   Cf. *ibidem*, pp. 74–77.

encouragement to develop his skills, despite everyday disappointments or failures, are important both at home and (especially) at school.

b) Guidance for Formators

All those who help form children (parents, teachers, etc.) should encourage the traits outlined below, which are listed in no particular order.

First, *self-esteem*. We have seen already that the child will develop it if he feels appreciated. This can be combined with correction, if necessary.

Developing *strength of will* is important. It will lead him to pursue diffi-cult or long-term goals. Initially, a child is motivated by immediate wants or the most basic impulses. He wants to feel good or cease feeling bad *right now*, even if it means doing wrong or ceasing to do good. These short-term solutions are very basic. Achieving them will not help him feel fulfilled as a person. On the other hand, when he realizes that, with patience and per-sonal effort, he has managed to finish a task, or complete a toy building, etc., he will think or say: "I did it by myself. I can do it."

Frustration tolerance will help him not to sink when he experiences a small failure. He will get up and try again. Some authors call this *resilience*, the ability to adapt to adverse situations in a positive manner.[6] It requires the educator to remain close by, to console, or gently to encourage him to begin again. It also means stepping back at the right time to allow the child to achieve his goals, which should be commensurate with his abilities. Needless to say, there will necessarily be frustrations along the way if the child is to develop frustration tolerance. If he is always "rescued" he will not be protected against life's setbacks.

In a conversation with a successful businessman, I once suggested that

6   The greatest proponent of this concept (though he did not originate it) is Boris Cyrulnik. whose main works are: *The Dawn of Meaning*, Mcgraw-Hill, New York (NY) 1992; *The Whispering of Ghosts: Trauma and Resilience*, Other Press, New York (NY) 2005; *Resilience: How Your Inner Strength Can Set You Free from the Past*, Penguin, New York (NY) 2009; *Talking of Love: How to Over-come Trauma and Remake Your Life Story*, Penguin Books, London 2009. He was Jewish and managed to hide from the Nazi regime during the Second World War, though his parents were deported and perished. After the war he studied medicine and specialized in psychiatry. There is a marked autobiogra-phical tone in his books.

he was too soft on his children. Much to my surprise, his answer was: "Look, I started from nothing, and my life has been very difficult. I achieved everything through will power. I want to spare my children all that I had to suffer." His concern for his children's well-being is unquestionable, but it was not easy for him to realize that the children would find it hard to develop that same will power if they did not go through some of the setbacks that he himself overcame.

A *sense of reality* is another trait worth encouraging. A certain amount of *magical thinking* is normal. This is a slight confusion between dreams, desires and reality, even in one's problem solving. For example, children often acquire an *imaginary friend* between the ages of two and three. The phenomenon should not generate surprise or alarm. It is a positive factor which helps them work through fears and conflicts and become creative. But the child should be helped to live in the real world, and especially be prevented from hiding behind his make-believe world to escape from the reality of frustrations and setbacks.

Parents are called to *develop the child's moral conscience*. When we say that a child has acquired reason, we mean that he is self-aware and aware that he is responsible for his actions. Initially, this awareness will be the result of what he has seen and lived at home. Erikson gives away his psychoanalytic background when he claims:

> during childhood, the parents' prohibitions and prescriptions are internalized to become part of the super ego; that is, an inner, higher-than-thou voice that makes you "mind"; or an ego ideal that makes you anxiously or proudly look up to your higher self and helps you later to find and trust mentors and "great" leaders.[7]

Little by little the infant learns to tell good from evil by listening to his conscience rather than by imitating what he hears from his parents. His judgment becomes self-governing. This allows him to develop a critical capacity about others (he begins to question his parents) and about himself (his conscience). He becomes aware of the meaning of moral evil. Children's

7   Erikson, *The Life Cycle Completed*, p. 53.

first confession often takes place between the ages of eight and ten. The child learns to distinguish what he has learned at home, good manners, and how things should work, from sin. In confession, very young children often accuse themselves of having fought with their brother, pulled their sister's hair, telling the odd lie, and picking their nose, but they make little distinction between all these things. They need someone who will patiently explain to them how these various actions should be assessed differently. It is also important to be aware that some children are very sensitive and have obsessive trends. If they are not taught to manage their insecurities or if they are ruled too rigidly, they may become scrupulous.

As they broaden the radius of significant relations, they should be encouraged to be *altruistic*. On this point I refer to the *extension of the sense of self* that Allport talks about. It will help the kid to overcome the egocentrism typical of children, which means the child's inability to see a situation from another's point of view. It is quite different from egotism or selfishness, which is more moral than psychological in resonance. As we mentioned earlier, the child will instinctively go for the biggest piece of cake, the ripest piece of fruit, the best candy bar, regardless of who and how many others also want some. Little by little, spontaneously and with encouragement, he will learn to look around and give up his personal preference (which is part of his *self*) for the sake of others. The foundations are thus set for a rich social and religious life, and to build a suitable hierarchy of values.

I would like to raise one final point about this stage. The child's brain is still rather immature from a *cognitive* viewpoint. He will think more concretely than abstractly. Indeed, a child is not taught to add by formulas like "two plus two equals four," but rather, "I have two apples, and I get two more apples, so now I have four apples." The same applies to the way we talk about God, both at home and in religious education. For instance, those who prepare children for their first Communion must "come up with analogies" for the child to understand God (we will see that during adolescence, the opposite tends to be the case). It is done intuitively when we teach children to pray. They are encouraged to talk to Jesus present in the Tabernacle, on a one-on-one basis, to treat God as a father, etc.

I would like to make a quick digression. A child raised in a stable family with a reasonable upbringing (not necessarily perfect) will have a pleasant, positive image of a father, and he can transfer this image to God with ease.

However, there is an increasing number of children from broken families, or children neglected by their parents. Though it may be more appropriate for the next section, I will mention the following anecdote, which shocked me as it occurred. A teenager approached me because he wanted to re-start his Christian life. We talked about prayer, the sacraments, virtues… and at the end I suggested that he talk to God trustingly, as he used to talk to his father. He stopped me in my tracks: "Look Father, if I had to talk to God the way I talk to my dad, I would rather be an atheist, because my dad is a bad man" (I've toned down the term he actually used). His father had left his mother and siblings—all very young—and ran away with his secretary. Furthermore, he had been very reluctant to help them financially (though he was in a position to do so) and forced them—especially his mother—to endure considerable hardship.

"How do I get out of this one?" I thought. Thankfully, the Holy Spirit came to my aid, and I managed to explain that his father may not have been good, but he knew how his father *should have* behaved. And that he knew the fathers of many friends who did care about their children. "Well, then," I said, "God is better than the best of fathers." He understood, and began to talk to God as if God were "the father he would have liked to have had."

We would do well to remember that we are not slaves to genetics, to our temperaments, or to our past lives. The following words of Pope Francis can help us here.

> Perhaps your experience of fatherhood has not been the best. Your earthly father may have been distant or absent, or harsh and domineering. Or maybe he was just not the father you needed. I don't know. But what I can tell you, with absolute certainty, is that you can find security in the embrace of your heavenly Father, of the God who first gave you life and continues to give it to you at every moment. He will be your firm support, but you will also realize that he fully respects your freedom.[8]

8   Francis, Post-Synodal Apostolic Exhortation *Christus vivit*, March 25, 2019, n. 113.

2. The Adolescent

a) The Ever-Present Generational Gap

> Today's youth is rotten to the core. Young people are bad and lazy, they will never be like the young people of the past. Today's young will not be able to maintain our culture. (Engraved in a clay vessel from ancient Babylon, year 3000 B.C.)

> The world as we know it has reached a critical stage, children no longer listen to their parents: the end of the world cannot be far away. (Priest of ancient Egypt, 2000 B.C.)

> There is no hope for the future of our country if today's youth were to take power tomorrow because this youth is unbearable, without any limit, it is terrible. (Hesiod, year 720 B.C.)

> Our young love luxury, they are rude, they mock authority and have no respect for the elderly. Today's children are tyrants; they don't get up when an old man enters a room, they respond badly to their parents. In a word, they are bad. (Socrates, 470 B.C.)

The internet is full of similar words of wisdom from antiquity, though I doubt that the quotations are authentic. (I have not managed to find the source of any of them.) Yet they reflect a reality. In every age the young have been ruthlessly criticized, and the criticism is usually followed by "it wasn't like that when I was a kid." If we ever think or say something similar, we shouldn't worry. It's only a sign that we're getting old!

Many people wonder whether today's adolescents are like those of previous generations, or whether they have specific characteristics. I would say that, by and large, adolescents of the early twenty-first century are basically the same as teenagers of past generations. There may be a few *quantitative* differences: they may be more or less solitary, tolerant, autonomous, constant, tough, self-sacrificial, altruistic, insecure, resilient. But there are some *qualitative* differences worth mentioning.

Young people today are *highly skilled*. Almost 100% of children in Western societies go to elementary school, and most adolescents have access to high school, followed by easy access to a university. Their academic record is often better than what their parents achieved. Not surprisingly, they may think things through to a greater extent. They want to make things their own, they are ambitious and want to feel free, autonomous, and in control of their future. On the other hand, more is expected of them—both from others and from themselves—and from a very early age they may feel great pressure to achieve, both professionally and socially.

A result of the above is a *crisis of authority*. Toward the end of the sixties the slogan "Forbidding is forbidden" was made popular by a small group of young people. At the time they were a marginal group, but the message has been taken up by several generations. The argument from authority ("because I say so," "it has always been this way") does not hold anymore. Rules are seen as arbitrary measures that should be flouted (like in *Harry Potter*), and the decisions of authority figures have to be justified. It's not a lack of trust, but a different way of thinking. However, rejecting authority comes with a price tag. There is no clear guidance, and adolescents can feel adrift in a sea of decisions. They do not know how to manage their freedom, and may have problems building their own identity.

People travel much more than in the past. *It becomes harder to establish stable relationships*, and settle in a neighborhood, school, city, or even country. This becomes one more factor that fosters individualism. Online contacts partially compensate for it, but online relationships are not the same as physical presence.

Immediacy is the fourth feature. Think of the world as seen by *digital natives* (people born in the age of the internet). Not too long ago, we had to wait for the morning paper to find out which team won. Today we look it up on the internet and have the information in seconds. But we have not learned to wait. The topic of delayed gratification was already discussed in earlier chapters.

Young people today represent the *civilization of images*. They have been raised in the audio-visual era and have become familiar with information and communication technologies from a young age. This has a bearing on how they think, learn, listen and relate to others.[9] For example, they often cannot cope with a professor giving a lecture from a podium, and lose focus after a few minutes. They need dynamic and interactive "learning experiences," preferably with videos, PowerPoint, Prezi, etc. It becomes a challenge for their teachers. Thorough knowledge of a subject is not enough, they also need to keep up with new teaching technologies (which may or may not be available to them).

A consequence of the above is *multitasking*, one final feature. Many other people have had to multitask, but for them it's innate. To write this chapter, I've opened four programs on my computer with material to be included, and for further information I search the web. I often fall into the temptation of checking items unrelated to what I am working on, and from time to time I also check my emails. My adolescent years are way behind me, but I can understand that the members of Generation Z (born between 1994 and 2010) may have problems concentrating on one specific task, when they have grown up in this environment from day one.

You might argue that those are merely *quantitative* features, but I do not think so. The mind, emotions, and behavior of today's adolescent have been forged with a different operating system. It places demands on their educators, who are not familiar with the style, because they were themselves educated in a different way. It is often difficult for them, and it contributes to generational conflict, somewhat like trying to work with iOS and Android at the same time.

b) Setting the Boundaries

Adolescence begins with puberty, an explosion of sexual hormones that begins around the age of 10 for girls and 13 for boys. If I were to describe the drama of adolescence with one word, it would be *imbalance*. The process of maturing has been reasonably smooth until now. But at this stage speed bumps can come into play in several areas:

9   Cf. L.A. Ruiz, "Comunicare la fede nel secolo XXI," in F.J. Insa Gómez, *Ti concedo un cuore saggio e intelligente. La dimensione intellettuale della formazione sacerdotale*, EDUSC, Rome 2020, pp. 197–216; M. McLuhan, Q. Fiore, *The Medium is the Massage. An Inventory of Effects*, Penguin Books, London 2008.

- *Physiological*: they can become parents barely two years after puberty.
- *Physical*: they have a virtually "brand new" body, and barely recognize themselves in it.
- *Psychological*: they are not ready to take on serious responsibilities, nor even to take care of themselves.
- *Social*: their role is still conditioned by the family, and it will take a long time for them to have the financial independence that enables them to leave their parents' home to set up their own.

This imbalance comes with insecurity, fear, and tensions within oneself and with others. The question they ask themselves, whether they realize it or not, is: *who am I?* They do not see themselves as children anymore, and they resent being treated as such, or given simple tasks. But they realize that they are not yet adults. They are attracted by serious responsibilities, but are afraid of them. They realize they are not ready to make decisions about their own lives, and they fear failure. They sometimes react to this insecurity by making rash decisions, purely by impulse. Furthermore, they still like some of their past toys and it's possible to find an adolescent secretly playing with them.

The end of adolescence is also variable. It is usually set at 19, more or less when they finish high school and either go to university or join the workforce. By then their bodies have matured to adulthood, they have a modicum of emotional balance, and begin to be financially independent. On the contrary, some of them become *eternal teenagers* or the *rebels without a cause*, who can be adolescents well into their thirties or even forties.

Erikson states that the defining feature of this period is *identity struggle*, the first component of the crisis of this period.[10] The other component of the dyad is *identity confusion* (Table 8). In a previous publication he had defined the identity of the self as the sum of two factors: awareness of internal equality (*inner sameness)* and continuity of one's significance in the eyes of others.[11] The adolescent needs to work out what he has been so far—a child—in order to accept some features and to reject others. And in what remains he needs to acknowledge the continuity with what he has

10   Cf. Erikson, *The Life Cycle Completed*, pp. 72–77.
11   Cf. idem, *Childhood and Society*, Penguin Books, Harmondsworth 1965², p. 253.

been so far—"I remain being myself though I have changed." He also needs others to continue to acknowledge him.

Age	Stage	Psychosocial crisis	Radius of significant relations	Basic strength	Core pathology
13-21 years	Adolescence	Identity vs. identity confusion	Peer groups and outgroups. models of leadership	Fidelity	Repudiation of the role

Table 8. Stages and developmental competencies of adolescence according to Erikson.[12]

Significant relationships here move beyond the family environment to *peer groups, outgroups and models of leadership*. There is a transfer of trust from parents to leaders or mentors, and the acceptance of a lifestyle, ideology or activism in groups, institutions, trends of thought, etc. The basic strength of this new setting is *fidelity* to new leaders. *Repudiation of the role* is the core pathology. This means rejecting all that cannot be included in one's identity. It can manifest itself as lack of trust, or as dogged systematic opposition, a kind of "negative identity" that lies at the bottom of adolescent rebelliousness.

However, repudiation of the role is also necessary to shape the identity of the adult. The name "core pathology" may suggest it (both here and in the rest of the developmental stages), but it is not some kind of "illness" or "delayer" of maturity, but a spur that helps us reach it, even when it begins with denial. Just as the adolescent needs some rebelliousness to be "himself" and break with stereotypes and with what others tell him he should be.

Arminda Aberastury and Maurice Knobel explain how the adolescent breaks from his past in three *basic duels*: a duel for the child's body, a duel for the child's role and identity, and a duel for the parents of childhood.[13]

c) Building Identity

During his journey to maturity new instruments become available to the adolescent over time.

12 Cf. Erikson, *The Life Cycle Completed*, p. 38.
13 Cf. A. Aberastury, M. Knobel, *La adolescencia normal. Un enfoque psicoanalítico*, Paidós, Buenos Aires 1984.

Children's concrete thinking paves the way for *abstract thinking*. It allows for greater introspection (critical self-reflection), opens him to the search for truth, the meaning of life, ideals, etc.

This opens the way for *reasoning skills*. He asks why things are the way they are (the "this is what I have been told" or "it has always been this way" does not hold anymore). The process is much harder, but the results are worth it. He makes the "why's" his own, and they become part of his set of values. But it comes with a price. Young people are very critical, can become inconsistent in thought processes or approaches to life, demand convincing arguments, etc.

The *egocentrism* or *self-centeredness* of the early years makes way for true concern for others and idealistic views that are sometimes naïve. The extremes co-exist for several years, and lead to paradoxical behavior. A teenager can go without lunch because he gave his away to a beggar in the street, and the next day he holds on to the coins he has to buy ice cream when a begging mother asks him for money to feed her hungry baby.

High emotional responsiveness is a prominent feature. It shows itself in frequent mood swings, irritability, emotional downturns, recurring inability to control impulses, etc. He must learn to control his reactions, to accomplish tasks when he doesn't feel like it. In short, to achieve *emotional security against segmental drives*, which was the third criterion of maturity in Allport.

There exists only now. Deferred rewards, long-term plans and distant goals, etc. do not attract him. He needs help projecting himself into the future, and to realize that the future depends on what he does now. He also needs to see the relative value of events. Having to repeat a year of high school or college, in addition to the academic setback, often means only one more year before they can earn money, become independent, get married... and a curse for life. He is surprised when someone tells him that no one wastes any time to work out how many years it took him to finish his degree when they see his CV.

At this time there is an *outbreak of sexuality*. It needs to be integrated—both in terms of emotional and physical pleasure—with love and the gift of self that sex is meant to express. In present-day society this is a particularly important challenge because access to explicit sexual content happens very early (often before puberty), mainly because of the widespread pornography on the internet. We will cover this topic extensively in the chapters that deal with the Christian virtue of chastity.

We have said that *uncertainty* is a feature of the adolescent. He lacks experience, is reluctant to receive it, and as a result every decision becomes a leap into the void. Yet he needs *to prove himself*, to explore limits. Not surprisingly he sometimes goes overboard. Punishment is a well-known teaching tool, but I would like to highlight the need to apply it consistently. It must fit the circumstances, be stable, and somewhat flexible. Too rigid an education discourages exploring and fosters timidity and insincerity. We will return to this topic at the end of the book, when we look at educational styles.

They feel very *attracted to consistency in life*. This is a very useful point which will help them to grow. As their *scheme of comprehensibility* becomes clearer in their minds it becomes possible to point out their inconsistencies, even if discreetly. If possible, it's better to do so in a way in which they reach the conclusion by themselves. It is also important to guide their critical judgment toward their own social group, to their "leaders and mentors," to the prevailing environment, and encourage them to live according to what they want to become, even if it means going against the world.

In the meantime, we need to be patient because it is a long path, and it is not always a straight line. As someone I know once asked: "You don't expect me to be consistent with what I think all the time, do you?" A way to foster consistency is that everyone at home—including parents and older brothers and sisters—take responsibility for their own actions. Anything you break you pay for, and if you make a mistake you apologize. We can always give ideas, repair the damage, or help ("we will do it together"), but the boy/girl should spend time and money to fix the problem he/she has caused.

The above is closely related to their search for *autonomy, authenticity, and inner freedom*. They detest anything artificial, phony or imposed, and they reject it instinctively. At this stage, they should not be left alone, but they need to have room to maneuver on their own, and be allowed to make mistakes. We just need to be there when they fall and give them a hand to get up. We can cause a lot of harm with an "I told you so" instead of a "don't worry, we can fix it together." We can give them moderate autonomy (schedule, some financial independence, etc.) and at the same time question them about what they plan to do with that autonomy. Their own answers to this question will point out to them where to find the authenticity they are looking for. It is a good way to promote their sense of identity and therefore self-assurance.

A way to develop one's identity is to assert it *against* or in opposition to other people. We have already acknowledged this mechanism in early childhood, but it becomes very obvious in the adolescent to the point of being infuriating. The following example shows it clearly. A couple told me how their teenage son said one Saturday evening that he wanted to go to Mass with them the following morning. It was a victory after months of hard negotiations, especially because it was his initiative. The following morning when it was about time to leave they asked him to hurry up so that they wouldn't be late. It led to the following dialogue:

> "You're putting pressure on me, so now I'm not going."
> "But you said yesterday you wanted to come."
> "Yeah, that's true. Wait for me to get changed and I'll come
> with you."
> "OK, but hurry up or we'll be late."
> "See? you're trying to force me again, I'm staying home."

Teenagers do need to distance themselves from their parents in order to be themselves, although they may not be able to do what they actually wanted to. Confusing, you may think, but welcome to the mind of a teenager already confused about his own identity. On the other hand, they have no problem identifying with their peer groups, a popular singer or athlete, etc., especially if they represent a note of rebelliousness. Therefore, it is important for them to have attractive, positive role models (neither boring nor prudish), and wholesome environments for them to spend their leisure time with others their own age: camps, boy scouts, youth groups, parish activities for the young, etc.

There are also ways of *involving them in family life* (and in school activities and in the different groups they have joined). One of them is to *count on them*: keep them informed of the decisions that need to be made, ask them for their opinions, and take it into account before resolutions are made. Another way is to give them responsibilities in the home. Areas that will depend on them for maintenance and with no one to replace them, unless they arrange it. The teenager will feel that he is entering the world of the adults, he will feel part of it, listened to, valued. As he realizes that they take him seriously, he will become more trustful of adults.

Respecting their privacy is a must, for the very same reason. Policing does no good: grilling, inspections, etc., may work in the short term to confirm what the boy has said or to prove him wrong, but they will feel betrayed. It takes a long time to regain a teenager's broken trust.

They need to grow in self-knowledge to be able to develop their identity, and to discover the reasons behind their goals, their reactions, moods, rebelliousness, comparisons. When parents have gained their trust, they will know when and how to ask the right questions at the right time. One way of doing it is showing them a "mirror" of the situation: describing particular situations objectively, without judging or interpreting the facts. In this way they help the young man to think rationally and come to his own conclusions, which most likely will be different from his parents'.

A final feature of this stage: *his faith life is a personal matter.* When he does a religious action because he wants to, his dealings with God become more mature, deep, and constant. Saying the rosary or going to Mass may be burdensome because they clash with his intended spontaneity. Making them compulsory does not help, but making them attractive might work. For example, going out for doughnuts after Mass. It may sound like a Pavlovian reflex, but it can be a pleasant inducement when they are not sure about going. Spending time with friends that have also attended Mass could be even more attractive. It may mean letting him go to church by himself (and trust him when he says he has been) or changing the family schedule.

Yet, the most convincing argument is the cheerfully consistent witness of Christian life of his parents and teachers. A young man told me that on one of the few occasions he was obedient he afterward went up to his mother, head bowed, and told her that he could not understand how she was so patient with him. Her reply was, "Honey, you're the reason I go to daily Mass. Otherwise, I would have lost my patience a long time ago!"

As the years go by things settle down, the boy gains some confidence and is able to start asking questions about his more immediate future: what he wants to study, where, potential professional openings, what values are important for his future life, practicing the faith, etc. According to Guardini, adolescence is

> the time when the strong feeling of the unconditioned provides the courage to make decisions that will determine a person's whole life. These include, for example, the choice of profession. This choice often shows a lot of daring, because it is a step that will determine the whole future before we are able to take a sober look at the reality of our own abilities and at the things around us. It is a particularly difficult step when external circumstances are opposed to the choice made, or when a wide range of talents and skills makes a decision difficult. On the other hand, it is often precisely the lack of realistic knowledge of the world that makes it possible to have the daring we were talking about. It can even become heroic when the decision is about something extraordinary. At this stage of his life, the young person may be engaged in projects that he would never dare to undertake later.[14]

Indeed, for many adolescents, this is the time when they discover a vocation of self-giving to God.

A final reminder is in order. A feature of the vital cycle is that all the stages and crises are necessary. Everyone has to go through the feared *adolescent rebellion*. I am sorry to worry those parents who are still hopeful that their son will bypass (and they will help him avoid) this crisis, which is often painful for everyone. But it is preferable that they are around when the boy goes through it. Unfortunately, it is not uncommon to meet young adults who were *good boys* during their teens, who hit the crisis ten or twelve years later when the environment was not so understanding, and the effects of their rebellion may be potentially irreversible.

If we think that psychological maturity is the balance between mind and heart (reason, will and emotions), the adolescent has a long way to go before he reaches such balance. Formation will entail finding reasons to

---

14 R. Guardini, *Die Lebensalter. Ihre ethische und pädagogische Bedeutung*, Matthias-Grünewald, Mainz 1986, pp. 26–27.

help him understand that it is a good thing to do things "because he wants to" as much as possible. It is also a matter of *educating their tastes for the good* so that they are attracted by it, and that their will is strengthened to seek it despite internal or external difficulties. This does not mean eliminating authority. But parents need to realize that acting out of duty does not necessarily create virtue, and gives no assurance that kids will follow the wishes of their parents when they eventually leave home.

ADULTHOOD

1. The Young Adult

a) Setting the Boundaries

Leaving behind the tsunami of adolescence, we enter adulthood. We will divide this stage into two periods: young adulthood and the fullness of life. We will cover the third stage (old age) in a separate chapter.

The young adult stage extends from the age of 19 (which usually marks the beginning of university studies or entry into the workforce) to 40. By then the individual is usually settled into life with its various aspects: emotional (marriage), professional, social, spiritual, etc. Important decisions are made in this period that either cannot be undone, or entail a commitment for the future.

For Erikson, young adulthood is the fifth psychosocial stage (Table 9).[1] The crisis of this age is not an internal matter, as it was in the previous stages. The crisis involves relationships. The individual has the chance to establish bonds that entail a commitment, and provide security, company and trust. The radius of significant relations expands further, and now includes *partners in friendship, sex, competition and cooperation*. It encompasses *intimacy*, another evolutionary competency The individual is also aware that acquiring *intimacy* will result in a loss of *autonomy*. The core pathology that threatens him is *isolation*.

Age	Stage	Psychosocial Crisis	Radius of significant relations	Basic strength	Core pathology
21-40 years	Young adulthood	Intimacy vs. isolation	Partners in friendship, sex, competition, cooperation	Love	Exclusivity

Table 9. Stages and competencies of the young adult according to Erikson.[2]

---

1   Cf. E. Erikson, *The Life Cycle Completed*, W.W. Norton, New York (NY)—London 1998, pp. 70–72.

2   Adapted from *ibidem*, pp. 38–39.

The person will be in a position to establish these relationships if he has adequately overcome the crises of the previous stages because he will have cemented his identity and will not fear *losing himself* in his dealing with others. He no longer needs to justify himself or oppose others in order to secure his ego. He is in a position to give *love,* which is the basic strength of the stage. Excessive openness has been noted by Erikson himself, which he calls *promiscuity,* the excessive ease to establish intimate relationships at the expense of appropriate depth. The term is not limited to partner relationships (let alone sexual encounters). Erikson applies it to friends and neighbors as well. At the other end of the spectrum, rejecting intimacy leads to loneliness and isolation, which can predispose someone to depression.

The core pathology of this stage is *exclusivity.* It means having only one relationship, to the exclusion of any others. Of course, a certain amount of this "pathology" is necessary, otherwise marriage would not be possible. We will now look at this stage in chronological order.

b) Entering the Work Force

A key event of this stage is leaving the family home. It is not so much the physical aspect of leaving the house. In many cultures the son remains in the parental home right up until his wedding. We are speaking of *de facto* independence from the house's rules, schedule, financial resources, etc., which is perfectly compatible with living in the family home during college or the first years spent in the workforce.

Joining the workforce gives real financial independence. There is no further need to ask parents for money or justify expenses. Many of us remember our first paycheck many decades later, and even the shopping we did with our initial earnings.

Work is very fulfilling at the beginning. The learning curve is very steep. The young adult has so little knowledge and experience that everything is novel, and he is enthusiastic about his job—the first case, the first client, the first patient. With the passing of time the novelty wears off, things become repetitive, and eventually monotony sets in.

Long hours of physical or intellectual work are not a problem and do not compromise their health, because the threshold for tiredness is high and young adults are physically strong. They recover quickly, which fits in very well with their intense work. A weekend—or even one day or a few hours—is enough to recover from a hard week's work and eagerly return on Monday.

Until they marry and start a family, young adults have no stable commitments, and are able to put more hours into work or take up further studies. They are ideal candidates for labor intensive jobs, but they don't mind it because it's a chance to go up the professional ladder, to earn more, and save for the future.

Usually, their level of responsibility at work is not high. Complex matters only come later, and at the beginning they can rely on the help of a supervisor. This helps to make up for the initial stress and help them grow in confidence as time goes by.

In addition, there is immediate gratification. With income comes acknowledgement from superiors and colleagues, promotions, opportunities in other fields, etc. The insecurity of the adolescent rapidly fades into the distance.

What we have described above is the ideal situation and rarely happens. In real life there are many hurdles that can make the first job difficult or frustrating. It may be hard to get a job, or the job is not what someone was looking for and does not meet his aspirations, or he is not suited for the task, clashes with bosses or colleagues, has an excessive workload or responsibilities, etc. His flexibility and capacity to adapt should be at a peak, but they will be seriously tested.

Having said that, this stage is usually a time for expansion, and the young person feels that he comprehends reality and masters it, probably because he is not that familiar with it. He has had few experiences of his own limitations and is not really aware of how complex a given environment is.[3]

c) Setting Up a New Home

From an emotional point of view the main feature of this stage is the establishment of stable relationships with a view to marriage sooner or later

3   Cf. R. Guardini, *Die Lebensalter. Ihre ethische und pädagogische Bedeutung*, Matthias-Grünewald, Mainz 1986, pp. 46–47.

(we will not consider other types of partner relationships because we are looking at formation within a Christian framework). Courtship is the stage in life where love leads to commitment, from loving a person to the idea of a common life project.

Whatever formation one has received will make the decision more or less difficult. Insecurity (one's own, in others, in life) will hinder the development of stable bonds. If the self-centeredness of adolescence remains, it will be a hurdle to the gift of self. The two members of the couple having different outlooks on sexuality (pre-marital sex, openness to children, etc.) will be a potential source of conflict. On the other hand, altruism and extension of the sense of self will help bring the other into one's life project, while respecting that person's "otherness." Flexibility will help establish agreements. Assertiveness will enable them to defend their rights from inappropriate demands from the other without damaging the relationship, etc.

I do not want to spend much time on the marital relationship because much has already been written in this regard.[4] I only want to point out something that, in my opinion, is essential. The decision to marry looks to the specific person we have before us, not the person we would like him or her to be or hope to become. How many marriages break down because they were based on a "he/she will change in time" model. Or even worse, the idea "I will change him/her." Of course, we should be confident that the sharp edges will be smoothed, but from a realist's perspective, future spouses (and we ourselves for that matter) will die with the same annoying defects they have now. They can even become worse, as Sancho Panza noted with his typical dose of common sense: "Each one is how God made him, many times even worse."[5]

---

4   Cf., among many, Francis, Post-Synodal Exhortation *Amoris laetitia*, March 19, 2016; J. Gray, *Men Are from Mars, Women Are from Venus. A Practical Guide for Improving Communication and Getting What You Want in Your Relationships*, HarperCollins, New York, New York (NY) 1993; M. Ceriotti Migliarese, *La famiglia imperfetta. Come trasformare ansie & problemi in sfide appassionanti*, Milano, Ares 2016; F.J. Insa Gómez (coord.), *Cómo acompañar en el camino matrimonial. La pastoral familiar a la luz de* Amoris laetitia, Rialp, Madrid 2020.

5   M. Cervantes, *Don Quixote of La Mancha*, II, 3.

d) The Crisis of the Thirties

The previous stage leads into the *crisis of the 30s*, when we witness the first clash between our intended plans and the real world. We could say that life tests the strength of the principles by which we have lived.

First come the demands of one's faith. It becomes more difficult to live by them, because there is an ever-increasing number of things to be done, and little time to do them. It is harder to fit in daily practices of piety, or dedicate time to personal formation or volunteering. Professional ethics can be quite challenging when we become aware of unscrupulous practices in the workplace, especially when opposing them can jeopardize our career. All these challenges need answers, which only can come through prayer.

On the other hand, the idyllic stage of falling in love wears out and the usual family issues begin to appear.[6] In the forefront lies the need to integrate professional life with the newly founded family. Those who bases their worth on professional standing may feel underestimated when spouses do not *adequately* recognize their professional achievements. *Adequately* is the key word because it may mean different things to either spouse. The choice of a life companion to start a family is rarely made on the basis of professional skills. The choice is made on the basis of character, capacity for self-giving, on affection, etc.

Many marriage crises begin when one of the spouses feels appreciated by everyone except the spouse, or when the family is viewed as an obstacle to professional aspirations. One spouse may reproach the other for giving the better part of the day to professional work, and leaving tiredness and complaints for the home. One spouse often becomes jealous, more or less justifiably, when the other puts effort into work to the detriment of the family. I refer not only to the wife reproaching the husband, which historically has been the most common scenario. I have witnessed worse jealousy

6   Mariolina Ceriotti Migliarese, a neuropsychologist and family therapist, discerns three stages in every marriage: idealization (falling in love), disappointment (beginning of life together) and re-organization (continuous renegotiation of rules and goals of life together to accommodate the ever changing circumstances). Cf. M. Ceriotti Migliarese, "La ayuda a las parejas en crisis," in Insa Gómez (coord.), *Cómo acompañar en el camino matrimonial*, pp. 111–127.

from husbands whose wife goes further ahead professionally, has more prestige, and above all when she earns more than him.

When women work outside the home, they usually have a greater load
because in addition to their professional commitments the domestic tasks
are not equally shared, and only women can be mothers.

To overcome this crisis, the first step is to *verbalize* the problem. Problems cannot be solved on the basis of feelings or impressions, and verbalizing is simply "to express an idea or a feeling with words." This crisis
highlights two topics that had remained in the background (and this may
be the root of the problem because they should have been discussed during
courtship).

The first question that each spouse has to answer is: What are my personal priorities? In other words, what *schematic of comprehensibility* have I
chosen—which the other has accepted before marriage—and for which I
am prepared to forego whatever becomes incompatible with it in any way?

The second question must be answered together: to what extent are we
prepared—the two of us—to sacrifice our profession for the sake of the
family, or the other way round? It is not as easy as saying that the family
has a priority over work, because everyone would agree on that. In fact,
family dynamics benefit from the work of both parents, because they shape
their financial and social status, the choice of school for the children, material comforts, holidays, etc. All these things may require one or even both
spouses to dedicate less time to the home. They will have to make it up
with more time and affection when they are physically present.

It is a most important question, and the answer is not always easy. It
usually requires trial and error, and needs to be open to review at all times.
Most importantly, the spouses must talk to *and* listen to each other, and
help each other so that they are not left alone to face their own challenges.
According to John Gray, "A relationship is healthy when both partners have
permission to ask for what they want and need, and they both have permission to say no if they choose."[7]

Most of the above can also be applied *mutatis mutandis* to an incipient
vocation within the Church. In such cases, dedication to the specific mission of the vocation would take the place of work, and life with those who

7   Gray, *Men Are from Mars, Women Are from Venus*, p. 298.

share the same vocation would be the equivalent of family life. We will cover this topic in the chapter on celibacy.

One final point: physical limitations begin to appear in one's 30s. Some people have called it "the decade of the *I never*": "I never had to warm up before playing sports," "I never had a bad night after a heavy dinner," "I never had back pain after carrying heavy gear," "I never was so tired on Friday after a long week at work," etc. The thresholds for tiredness, physical endurance and resilience are not what they were in one's 20s, hence the need to pace oneself.

2. The Fullness of Life

a) Setting the Boundaries

This next stage extends from the time when there is a reasonable level of stability in the family, at work, etc., until retirement.

In practice it dovetails with adulthood, the psychosocial stage that Erikson places between the ages of 40 and 60 (Table 10).[8] The radius of significant relations is shared by the *divided labor* and the *shared household*, the two major environments of this life stage. The crisis of this stage is primarily one of *generativity*, at three different levels. Procreativity (beings), productivity (things) and creativity (ideas). I think each of these levels can be related to the aphorism of uncertain origin, "there are three things every person should do with his life: have a child, plant a tree, and write a book." Everyone needs to feel useful and needed by others. All of us seek to project ourselves into the future to leave behind a legacy to our family and to the world. It is achieved firstly by having and raising the children, guiding them to achieve in life. It is a kind of prolongation of one's own life. In other domains the projection of self can be achieved through work, writing, science, art or social activism. The other element of the crisis is *stagnation*, giving up the idea of leaving a legacy, possibly because the contribution to history will not match the dream. Disappointment may result in questioning oneself: "What am I doing here? Why am I struggling and giving up so much?"

8   Cf. Erikson, *The Life Cycle Completed*, pp. 66–70.

Age	Stage	Psychosocial crisis	Radius of significant relations	Basic strength	Core Pathology
40-60 years	Adulthood	Generativity vs. stagnation	Divided labor and shared household	Care	Rejectivity

Table 10. Stages and evolutionary competencies in adulthood according to Erikson.[9]

The basic virtue that emerges from this antithesis is *care*. Bringing children (or ideas, goods, etc.) into the world is not enough; they can only develop to their potential if we are committed to them. The core pathology is "*rejectivity*, that is, the unwillingness to include specified persons or groups in one's generative concern—one *does not care to care* for them."[10] Obviously, some level of exclusion or selection of the elements to be adopted is necessary. Not everything can be included in one's generativity, only those things that are or can become "familiar." In a strict sense, pathological rejectivity is the refusal to take care of anything that one would be expected to care for, whether in the family circle or within the community.

This stage covers almost one third of the individual's life expectancy, and it is looked upon as the *fullness of life*, the time when the individual's potential is most developed, and the conditions are most favorable to realize such potential. The previous stages do have their own significance, but they have been a kind of preparation, and whatever follows later will be an epilogue. However, as those who have reached the stage know too well, it is not a peak that can be quietly enjoyed forever when it is reached. It is but one more evolutionary phase, with its own specific conflicts.

We will run through the decades that make up this stage over the following paragraphs and highlight the main challenges for each of them. As a summary, the individual needs to balance *productivity* (more in the family environment than in the workplace) and the frustrations that will be encountered along the way.

I would like to make a final comment. From a Christian perspective,

9   Adapted from *ibidem*, p. 39.
10   *Ibidem*, p. 26.

the tension between generativity and stagnation, a feature of this stage, gives us a glimpse of the human heart's desire for transcendence.

b) The Forties: Stability vs. Search for Novelty

Those who have successfully overcome the previous stage reach their 40s with a stable family, a stable job, a balanced personality ... and even the definitive home! It looks like these people only need to coast along or at most to hold on to what they have achieved against the difficulties that no doubt will come up. Could this be enough to ensure a satisfied life? The answer is a decisive NO.

Marriage enters a new stage: children come, each requiring financial support and a lot of time and attention. Life as a whole needs to be negotiated once more, not only work time (including travel and promotions), but even within the family dynamics—the responsibilities of each spouse, holidays, date nights, going to the movies, etc.—because the time available as a couple becomes scarce, and this time needs *to be treasured.*

A friend of mine who was in the middle of this stage told me that he had a heavy workload and that both he and his wife had to work a bit on weekends to keep up. They have two lively young children, and I ventured to say that they were splitting Saturdays, so that each of them has half the day free to work while the other can take care of the children. He gave me a look and said: "Look, from Monday to Friday my wife and I return home more or less at the same time as the children. We barely have time to help them with homework, cook dinner, give them baths and put them to bed... and then we go to bed, exhausted. We have virtually no time to talk about how our day went. If we did what you just said, we wouldn't be able to talk on the weekends either. What we do is go out with the children all day; while they play in the park, we talk about our things. Work? We do that when we get home, while the kids watch TV, or play, or run around us. If not, at night. We're agreed that this is the best system to ensure that we have good communication in our marriage."

In the *area of work*, the *exponential growth* of the early years *flattens out.* Surprises, achievements, promotions do not happen so often or are no longer the novelty they once were.

Here comes into play one of the *big five* of the traits of personality we saw earlier: *openness* to change comes with the *search for novelty.* A restless, creative individual needs to "create," and gets bored when things become monotonous. He will try to break the *homeostasis* or *status quo* soon after he reaches it.

Once I came across a university professor who enjoyed a lot of prestige among his students and his colleagues. He asked his department to change the subject he had taught successfully for twenty years. His proposal was peculiar to say the least. He would have to become familiar with a new subject, to prepare all the teaching material from scratch, etc., even though he could teach his present subject almost in his sleep. He explained that he needed a change. He was tired of saying the same things every year, using the same examples, telling the same jokes, and getting the same questions. He needed a change, even though it meant increasing his workload substantially.

If we reach this stage, it may be feasible to satisfy this need by changing jobs, or by moving to a new position within the same business. However, sometimes that's not an option. What about lifelong choices, such as marriage or a vocation? In these cases, creativity means to look for desired renewal *from within*, to give a *new hue* to the same old relationship (which some people do by changing their *look*). For a marriage to stay alive day in and day out, it may mean a *change of approach* (of course, it should be a shared decision) to bring back the pleasant flavor of newness. If people change, relationships (rules, pacts, boundaries) must also fit the new reality.

In all features of personality, the dictum *in medio virtus* holds true. Openness to change should be managed with care. Too much may lead to an insatiable appetite for change, excessive dependence on new sensations, or maladjustment, which is usually a sign of personality defects. These are people who are never happy wherever they are. What bothers them is not outside, but within themselves. Were they to change places or jobs, they would still be uncomfortable, because the real problem lies within their own selves. It's like the worker who applies for a transfer because he does not get along with his boss, but the same thing happens in every new position. Ultimately, we all need to learn to enjoy the present, the today; our ordinary occupation, learning how to travel in "cruise control."

At the opposite end of the spectrum we find people who are more conservative. Their achievements afford them a relative peace, and they can fall into conformity, routine, an absence of dreams and challenges—in other words, stagnation. Life loses its spark, and they fall into a *bourgeois* outlook or early "old age of the mind," a kind of interior gentrification. To paraphrase a well-known sportsman, "You move from bourgeoisie to 'hamburgersie' when you get used to winning."

On the other hand, stability should not drift into selfishness or lack of concern for social issues, or limiting one's interests and concerns to "my people." We should have the daring to *complicate our lives* for the sake of other people, especially those in need, who are further removed from us. It's about sharing the goods we have earned with our endeavors.

One final idea regarding the *search for novelty*. It was already mentioned in the first chapter, but it does not hurt to mention again that this personality trait must factor into our decision to follow a given profession, or—in the case of formators and friends—our advice that we offer others.

The peak of the tension between stability and the search for novelty tends to happen during the so-called midlife crisis, also known as the *now or never* moment. Time goes by relentlessly, and the individual is well aware that half of his life has gone, and that he is now at the peak of his physical strength, or has just begun to decline. He will no longer be capable of carrying out all the projects he would have liked, but there is still time for a hard change of course, a sea change, and time is of the essence. It is now or never. But just what should be changed? This is the 24 million dollar question because anything and everything could go: work, family, vocation. St. Josemaría used to mention the advice a friend gave him when he was a young priest:

> don't forget that when people turn 40, those who are married want to *unmarry*; monks want to become priests, doctors, lawyers; lawyers, engineers; and everything is like this: a real spiritual catastrophe.[11]

Once more, the strength of our deepest convictions is put to the test. Men and women go through this crisis in different ways. For women

11 San Josemaría Escrivá, *Carta 1*, n. 22, in idem, *Cartas*, Vol. I (ed. Luis Cano), Rialp, Madrid 2020, p. 105.

it is the decade of menopause and all the changes that come with it: biological (physiological, hormonal) and psychological (emotionally they become more volatile). The loss of potential motherhood can be very stressful, especially in a time when women often get married later in life. Changes in physical appearance are more dramatic for women, and the answer is usually to increase the use of cosmetics. These changes can be highly frustrating for some: they notice a loss of appeal, even from their own husbands, sex is less pleasant or downright uncomfortable, to the point of occasionally feeling that "I am no longer a woman" (although this would denote a limited understanding of what it means to be a woman).

Things are different for men: they have lost little of the vigor of youth, both in terms of physical strength and sexual desire. The latter can be an area of conflict or frustration if the wife (whose sexual desire may have waned) does not realize that the husband needs the displays of affection he has enjoyed so far, including sex.

When love is allowed to grow cold, when there is little mutual understanding and appreciation, when displays of affection had been based mostly on bodily expressions, when there is no dialogue where both give in to the wishes and needs of the other, the foundations are set to becoming estranged. And when one drifts away, he or she may find in someone else what the spouse is not able to provide. The husband may find a younger, more attractive woman, who appreciates his masculinity (physical strength, psychological safety, and possibly financial security to boot) and knows how to give what he is craving—care and sexual fulfillment. The opposite may also occur, but usually not as frequently: the woman may also look for an extramarital relationship, wanting to feel younger and appreciated. Much infidelity and quite a few marriage breakups begin when the spouses have not grasped how important the dynamics of communication are.

It is important to be honest with oneself from the start, when one begins to open the heart to another person. There may be lurking in the background a desire

> *to check* whether we still have it, if we can provide some support
> to a woman in distress because of a violent or indifferent husband, or tenderness to a man whose wife never understood him,
> or left him for another man. It may truly be a desire to console

the person who suffers or is distressed. But in any case it is not the soft-hearted, the infatuated or fragile, the dreamer or the naïve who should do it. The outcome tells us the answer: the affection that began as friendship ends up being lust: a matter of not starting, not simply *stopping*, before a path that is not *my path*.[12]

One final consideration to finish this section. We stated earlier that throughout the life cycle all the phases and the corresponding crises are necessary. This means we also need to go through a midlife crisis, although its intensity and anxiety will vary. Those who have a strong *search for novelty* are more at risk than those others who are more sedentary and conformist. Knowing oneself—and knowing one's spouse—will help to see them coming, and adopt the appropriate measures. Prevention is better than cure.

c) The Fifties: Stability Without Rigidity

We now reach "maturity within maturity." Plato himself stated that you need to be fifty to be able to rule.[13] The time has come to enjoy all that has been accomplished (character, virtues, professional achievements, family, friends) and build on it. However, it is the time when we regret the absence of habits that we did not manage to acquire, that would have made life more fulfilling and facilitate better relationships with oneself and with others.

Can anyone change his or her personality after reaching maturity? Is it possible to improve one's character with the passing of the years? The answer is yes. The struggle to improve the way we are, enhance our habits, and acquire new ones is not only possible, but necessary. Otherwise, stability can become *rigidity*.

Let's go back to the *big five*. Anyone can slip up on any of the five lines set for each one of the pairs of traits: creative vs. conscientious, extroverted vs. introverted, agreeable vs. detached, neurotic vs. resilient. It is a matter of staying away from the maladapted extremes and fostering the dimensions

12 M.A. Fuentes, *La castidad. ¿Posible?*, Ediciones Verbo Encarnado, San Rafael (Mendoza, Argentina) 2006, pp. 182–183.

13 Cf. Plato, *The Republic*, VII, 18.

that are less developed. This task should be undertaken realistically. We should not pretend to achieve radical changes that prove themselves impossible to achieve. It is rather a matter of avoiding the typical *risks* of our character without losing the obvious *strengths*.

It is fair to say that as time goes by it is harder to make this change. Habits become more entrenched, and reactions become almost automatic. But it is always possible to resist the inertia, or at least realize *a posteriori* that a particular response was not the best, and to apologize to those we have hurt, and work out a better alternative for the next time. This is the *youthful spirit* we should never lose. It helps us to be more flexible, optimistic, and tolerant of others in all circumstances.

I once worked on a document that other people had to approve. One of them proposed several changes that were not strictly necessary. Three of us were working on the final draft, when one of them suggested we include those changes. They would not improve the final result, but neither was it any worse for them, and the person who made the proposal would not feel ignored. The other person in the team said: "This is exactly what I do with my husband; I agree with him in all the things that make no difference to me." How shrewd! How often do we stick to our guns even when we would lose nothing by giving in, and would make the other person happy in the process.

However, we cannot avoid little habits becoming entrenched, and we develop the feared *manias* (feared by others, of course). I once listened to an old priest who had much experience and great common sense, who commented that he had often heard that people should absolutely avoid developing obsessions or manias. He thought that that was not a realistic goal, and he coined the motto, "manias: few and constant." He supposed that they are unavoidable, but having many becomes unbearable for those with whom one lives, and if the manias change they *go berserk*. He used the example of windows. Some people prefer to leave them open to air out the room, others want them closed to keep out the cold. It is always possible to reach an agreement, if everyone is consistent with their preferred option.

Here Christian life comes to the rescue of psychology because the virtues (headed by charity, followed by humility, fortitude, temperance) become the solid foundation to improve one's character. On the other hand, some acts of piety such as the daily examination of conscience will help us recognize poor behavior and make the resolution to change them. That makes life more pleasant for those around us, makes us feel happier and more relaxed, keeps stress levels down, and even lowers the risk of stress-related illnesses.

There are also challenges regarding professional work and other activities. Awareness of our skills and professional achievements can lead to exaggerated self-reliance, to more or less consciously preventing ourselves from learning from others, especially those with less experience. And for the same reason we may find it hard to ask for help and to let ourselves be helped.

With the passing of time we develop a collection of projects that are either unfinished, failed, or not even started. It is easy to despise what we could not get (the dreams we cherished for so long) like *the fox and the grapes*; however, sour grapes can make people bitter. Cynicism is even worse. We defined it earlier as *laughing at the things we love … at the cost of not loving them anymore*. It dries up the heart.

Guardini calls it the "crisis of the experience of limitations." The person is forced to accept boundaries, inadequacies, and hardships in his own life and in the lives of others. Every person will come out of it stronger if he overcomes it without cynicism or resignation. They will also be in a better position to service, because

> existence relies on these people. They are capable of doing what is truly worthwhile and enduring precisely because they no longer harbor the illusion of great successes and splendid victories. This is what the statesman, the doctor, the educator should be like.[14]

The physical aspect is most noticeable with the passage of time. The realization that "I am no longer maturing; I am just getting old," is a serious blow. The ailments associated with age come thick and fast, we have to give up sports and other physical activities that are more demanding, and we have to adjust the pace of work and rest. It also has an impact on psychological function. It is harder to learn new things, especially if they are related

14   Guardini, *Die Lebensalter*, p. 51.

to technology, which is now ubiquitous. A design expert sees that any youngster performs better with his computer than he does by pen and paper, as if by magic. In some areas, experience can more than make up for it. Indeed, in many intellectual, artistic and craft-related matters the peak is reached at an older age. But this is not the case for those who do physical work. They will suffer the limitations of their age, and have no alternatives.

Besides, we have to come to terms with the fact that death is no longer remote. Old age for an adolescent begins at thirty, and death is a very long way off. When we reach thirty, we feel so healthy that old age will not come before 50, and yet the process continues until we realize that repeated ailments mean that we can no longer delay our entry into old age. On the other hand, contact with "premature natural deaths" (such as cancer, heart attacks, car accidents) of people we knew and love, makes us think that our turn may come sooner than expected.

d) The Empty Nest Syndrome

The timing of *empty nest syndrome* depends on when the youngest children were born. Usually, the syndrome arrives in one's 50s or 60s. The children have left home (or they are grown up and have become autonomous), and the two spouses are left on their own, much like when they began life in common. The rest of the house is empty, they eat on their own as a rule, the conversation topics are more restricted, etc.

If the couple has not taken good care of their life as a couple (remember my friend who insisted on taking the kids to the park to talk to his wife), they may find themselves looking at each other as two strangers. Their concerns have gone in such separate ways that they are no longer shared, they have grown apart, and love has grown cold.

Sometimes the couple's distancing is not due to simple oversight. The children are often the excuse to cover up the little obstacles encountered in their life as a couple. The multiple issues related to the children (schools, friends, holiday plans) are raised to avoid conflict or to dodge intimacy. When this happens the concerns and problems of the couple are not faced, and therefore not solved.

If it comes to that, it is urgent to reassess the family dynamics, the roles in the home, holiday plans, and life in common. It would be much easier if they had tried to be flexible and prevented—or tried to prevent—manias

128

from taking over. The idea is to re-discover the beloved with his/her old and newly acquired positive features and thus make their love young again.

Married love needs to be nurtured at all times to keep it alive. But on occasions like this, twigs and leaves are not enough to kindle the fire. A proper log must be thrown in to get it going again. It requires thought and ingenuity. Looking back can provide the clue as to what to do now: Why did we get married? What did I find in him or her that made me give myself for life? What did we enjoy doing together? It is the time to recover *our* little things that we so enjoyed thirty years ago, which we had to give up for the sake of the children: our favorite outings, restaurants, movie theaters, songs or holiday destinations, etc.

Thus we set the foundations to enter the next, and last, stage in life hand-in-hand. It will also allow us to move toward the heavenly goal, also hand-in-hand. Friends of mine asked me to celebrate Mass on their golden wedding anniversary. The little church was packed with the harvest of their fruitful love: three generations were present, a perfect picture of the "generational conflict." The little ones ran around, the occasional teenager looking bored on his mobile phone, mothers trying to sort things out, fathers letting mothers sort things out, and in the central aisle the two main characters. I started the homily by thanking them. Thanks for their fidelity, at a time when divorce is the order of the day; thanks for showing us that the promises made on the day of your wedding can be kept. And it wasn't, I added, for lack of difficulties, which you managed to overcome together (they gave each other a nod and a knowing look), also the difficulties caused by the other person's character (they looked up to heaven with a gesture that said "you have no idea") and despite the many chances you both had to be unfaithful (they nodded slightly), which you were able to overcome because you loved each other (they looked at each other again, with a smile).

In the words of Pope Francis,

> There is beauty in the wife, slightly disheveled and no longer young, who continues to care for her sick husband despite her own failing health. Long after the springtime of their courtship has passed, there is beauty in the fidelity of those couples who still love one another in the autumn of life, those elderly people who still hold hands as they walk. [...] To find, to disclose and

to highlight this beauty, which is like that of Christ on the cross, is to lay the foundations of genuine social solidarity and the culture of encounter.[15]

With quintessential British humor, Lord Byron said that *it is easier to die for the woman you love than to live with her.* I think that if you were to ask the ladies they would agree that the reverse is also true. The day-to-day of life together is a permanent challenge for all spouses. Fortunately, they have the grace of God that they received in the sacrament of matrimony.

After the children leave the parental home they need to be treated in a different way. We earlier saw that parents project themselves in their offspring. They want the child to be like them but without their limitations, and reach where they themselves could not reach. The only problem is that these expectations are seldom realized. Children may not like their father's profession, life took them in a different direction, or they did not work hard enough—children are free, and make their own decisions, which the parents may or may not agree with. Leaving home may be one more source of conflict for many reasons—because they leave without the parents' blessing, because they still ask for money, because they do not approve of the choice of spouse or the lifestyle embarked upon. In any case, when children become adults, the relationship changes. It will always be a parent and child relationship, but earned moral authority is the only kind that remains. Now they have become adults, and they must be treated as adults, as equals.

The final challenge of the adult stage is *to allow,* and more than that, *to enhance the generational handover,* both within the family and at work. It is the best way to live generativity, which Erikson proposed as the *evolutionary competency* to reach, the best way to leave a mark on life. And with this achievement comes the role reversal that occurs in old age, when the parent moves from being caregiver to being cared for.

This completes a quick overview of adulthood. It may look like an obstacle course, but we should rather think of it as a fascinating adventure, with all its difficulties, challenges, and rewards.

15 Francis, Post-Synodal Apostolic Exhortation *Christus vivit*, March 25, 2019, n. 183.

IMPROVING CHARACTER IN ADULTHOOD: TAKING CARE OF RELATIONSHIPS

Before we move on to the third stage, I would like to look deeper at the idea of self-improvement mentioned in the previous chapter. How can we achieve this? By taking good care of relationships, or even better, opening ourselves up as much as possible in three areas: family, work, and friends.

1. The Family

The family is first, because it is within the family that a person can develop the need to love and be loved to the full. In this context family includes the obvious—husband and wife, children, and extended family—but also other forms of living under the same roof by reason of a common vocation or other circumstances. All of them have particular features.

Bonds are irreversible. Being a father, a spouse, or a son is for life. The starting premise for this book is a Christian perspective, therefore divorce is not considered. In the case of separation, when very serious circumstances make it necessary, the spouses are aware that the marriage bond remains.

The other is not chosen, with the exception of the spouse, of course. Once married, everyone that comes along must be accepted: children, brothers and sisters, cousins, uncles and aunts, in-laws, etc.

Having said that, *affinity is not always the same.* We do not all have the same character, tastes, interests, etc.

Yet, they all are *unconditionally accepted.* Although we have no choice and there may be little in common with some of them, family ties mean that they are all an integral part of both the nuclear and extended families. St. John Paul II used to say, "the other is not loved because of his usefulness or pleasure: he is loved in himself and by himself."[1]

---

1   St. John Paul II, *Homily at the Mass for Families,* Madrid, November 2, 1982.

There is a *close living relationship* in the nuclear family. After work, school, or spending time with friends, we return home to the family. There are no holidays from the family. If there is a need to escape, there is a problem in the family dynamics that should be sorted out. Needless to say, it is not necessary to do everything together at all times. Many activities are carried out with other people, and can be useful as a "rest" from the family for a short while, so as to return with greater enthusiasm.

The way to make living with others easier is *to love them with their defects*. When he spoke to married couples, St. Josemaría used to ask spouses if they loved the other. The answer was an obvious, "Yes." He then asked the key question: "But do you love your spouse with his (or her) defects? Because if you don't, you do not really love him (or her)." To love truly means accepting the limitations of the other, even when we have the feeling that they are not doing enough to overcome them. Because of these shortcomings we feel that the other is vulnerable and needs our care, our help to endure those defects and to correct them, while not obsessing about them. They can provide a chance to show our sense of humor, which Allport described as "the ability to laugh at the things one loves (including, of course, oneself and all that pertains to oneself), and still love them."[2]

Therefore, family helps people *to come out of themselves*. Living closely with people we didn't necessarily choose but whom we love because they are different from us, and with whom we have to keep on living with, forces us to leave our own preferences behind and give in. We do so first of all out of love for our spouse, children, siblings, etc., but also because we are conscious that family harmony and unity requires that we forego these preferences, and it is worth it to do so.

Finally, *it will always be there*. This is the most beautiful thing about the family. When the hard times come, we know who to turn to, because we know that they will take us in *unconditionally*.

No doubt this is beautiful, but is it realistic? I think so. Moreover, my experience tells me so, as long as the expectations of what Dr. Ceriotti Migliarese calls *the imperfect couple* and *the imperfect family*[3] are met. At the

---

2   G.W. Allport, *Pattern and Growth in Personality*, Holt, Rinehart and Winton, New York (NY), p. 292.

3   Cf. M. Ceriotti Migliarese, *La coppia imperfetta. E se anche i difetti fossero un*

expense of repeating myself, one goal of this book is to learn to live in an imperfect world, surrounded by imperfect people, being ourselves imperfect, but with a serene eagerness to improve and above all to be happy, and in addition to make our loved ones happy.

Marriage can at times be difficult, like every path in life, but it has the remedy within: mutual support. The experience of a married couple, friends of mine, made it clear to me. He was diagnosed with a progressive neurological condition, and was recommended to do physical therapy to maintain his mobility. As a good doctor, he ignored his colleagues' advice... until his wife had an operation in her arm a few months later, and also was recommended physical therapy. Now it was the husband who encouraged her to go, but she was busy and not keen on going. In the end they decided to go together, aware that that's how they would force each other to go. Often during the rehabilitation period, one of them would find an excuse to skip a session (work, tiredness, care of the children, etc.) and encouraged the other to go alone. The other person, however, would find an excuse and reply, "Don't worry, we'll both stay home." Invariably, it spurred the other to go and do the exercises. The result was that for many months they both kept their appointments without fail because they knew that the other's wellbeing was at stake.

Spouses are like a house of cards. On their own they may be weak or unstable, but when they realize that each is the support of the other most of their excuses disappear. They even diminish the criticisms of the other's defects because they see themselves as the support the other needs to overcome them.

2. The Workplace

A sizeable part of the day is spent at work, at least from Monday to Friday. It is the source of another kind of relationship—namely, that of colleagues, and it has its own specific features.

The source of unity there is a *common enterprise*, the completion of a specific task. It requires *cooperation*, putting together various strengths that ideally

ingrediente dell'amore?, Ares, Milano 2012; idem, *La famiglia imperfetta. Come trasformare ansie & problemi in sfide appassionanti*, Milano, Ares 2016.

create synergy, where the sum total of individual efforts is greater than what individuals could do on their own. One plus one is greater than two.

Work relationships are not established by choice. We usually join a pre-existing team, and other elements are added on to it. This requires an effort to adapt to others' ways of being and trying to integrate.

Therefore, it demands a *respect for other people.* Workplace relationships, unlike those in the family, are not based on love (of course, charity must be lived at all times), but on respect. It is very desirable to get along well, to have a relaxed work environment, to avoid disputes, but the main goal in a business is to meet sales targets, provide customer service, etc. This requires being flexible, listening to the opinions of others, being prepared to give in, holding a position we do not particularly like but that will facilitate a better outcome, etc.

Finally, the workplace is a natural environment to make friends. Many hours sharing a common goal, working side to side, is often the breeding ground to develop friendships, and even in some cases the love that leads to marriage.

3. Friends

The last area to look at is friendship, that personal, pure, and disinterested affection, shared with another person, which is born from and strengthened by the relationship. We can highlight the following features.

It is based on *affective attunement.* It begins with something that is shared (a job, a hobby, a sports team). A special affinity is uncovered that leads to being at ease with that person, and feeling listened to and understood. The philosopher Josef Pieper said that love leads one to say: "It's a Good thing that you exist, it's good that you are in this world!"[4]

It is a space to share *intimacy.* Cicero wrote that a friend is one

> to whom you neither fear to confess any fault nor blush at revealing any spiritual progress, to whom you may entrust all the secrets of your heart and confide all your plans.[5]

4   J. Pieper, *About Love,* Franciscan Herald Press, Chicago (IL) 1974, p. 19.
5   Cicero, *On Friendship,* 6, 22.

Friendship is *free of charge*. According to Aristotle, the friend is "another self."[6] Indeed, he described twenty-four centuries ago what Allport calls the *extension of the sense of self*. As it is part of oneself, one gives what the other needs without keeping score. Thus, the Philosopher adds, "The man who is to be happy will therefore need virtuous friends."[7]

Not all friendships are the same because *there are degrees*. They will depend on the intensity of the affection and the importance of what they share. This is the reason why the deepest friendships emerge when particularly important things are shared: vital events with a heavy emotional component, intimate concerns, common ideals, the same vocation, etc.

Friendship is found and accepted. A decision of the will (I will become a friend of such and such a person) is not enough. We can prepare ourselves, we can meet frequently with someone, but the feeling of friendship has to come *by itself*, it cannot be manufactured. On the other hand, it needs to be reciprocal. Friendship always goes *both ways*.

Friendship suffers from *disuse atrophy*. It grows with contact and shrinks with distance. Fortunately, technology comes to the assistance to keep in touch, but we should not fool ourselves: looking somebody in the eye in the light of day is far better than the alternative (a pixelated image on a computer, tablet, or cell phone).

Friendship can flourish within the family and in the workplace, the two environments where we spend most of our time. They say that touch makes love. It is easy to understand in the workplace, but it requires an explanation when we talk about the family. Some siblings are *also* friends, but others are only siblings. In other words, when siblings are also friends they reach a level of affinity and trust that leads to preferential treatment.

The last statement brings up an interesting concept regarding healthy friendships: preferential does not mean exclusive or excluding of others. C. S. Lewis says that "friendship is the least jealous of the loves."[8] Friendships that are sealed off from others—as happens to some adolescents—are not healthy. Two people who seek each other out at all times, on their own, to share the whole of their inner world with a definite lack of modesty, to

6   Aristotle, *Nicomachean Ethics*, IX, 9.
7   *Ibidem*.
8   C. S. Lewis, *The Four Loves*, G. Bles, London 1960, p. 73.

pledge to each other's secrets etc., reveals immaturity. They are unconsciously using each other to make up for their fear of the outside world.

A controversial point is whether friendship can only take place among equals. As a matter of fact, I had initially included another feature: *symmetry*. Is *asymmetrical* friendship possible? For instance, between two people with a great age difference? Yes… and no. There can be a great degree of affinity and trust between them, and so we could think of a true friendship… but only to a point.

In my opinion the highest levels of friendship require reasonable parity. The different affective and maturational development of two persons of vastly different ages make it difficult to be on the same page to form a deep friendship. Tastes and interests, and especially how they are lived out, are different between people whose ages differ by scores of years. If we return to Aristotle, if my friend, my "other self" has such a great difference in age from me, it may mean that I am not in the stage of the life cycle that I should be in. In my opinion the father-son relationship would be the right model for a relationship that has a big age difference.

Having said that, is it possible for a parent and child to be friends? We often hear people say that "parents should be the best friends of their children." I would agree, with the caveat that the word friendship is slightly inaccurate here. What it means is that children should trust their parents the way the trust their friends, which only happens if parents can inspire such trust. The bottom line is that *parents should be parents*. That means fostering an environment of trust and affection so that that kids *want* to confide their problems to mom and dad first. But the role of a father—and his responsibility—goes much further than being a friend. It includes raising and teaching them, and that means exercising authority (which a friend does not have), pointing out the good and the bad, rewarding the former and punishing the latter. We already said that a friend is an equal. A father is not an equal but a reference point, and as such he is on another plane, although that certainly includes an affective dimension.

One final point regarding asymmetric friendships. There are some people whose friendships—that is, the persons with whom they are truly at ease—are with people with a great age difference from themselves, and they lack the social skills to establish contact with their peers. In this case the asymmetrical relationship would be a refuge from such difficulties, by seeking someone weaker (a younger person) who accepts and values them uncritically, or at the other end of the spectrum, someone who provides security.

Two specific scenarios deserve a separate mention because they have specific features: marriage and apostolic celibacy.

Marriage has been defined by many as a particular form of friendship, where the spouses make the decision to give to each other completely and for life; this gives rise to a "intimate partnership of married life and love"[9] that will naturally grow when children come. Strictly speaking, the spousal relationship is different from mere friendship, as C. S. Lewis describes in *The Four Loves*, because of its indissoluble nature, its openness to life, and its erotic component.

But rather than talk about the relationships between the spouses I would like to focus on the relationships that spouses can have outside of marriage. The spouses share a home, projects, dreams, their bed … should they also share their friends? In other words, is it good for each one to have their own friends and spend time with them, or is it better that they always be together, and if necessary drop those friendships in which the other spouse does not click?

I would answer with this statement: *for a marriage to work otherness must be respected.* Community of life is not the same as having identical tastes, hobbies, and personal links. The differences are more patent when we take into account the differing sensitivity of men and women. This was clearly shown in a TV commercial: a woman is showing her new home to her friends, and they all scream with excitement when she opens a closet full of clothes … and they are silenced by the louder screams of the husband and his friends when they come across a fridge full of beer.

Many times the willing sacrifice of either of them to adapt to the other spouse will lead to increase the range of activities that they can do together. Other times it will not be necessary to make the effort, and indeed it will be more appropriate that, without neglecting family obligations, each one goes out with the friends that he or she has made, before or after getting married, for an outing, cultural excursion, sports, etc. It is not a matter of "having a break from the other" (words that may be commonly used, and are not a problem if properly understood), but a matter of not neglecting one's own relational needs because they are not exhausted in family life. By

9   Vatican II, Pastoral Constitution *Gaudium et spes*, December 7, 1965, n. 48.

contrast, if they take reasonable care of these relationships, both spouses will feel better sharing the many things that they have in common, and eventually they may even share these friendships.

The second special scenario is that of people who have given their lives entirely to God in apostolic celibacy. We will dedicate a whole chapter to this topic, but I just want to mention one thing. Giving oneself to God and to others does not get rid of the need for friendship, and that means friends among and beyond those who share the same vocation, and friends beyond the group of those who benefit from their apostolic work. If we look at these categories within the three-fold division, those who share the vocation would fall into the family category, and those who benefit from their work would fall into the workplace group. True friendships can develop in both areas, but it should not be taken for granted.

Celibacy implies foregoing a life project with someone else and foregoing intimacy of body and soul with that person. But it does not imply that the need to share hobbies, tastes, and dreams with others in a trusting environment disappears. It could be argued that this is already done in spiritual accompaniment or direction. It does happen there, and it is also true that spiritual direction usually happens in a relaxed and trusting environment. However, friendship is something else: it is the *spontaneous sharing of some of one's significant affective interiority within an environment of parity.* Spiritual accompaniment does not contain these features: there is no reciprocity or parity in the sharing, it is not spontaneous (it only happens at the time of the appointment) and the contents and how they are talked about are different.

Maurizio Faggioni makes a point about priests, but the same can be applied to other kinds of celibacy, including that of women. Friendship makes it possible that

> One day, he will be immersed in the demanding routine of pastoral ministry. His friends—whether they are brother priests or lay people, men or women, single or married—will offer him affective and human support. The priest, like any married man, may need that from time to time. Now, the celibate person can't expect a friend to provide the affective support that a wife would give, because friendship is different from conjugal love. But he

138

knows that despite distances, the passage of time and the vicissitudes of life, the friend will always be there.[10]

I think it's worth adding a postscript that applies to both marriage and celibacy. We have seen that friendship *is found and accepted*, and fostered through interaction. It therefore has points in common with the process of falling in love and courtship that results in engagement. This, however, has an important feature that makes it different from friendship: the erotic component. In falling in love, the other person is liked *as belonging to the opposite sex* and *in view of a common life project*. Moreover, the erotic component can arise spontaneously in a friendship relationship: many marriages develop from a friendship born without any other pretension. This is precisely the reason why people who do not want to fall in love (for example, those who are already married or who follow a path of celibacy) must live out a "custody of the heart" when dealing with people of the opposite sex—that is, not to allow situations that could encourage romance. Even more important in these cases is to be attentive and sincere with respect to one's own feelings—without tension, fear or scandal in the face of what one feels or could feel—to limit the times spent with certain people, not being alone with them, etc. In the part dedicated to chastity and celibacy we will go into these themes in greater depth.

We end this section with a quote from Aristotle that summarizes this whole section: friendship "is one of the most indispensable requirements of life. For no one would choose to live without friends, but possessing all other good things."[11]

4. No Confusion and Having a Clear Hierarchy

We have looked at three basic kinds of relationships. Everybody needs to feel that they belong to a family,[12] a job where they can develop their skills

10 M.P. Faggioni, "The Value of Friendship in Celibate Life," in F. Insa, D. Parker (eds.), *Loving and Teaching Others to Love. The Formation of Affectivity in Priestly Life*, Independently Published 2021, pp. 151.

11 Aristotle, *Nicomachean Ethics*, VIII, 1.

12 As already stated, I also call "families" those groups that arise from a spiritual bond among individuals who live a specific vocation within an institution of the Church.

in cooperation with others and friends with whom enjoy and share hobbies and interiority.

These three areas are not watertight compartments, they can overlap: it is possible to work with a brother in a family business, and have such a good relationship with him that he can be looked upon as a friend.

However, they are three different areas, and they should not be mixed. Each has its own typical features, and confusing them may result in awkward situations. "My wife is my boss," words that usually imply a complaint, would be the most common example. We can replace the word "wife" with husband, brother, sister, friend, spiritual director, the superior in a religious order, etc. When this happens, crossing boundaries becomes easy: a work-related request during a family meal, sports, or a conversation of spiritual accompaniment, or from the director of a religious institution.

By and large it is unwise to cross these boundaries because it can break the harmony between the two relationships involved. Occasionally they may be appropriate, but the "boss" should be particularly careful, and the "subordinate" should be assertive enough to protect the separation of the two areas when inappropriate requests are made.

In so far as it is possible, the same person should not hold multiple roles—for instance, being the spiritual director and boss of a spiritual brother.

A final issue arises when there is a conflict between the demands of two different areas, or when the conflict happens within the individual's value system. We have already referred to the crises that may arise from mixing work and family. Now I would like to look at possible contrasts between the lifestyle of friends and one's own. We have seen that there are degrees of friendship. Some people are better friends than others, because of the *quality* of what is shared rather than the *quantity*. In other words, the subjective importance given to the things that are shared. This is why the best friendships are not merely people on the same football team but those who share *life's great ideals*. Yet, it is possible that the example or the contact with a friend creates pressure to give in on one's ideals (such as a consistent Christian life). As the saying goes "a man is known by the company he keeps." This is the time to review the value system and the scheme of comprehensibility because it may be in danger. Usually there is no need to break up the friendship, but it would be prudent to keep some distance, avoid some topics of discussion, and not spend time together in certain places, even at the cost of cooling off the relationship. A true friend will accept it, and the relationship might even become stronger. There are other things to be shared. And respect for the other, a key feature of friendship, will come into special relief.

Positive effects can result from situations like the above. Firstly, the desire to share great ideals will lead to seeking out those who are already living these ideals, especially if they have helped others to do the same; they are the so-called *good friendships*. It will also contribute to talking with friends about one's own value system, such as living an authentic Christian life, that provides the motivation to become better people. For those who do not share the same values we can explain why we do or do not do certain things in a way they can understand, aware of St. Peter's words "always be ready to make your defense to anyone who demands from you an accounting for the hope that is in you" (1 Pet 3:15). This explanation, possibly followed by an invitation to savor all that gives us peace and happiness—while respecting the freedom of the friend—is the foundation of Christian *apostolate*.

In short, if these three areas are clearly identified and combined in our own value system, it will be easier to establish a hierarchy that will enable us to avoid conflicts or solve them should they emerge. This hierarchy will lead to unity of life, to grow both humanly and supernaturally in all of them and to attain sanctity, the goal of the Christian vocation.

OLD AGE

1. Who Says When Old Age Begins?

When does old age begin? It is difficult to set a date; we often meet elderly people who remain physically and intellectually very active. Improvements in living conditions, the advances of medical science and the dynamics of many professions allow people to function very well at an age that people once considered quite advanced.

Rather than judging from a timeline, I will mark the last period of life from the moment of retirement. In most Western countries, people retire between the ages of 65 and 70. It is an objective event that marks the beginning of a new way of life, and carries many personal, familial, and social repercussions. It is not always clear-cut. Sometimes people retire because of issues in the workplace, opportune retirement packages, chronic but non-debilitating illnesses, the high risk of certain jobs, etc. On the other hand, some people keep working until much later, especially those engaged in intellectual types of work.

The idea of a *third age* (old age) is not related to a specific number of years or situation. Rather it includes a set of personal and social characteristics that can surface at other times, and go mostly unnoticed. The beginning of old age also depends on other factors, such as healthcare facilities in the area, the socioeconomic level of the individual, work related wear or even burnout, the country and historical circumstances in question, etc.

Some authors even talk of a *fourth age*, that begins when physical limitations have an impact on personal autonomy, usually around age 80. Someone is needed to take care of domestic tasks (cleaning, laundry, cooking, etc.) and later personal care: hygiene, dress, and eating. By then chronic and degenerative illnesses take their toll. These diseases were rarer in times of lower life-expectancy, but improvements in the quality of life and medical advances have postponed their appearance.

Other terms that refer to this period of time have their own nuances (old age, senescence, senility, etc.), but we will not consider them here.

142

Death is the obvious endpoint of this stage. According to the World Health Organization, life expectancy in 2019 in the United States was 76.3 years for men and 80.7 for women.[1] This means that we could live in retirement for many years, and these years should have their own specific purpose. Everyone deserves a significant end, like a crowning of his passing through life, though it would be strange to think that one fifth of life should be spent preparing for death. The idea would be for everyone to have the chance to look back and say, "my life was worthwhile," and to look ahead quietly, aware that

> for your faithful, Lord, life is changed not ended, and, when this earthly dwelling turns to dust, an eternal dwelling is made ready for them in heaven.[2]

2. Setting the Boundaries

Old age is Erikson's eighth and last psychosocial stage (Table 11).[3] The radius of significant relations expands to the max, and includes *the human species, my species*. The two extremes of the corresponding psychosocial crisis are *integrity* vs. *despair*. According to Erikson, integrity is a sense of consistency and totality in the somatic, psychological, and social levels; they are precisely the three elements we used in the first chapter to describe personality. All three run the risk of disintegrating over the years, and the opposite of integrity is despair.

Age	Stage	Psychosocial crises	Radius of significant relations	Basic strength	Core pathology
60 years–	Old age	Integrity vs. despair	"Mankind," "my kind"	Wisdom	Disdain

Table 11. Stages and competencies of old age according to Erikson.[4]

1   https://apps.who.int/gho/data/view.main.SDG2016LEXv?lang=en. (Accessed August 7, 2021)
2   *Roman Missal*, Preface I for the Dead.
3   Cf. E. Erikson, *The Life Cycle Completed*, W.W. Norton, New York–London 1998, pp. 61–66.
4   Adapted from *ibidem*, pp. 32–33.

The search for integrity will lead people to remain faithful to the lifestyle they have led until then, to what they have been and wanted to be, to act in accordance with their value system and always to seek the goals they set for themselves. It also implies accepting his own past, and the fact that death is a part of life. We already mentioned in the first chapter that a feature common to all stages is that they are all necessary. Acquiring this competency prepares the individual to leave this life peacefully.

The basic strength of the stage is *wisdom*, the "informed and detached concern with life itself in the face of death itself."[5] The old person knows about life and he is detached from it. The opposite pathology is *disdain*, a reaction of contempt when one senses that the end is nigh and he feels confusion and abandonment (and the fact that others see him in the same way). Disdain shows itself in many ways, like the loss of interest in new things, the view that "old is better," indifference to the surroundings, reducing one's social circle, neglect of physical care and appearance, and a long list of other things.

Romano Guardini agrees with Erikson that the antithetical terms of old age are wisdom and despair. He states that "a calm dignity that results from oneself, not from one's achievements"[6] emanates from accomplished old age. He adds a further ethical task:

> to accept that one is growing old and to identify himself with his lot in life. In this way he will not be angry because life is ebbing away, or jealous of those who have it to the full. He will acknowledge young people, and will even love them and try to help them. The motive should not be the desire to control them, because it would be a way to conceal envy, but out of solidarity with the cause of life, and the desire to help life to be what it should be, despite all the dangers, bewilderment and confusion that surround it.[7]

---

5   *Ibidem*, p. 61.
6   Cf. R. Guardini, *Die Lebensalter. Ihre ethische und pädagogische Bedeutung*, Matthias-Grünewald, Mainz 1986, pp. 61.
7   *Ibidem*, p. 94.

This is the great contribution the elderly can make, and the best memory they can leave behind.

3. The Signs of Aging

a) The Need to Anticipate

The purpose of what follows is to suggest some ideas to help the third age be a time of human and spiritual growth. We can summarize them with one single word: *anticipate*. We might think of an 80-year-old man who falls and breaks his hip; he undergoes surgery and recovers, ready for discharge. But home is a second-floor apartment, there is no elevator, he only has a bathtub with no walk-in shower, and the shops are a 15-minute walk away. He lives on his own and urgently needs home assistance. Clearly, this should have been thought out much earlier to prevent what is now an emergency. Things are not always so dramatic, but foresight is definitely critical.

In order to stay ahead of the curve, we need to know what to expect, mainly in two areas: personal limitations and social interaction. The way they present themselves varies from person to person, both in timing and how the initial symptoms appear.[8] There are many common issues, and the boundaries are not always clear cut.

b) Physical and Cognitive Changes

We have mentioned in previous chapters that the body begins to wear out in the 30s (described as the decade of the "I never") with regards to *physical activity*. The peak of a man's physical performance takes place in the first half of his total life expectancy. It can be observed in elite sportspeople, most of whom retire before they reach the fortieth birthday.

The third age brings a new factor into play: the loss of general strength

8   There are many online sites with practical information. The author recommends the American Geriatrics Society website, which has many articles on the assessment and the physical and cognitive stimulation of the elderly: https://www.americangeriatrics.org/publications-tools/patient-education (accessed: May 29, 2021).

can be such that day-to-day activities become impossible or difficult to manage. There is a loss of strength, and the elderly slow down, get tired more easily, and become clumsy, to name just a few psychomotor shortcomings.

However, the *loss of sensory function* can restrict them even more. Presbyopia appears in the 40s, but at first it is easily managed with glasses. An old person's sight worsens both because of general deterioration of vision (more than half of those over 80 have cataracts, which can be fixed, albeit with a more invasive procedure) and retinal degeneration, which is more difficult to manage.

What really limits old people in most cases is the loss of hearing because it leads to isolation, especially when relatives and friends become impatient. Treatment for this condition is expensive, bothersome, and the results are not great.

Aging impairs *cognition*: understanding and reasoning become slow, their abstract reasoning diminishes (with a consequent loss of their sense of humor, because they do not get double meanings) and so does their memory (that is, their ability to keep and recall information). These limitations are a severe handicap to learning the new skills required to cope with their changing circumstances. The chance of developing some kind of dementia also increases with age. Alzheimer's disease is the most prevalent: it is estimated that 1% of the population between the ages of 65 and 75, and up to 25% of those above 85, suffer from Alzheimer's.

It is important to notice the first symptoms of dementia. Forgetting names of people and even of things is a common early sign. The individual will often try to hide it—not always consciously—by blaming others ("who misplaced the keys?"). We call this *confabulation*. A visit to the doctor will facilitate an early diagnosis and initial treatment (medication and/or cognitive stimulation) that can delay the progression of the illness.

Lack of sleep is a frequent complaint. It becomes harder to fall asleep, and sleep itself is often broken and of poor quality. It often reappears as day-time somnolence. A friend of mine described it with a good dose of humor: "As I grow older, I sleep less and doze more." A Spanish contribution to mankind comes in very handy here: the word "siesta" needs no translation. A 30 to 60 minute rest after lunch (sometimes a shorter one before lunch) can help overcome nighttime problems and afford better functioning during the day. This nap must be short, otherwise it can make it difficult to sleep at night.

The elderly can become uninhibited, and their raw *character* becomes more obvious. They can seem more impatient, impulsive, irritable, demanding, rigid, precocious, depressed, greedy, and controlling. To a large extent, one reaps what one has sown. Those who tried throughout life to be patient, kind, caring, cheerful, and optimistic, etc., should not fear the lack of inhibition. The loss of "openness to change" is typical of this stage. Occasionally it degenerates into suspicion and the mistrust of anything new. We will see later that it is mainly due to a feeling of alienation from the world they live in, and longing for the world where they felt at ease. They can become extremely protective of their autonomy and independence even when they can no longer look after themselves.

Their *sense of time* is also different. It is true that they do not have much to do, and take longer on the phone or doing simple activities, but there is also a cognitive element at play. The general slowing down leads them to developing a different sense of time: they feel more at ease doing things slowly, and much prefer to take their time.

With regards to *sexuality*, they find it difficult to perform the conjugal act or are unable to do it altogether. When we spoke of the 40s we looked at the psychological effects of menopause in women. Now it is the man's turn. They may seek medical or paramedical remedies to maintain sexual function—which is important in the context of marriage—but the solutions are not always successful or safe. An acquaintance of mine who had begun to notice these changes composed the following prayer: "My God, if you remove the power, please remove the desire as well."

Lastly, *chronic illnesses* accumulate (hypertension, diabetes, arthritis, hypercholesterolemia, etc.). They can cause pain and lifestyle restrictions, require special diets and limit physical activity. They simply mean that the body is *wearing out*.

c) Social Changes

Work commitments cease after retirement, and with them the daily and weekly structure. Every day is the same, "every day is Sunday," and the external motivation to carry out the tasks that they could or should do may no longer be there. They then tend to delay tasks indefinitely, although if they have too much of anything, it is time itself.

In addition to the absence of activity there is a loss of the *role in life* itself, which is greater the more the individual identified himself with his professional work: "I am a professor, a doctor, an engineer, a businessman, a farmer, a tradesman...." The role can be projected—with or without motive—on society: "I used to be *their* doctor, this is why they valued me." Ultimately, the old man is no longer the reference point, the consultant. He is still fit and able (ability does not disappear on the day of retirement), but he is not "out there," and little by little he is forgotten. The desire—with a touch of narcissism—to be called upon to solve problems and give suggestions at work often leads to frustration when the calls do not come. The typical questions after retirement become: "What am I now?" "What am I good for?" Being ahead of the curve here means promoting areas other than work while still in the workforce, so that one's identity is not undermined at the time of leaving professional work.

We have also mentioned the *empty nest syndrome* and its effect on the life of a couple. If the marriage relationship has not adapted to this situation, life together can be even more troublesome, because the two will spend more time together. If only the husband worked outside, the wife may find her space invaded and routines altered. Up till then the house was "hers and hers alone" all morning, and she had her routine to enjoy, cleaning and looking after it. The retiree husband, on the other hand, may feel like a stranger in his own home. The rules of life together have to be renegotiated, just like yesteryear: schedules (when to get up, bedtime, meals, etc.), going out, sharing domestic chores, use of goods and rooms, television, etc.

When one spouse dies, the other may have to live on his/her own. This is especially hard for men, who often are incapable of running a household. Wanting to remain independent and not wanting to *invade* the children's homes will explain why they delay hiring a caregiver or moving to supervised residential accommodation for as long as possible.

The *financial aspect* is another source of stress. Pensions are not enough to keep the previous standard of living, and may not be enough to cover all their needs. It is wise to save for a rainy day because the future is uncertain. For some people this is a big worry and they become excessively frugal. Reality hits hard when past dreams such as travelling are no longer possible.

Following retirement, one's *social life* also takes a hit. The chance of meeting and socializing with many people is suddenly cut short. Overnight it seems the elderly find themselves "playing in a lower division," and one needs to fill the time by himself because his friends and acquaintances remain at work. The physical and mental wear makes going out more onerous, and the elderly tend to limit social contacts to immediate family. On the other hand, old friends die, and their absence contributes to the increasing sense of isolation (fewer people to go out with). The feeling that one's own time is ever nearer involves a kind of psychological stress. Miguel Delibes, a twentieth century Spanish novelist, describes it very well in one of his works: Eloy is a 75-year-old retiree that comes back home from the burial of his last remaining friend. As he walks back with the priest he tells him, bitterly, as he points to the cemetery walls, that he has more friends behind these walls than in town.[9]

Sensory and cognitive losses can make crowded places uncomfortable (for instance, large family functions). It is a good idea to provide them with a space where they feel comfortable and part of the scene, where they can listen and contribute to the conversation. This means that the relatives should understand that sometimes they will repeat old stories, or ask again and again what they missed in the conversation.

Finally, as the world's pace accelerates, it is easy for the elderly to become disconnected, particularly in technological matters. Losing some of their ability to retain information (memory loss) and to learn new things makes it harder to keep up to date with the news, politics, sports, etc. In a relatively short time, they can feel that "this is no longer my era." Hence, they like to talk about the past and they find refuge in "the good old days," the world they can relate to, where they were acknowledged and respected, the world they remember fondly and may even long for.

Others have the opposite reaction. They hang on to this life and deny the passing of time as if they wanted to show that advancing age has no effect on them. It is important to be understanding and understand that the elderly

> seem to be mourning not only for time forfeited and space depleted but also [...] for autonomy weakened, initiative lost, intimacy missed, generativity neglected.[10]

9   Cf. M. Delibes, *La hoja roja*, Argos Vergara, Barcelona 1979, p. 156.
10   Erikson, *The Life Cycle Completed*, p. 63.

We cannot forget that

> the senile person is weak and feels threatened. He defends him-
> self by asserting what he is and what he has: his properties, his
> rights, his habits, opinions and assessments. Senile stubbornness
> comes to the fore: the dogged determination to hang on to some
> things and to resist others, even to the smallest minutiae. It is
> not easy to counteract this kind of age hardening, because the
> mind and the feelings have lost their ability to stand to reason
> and to understand the nature of the arguments at hand.[11]

Maladaptation can lead to depression, often underdiagnosed in the elderly because it is confused with their inactivity. At this point I will not treat
senile depression because of its similarity to the depression stage of mourning, which will appear in the next chapter.

Given this long list of problems, old age may not be something to look
forward to. Yet from the psychological perspective the progressive decline
of old age has some positive features. It becomes obvious that "here we have
no lasting city" (Heb 13:14) and that helps detach us from the goods of
this world. We could say that the end of the life cycle is the reverse of its
beginning. A child's life begins with attachment to the mother, and the elderly's ends with a certain detachment (but not scorn) of a world that feels
somewhat foreign. This facilitates yearning for a life to come where "Death
will be no more; mourning and crying and pain will be no more" (Rev
21:4).

Having said all this, it is possible to manage many of the issues raised
successfully. That will be our next topic, after a short reflection.

4. Excursus: When There Is No Retirement

We have only considered the case of those who retire from a "normal" job.
For an employee retirement means a sudden change of circumstances, with
a clear "before and after." One positive takeaway is the realization that time
passes, whether we like it or not.

---

11 Guardini, *Die Lebensalter. Ihre ethische und pädagogische Bedeutung*, p. 66.

Some people do not have a professional job in the usual sense: a paid job, a contract, or professions with a definite endpoint. I am thinking of housewives, priests, etc. We can also include those who partially retire, or professions in the liberal arts, where work is self-directed and can continue until the end of one's life. The passage of time has an impact on these people as well, but they may lack that concrete point in time when they realize that they have reached old age. The danger is that these individuals or those who live or work with them may not realize that they have a growing number of issues. They may not make the necessary adjustments to fit their decreasing skills. It's like seeing a relative after a long time away and noticing physical and psychological changes that have escaped the attention of those living with him.

In these cases, it is important for friends and family members to notice signs of aging that the person in question may not even be aware of, such as unusual tiredness, forgetfulness, aches and pains, etc.

5. Getting Ready for Old Age

Sooner or later and to a greater or lesser degree we'll all end up with some of the limitations we have described. But there's a lot we can do to reduce their impact on our daily life.

We have already mentioned that the key is to *anticipate*, to foresee future problems and be ahead of the curve. Many authors recommend that we think of old age beginning ten years earlier. At that time—say 55 years of age—people should use the physical and mental agility they still enjoy, and the great amount of time they have left, to think out a game plan for the significant changes that will eventually occur. We will list here a few possibilities. Ultimately, they are about thinking about the relationships and activities that will replace professional work when retirement comes.

Given that *work-related relationships* will cease, one step will be developing the other two big relationship "blocks": friends and family. Part of this is putting work into perspective. One should question whether the last few years of work should be seen as a *final sprint* in the professional race, at the cost of neglecting those who will remain with us afterwards.

Healthy habits—which we should start practicing early in life—not only help prolong life but also improve its quality. A stroke or a heart attack may cause death, but it may also result in serious impairments. It goes without saying that we ought to avoid unhealthy habits such as smoking, leading a sedentary lifestyle, and carrying excess weight, and ought to get in regular exercise and find a reasonable balance between work, rest, sleep, etc. Regular medical checkups are also key: they can detect illnesses at their early stages, before they can no longer be controlled.

Then there's the need to *improve one's character* throughout all of life's stages: becoming more flexible, blunting the sharp edges, preventing quirks, developing a good sense of humor (without becoming cynical), being understanding with the failures of others (and our own as well) and not becoming agitated, respecting other people's personalities and habits that are different from one's own, and adapting to other people's rhythms. A friend of mine once said that "at fifty you have to decide whether you want to become a gentle grandfather or a grumpy old man." Sometimes it can be useful to ask oneself the following question: "What sort of person would I be if I had dementia and became uninhibited?"

Learning to ask for help and allowing others to do so is a good asset when we become elderly. It's only a matter of time. If we live long enough, we will be physically more dependent on others. Old age confirms the idea that "someone else will fasten a belt around you and take you where you do not wish to go" (Jn 21:18). An excessive yearning for autonomy, or thinking that others underestimate our abilities as they try to help us, will make it very hard to cope with the limitations that come with old age.

It is necessary not only to allow for, but to foster *generational succession*, by looking forward to other people taking over our projects and starting where we left off rather than beginning again from scratch. This will enable young people to develop them further and make the adult's drive for *generativity* a reality. It will also make *role inversion* easier when the caregiver becomes cared for.

As far as possible we should *prepare the home* we expect to be living in when we turn 80. This means removing physical obstacles, making the necessary changes to bathrooms and stairs, and finding easy access to basic needs (shops, public transport, etc.). A smaller home or a condo is often a good solution after the children have left home, but with the limited income of a pension the house and its maintenance must be affordable.

Finally, it is worth reminding ourselves of the importance *of living out one's life project consistently.* The values we have espoused all our lives should be the values we want to have when we die. Exceptions make no sense; as the dictum goes: "We either live the way we think, or we end up thinking the way we live." Unity of life, both from a psychological and Christian point of view, provides a sense of identity—or integrity, to use Erikson's word. That will help us face the difficulties that come along, to look back on them with serenity and look to the future with hope.

6. A Stage to Continue Growing

This section contains a few pointers that can help to make the third age an enriching experience. They can be applied to oneself and suggested to relatives and friends, as well as to those who come to us for spiritual direction.

Guardini, considering the "ethical task" of old age, wrote that "only those who have accepted their aging interiorly can age in the right way."[12] This is in reference to embracing the limitations imposed by nature and not simply enduring them. Old age is part of life too, even if it has its curiosities. Therefore, the wise person

> knows about the end and accepts it. We do not mean being happy about it, although it does happen in some exceptional cases. We refer to the increasingly sincere preparedness to accept what will necessarily happen.[13]

Relatives and friends should articulate and clarify the fears that usually accompany old age, because sometimes the elderly may not be fully aware of their existence: loss of autonomy, financial issues, isolation, becoming a burden on the family, being forsaken, ending up in a nursing home, pain, illness, death. It is often difficult to talk about these issues, and people act as if not mentioning them would make them disappear. When they do come up, we should be sensitive to how the individual "reads" his own decay. The way he has looked upon his own abilities throughout life will

12 *Ibidem*, p. 92.
13 *Ibidem*, p. 56.

determine whether he sees the process as a humiliation, a painful loss, an opportunity to grow, etc.

It is not possible to find a solution to every problem, but sharing these concerns will help the elderly unburden themselves, and realize that it is silly to let possible future problems upset their present well-being. A friend of mine told me a story that illustrates the point. His elderly mother was admitted to the hospital for a few days. While there she witnessed her room-mate fall down in a dramatic fashion, and it resulted in a broken hip. When she was discharged, she developed such fear of falling that she reduced her activity as much as if she had had the fall herself. The solution was not easy, but some calm conversations with her children helped her to return to her normal daily activities, open up to the world once more, and to think again about what she could still do for others.

"Do business with these until I come back" (Lk 19:13). This advice is for everyone. The Lord has not come back yet—no matter how close he may appear to be—and therefore the duty to make one's talents bear fruit continues. No one can think, "I have done everything in life that I had to do," because he would then earn a scolding, like the servant who hid his talent rather than trade with it (cf. Lk 19:20–26).

The first step would be to ponder: "What talents do I have, today and now?" "How can I use them to serve God and others?" Notwithstanding physical and psychological decline, we all have one talent right to the end: time, twenty-four hours each day. It is never too late, as the Lord shows in the parable of the vine workers (cf. Mt 20:1–16). The eleventh-hour late-comer received the same pay as the others, to the great confusion of the other workers. Several books from the reference list at the end of this book can be handy sources for personal reflection. It can be a great source of in-spiration to read the biographies of people who managed to live a full life in their old age, based on service to others, even when struck by illness, physical impairment, and old age.

We will mention later many activities that can be undertaken during this period, yet I do not want to leave the impression that the goal is to fill the day doing things, even if it is for others. Erikson's adult competency of *generativity* gives way to *integrity*. Therefore, we first need to look within, and the first task is to grow in interiority. This could partly explain why the elderly are slow. It is not only a matter of physical or psychological decline, but the fact that there is less external pressure to do things and this helps them to think things through more carefully. Together with their life experience it gives them the wisdom typical of the age.

We have acknowledged many times that a person grows in relationships more than in anything else. Therefore, it is necessary to prevent isolation and to maintain contact with others, within the family and outside the family circle, and so overcome the increasing resistance to leave the house.

As we are talking about family life in the third age, I would like to make a comment on the topic of friendship. It is true that over time we lose contact with people, but the elderly can partially recover the loss by getting back in touch with old friends and above all by making new ones. That requires connecting with activities where they can meet people: the parish, volunteer work, a tennis club, a veterans' organization, etc.

It is also time to adopt a secondary role in one's dealings with others—trying to adapt to others and not force them to give what they cannot or will not give. It also means thinking proactively: "What do I have to change to improve my lot, with the means available to me and with the people around me?"

One great challenge for the elderly at this point is *time*. Their schedule must be filled, and they must feel—and be—useful. It requires a daily plan of activities that is both realistic and somewhat demanding. That means a set time to rise and attend to personal care. Physical appearance remains an important issue (cleanliness, changes of clothes, etc.). They ought to carry out as many activities as possible, although they may require assistance for some domestic tasks. They should make their own beds, help with the cleaning and cooking, etc. We have already mentioned the possible need for a period of rest, before or after lunch (up to one hour) to compensate for the lack of sleep at night.

Daily physical activity, adapted to their age and condition, is highly recommended. They may be able to play their favorite sport for an extended period of time, but the moment will come when it has to be curtailed or replaced with something less demanding, like walks, even with an aide or with someone pushing the wheelchair (then it is the pusher who enjoys the exercise).

Side-by-side with these activities, means should be taken to avoid sporting injuries, falls, forgetting to switch off the gas or stove after cooking a meal…. It is indeed an uneasy balance. As a general principle, "it is better for the individual to do it, even if it is not done very well, or it takes longer to do." We should bear in mind that the principle "use it or lose it" applies to all kind of skills. Once lost, it is not only more difficult to regain them, but the loss can also involve carry away other related skills.

Some people need to be encouraged to reduce the rhythm and intensity of their activity, and adapt to the possibilities and lower demands of their new state in life. It is quite possible that they have always been under pressure (from themselves or from others) to produce results. Now they need to learn to enjoy what they do, regardless of the results.

Tasks will certainly be less socially relevant, and probably not as fulfilling. On the other hand, retirees can spend more time doing what they like. The time has come to take up hobbies that had been abandoned because of a lack of time: reading, writing, playing a musical instrument, handiwork, sight-seeing, visiting museums, learning a language, tech courses, or online classes at a university. It is a good time to become more tech savvy, which will help them to better connect with the world. All these activities help keep the mind active and delay the onset of dementia. It is not just *occupational therapy*, but engagement in pleasant activities that help enrich the person holistically. Crosswords or sudoku are fine, but the idea is to be more ambitious.

Thus far I have tried not to be exhaustive, but I cannot resist quoting from a long list of tasks proposed by one of the authors of the bibliography included at the end of the book:

> handicrafts, accounting or statistical projects, home maintenance, replacing fixtures, gardening, embroidery, sewing, suit and dress alterations, maintenance tasks, simple mechanics, cooking, bread or cake making, carpentry, marquetry, classifying and sorting documents, books, tapes, records and magazines; archive upkeep, oil and watercolor painting, photography, film development, typing and other computer tasks, setting up notices, sending cards and other promotional material, translations, temporary nursing arrangements, recreational activities, occasional teaching, organizing travel or excursions, handling telephone calls, working in call centers, market research, surveys,

data recording, cosmetics, market research, hairdressing, tailoring, suit and dress rentals, shoe repairs, doll repairs, home vending: buttons, buckles, lace, pencils, exercise books, etc.; ice cream, soft drinks vending, packaging for presents, accompanying and/or supervision of children, assisting invalids or elderly people who have no relatives available to take care of them....[14]

It is a long list of activities, but by no means exhaustive. We could also add: caring for grandchildren (so many homes can manage thanks to the assistance of grandparents), helping out in parishes or youth clubs, volunteering, etc. There is a wide range of options: providing catechism and Christian formation classes, helping out at a front desk, monitoring study or sport sessions, even using some of one's professional talents: accounting, maintenance, repairs, etc.

Sorting out one's medication and domestic finances is important. Forgetfulness in these areas can be particularly harmful, and having someone supervise that the right medication is taken at the right times is recommended. The same applies to financial matters. A trusted person who knows the passwords can manage the bank accounts, be given power of attorney, and can also manage the portfolio of shares, property and other goods. A certain amount of money should be made available for day-to-day purchases. Making a last will and testament early is a good practice. Close relatives should be made aware of this, and respect the wishes of the individual. The elderly will have to stop driving sooner or later, usually because of loss of vision or of one's reflexes.

Loss of sphincter control is a distressing event. Hygiene may require the use of pads, especially at night. It also prevents having to get up during the night, with the inherent risk of falls.

In the more advanced stages, when one is confined to bed, there is something that can always be done—namely, praying. It is no small matter, nor pure consolation when one cannot "truly" cooperate in other projects. It is a way of serving others with one's mind, heart and will. Significantly, St. Therese of Lisieux is the patron saint of the missions, although from the

14   A. Delgado Cardona, *Aprender a envejecer*, Corporación CED, Medellín 2006, pp. 95–96

age of fifteen until her death nine years later she never left her Carmelite convent. She offered abundant prayers and sacrifices and thus sustained the activity of many missionaries around the world with her zeal for souls.

There is a time when physical impairment is such that the level of care and supervision required makes it dangerous for people to live on their own. It is of course a hard decision to make, both for the person (he realizes that he is losing autonomy) and for the immediate relatives. Moving to the home of one of the children can be a good option, provided that the decision is made together by the husband and wife (and with the children's input sometimes), and that the home is large enough and equipped to take care of the newcomer. Matters become more difficult when the level of care becomes more intense: feeding, personal and/or medical care, or when twenty-four hour/day direct supervision becomes necessary. Occasionally someone can be hired, but the impairment may be severe enough that transfer to a specialized center is required. Both options are costly and need to be assessed properly. Admission to a nursing home or retirement village can be distressing for all. It may be interpreted by the elderly person as abandonment by their relatives, when in fact it means that proper care and attention are given when the person needs it.

The task of the relative and/or caregiver is not easy. It requires a combination of patience and fortitude, and it is not always obvious when to apply them. It is also a matter for the closer relatives to distribute the various tasks in a reasonably balanced manner. It is not fair to overburden the person "who is good at it" or who lives closer by or who has a better relationship with the elderly person. It is always possible to take some of the easier-to-manage tasks from the overburdened caregiver, and provide "respite breaks" from time to time. Although it may be difficult, the relatives ought to care for and respect their elders at all times, as St. Paul recommends to Timothy: "Do not speak harshly to an older man, but speak to him as to a father [...] to older women as mothers" (1 Tim 5:1–2).

7. Getting Ready to Leap Across to the Eternal Home

Last but not least we come to deal with the main task of this stage: getting ready to leap across to heaven. We have emphasized all throughout the chapters on the life cycle that each stage has a meaning of its own, and that each stage must be lived in preparation for the stage that follows. Old age needs to be lived in preparation for the next and final stage: the call to eternity.

> To become old means getting closer to death, and the older we are the closer we get to it. In that close proximity we even manage to touch the bottom of our existence. We ask ourselves the ultimate questions: 'is death a dismantling into a void, or the way to what is truly real?' Religion alone can answer these questions. Becoming old without faith in God is a bad thing. Verbiage is of no use. The core of the old man's life can be no other than prayer, of whatever kind.[15]

If we have lived life as a gift from God, it is easier to accept that the gift is about to end, and usher in another gift that is even greater and lasting.

Among the many tasks to be undertaken, dealing with God plays a prominent role. That must be expressed in a time for daily prayer and receiving the sacraments often. The best way to ensure that God will welcome us is to receive him in the Eucharist every day. The anointing of the sick may be an appropriate course of action, bearing in mind that

> it is not a sacrament for those only who are at the point of death. Hence, as soon as anyone of the faithful begins to be in danger of death from sickness or old age, the fitting time for him to receive this sacrament has certainly already arrived.[16]

At the time of taking stock of one's life, its lights and shadows, the aspiration often repeated by Blessed Álvaro del Portillo can come in handy: "Thank you, sorry, help me more." It acknowledges whatever good we have done, the imperfect nature of our works, and the trust in divine assistance for the time that is left.

One of the principal reasons to give thanks is the perseverance in our

---

15 Guardini, *Die Lebensalter. Ihre ethische und pädagogische Bedeutung*, p. 73.
16 *Catechism of the Catholic Church*, n. 1514.

Christian vocation, a manifestation of God's love that has guided our whole life. Benedict XVI reminded a group of priests, religious, seminarians, and deacons of something that can also be applied to lay people, especially those who are married: "Faithfulness over time is the name of love, of a consistent, true and profound love for Christ the Priest."[17] When we come close to the moment "to depart from this world and go to the Father" (Jn 13:1), the Pope's thought will give us the serenity and the hope that St. Paul conveyed with these words: "I have fought the good fight, I have finished the race, I have kept the faith" (2 Tim 4:7).

The humble acknowledgment of the good we have done—real, but never enough—of the fruits of our own life, of the deeds that will survive us and of the children—physical and spiritual—will confirm that our life has been fruitful. Awareness that we could have done more will be another test for our frustration tolerance (necessary from early child-hood, as we have seen) and will help us to use whatever time we have left to persevere in doing good works. The desire to leave a good memory to our loved ones and "leave to the young a noble example," like old Eleazar (cf. 2 Macc 6:18–31), will motivate us to show patience, have a sense of humor, and view things from a fully Christian outlook to cope with the ailments of old age and the pains of illness. Such an attitude conforms to the dictum *juvenes videntur sancti sed non sunt: senes non videntur sed sunt*, the young seem holy but are not, the old do not seem holy but they are.

Occasionally a painful feeling of uselessness, despair, and remorse may come to the fore on account of mistakes made, or for having wasted one's life entirely. In the latter case it is quite possible to feel that life should not end yet because there is no legacy left. The *generativity* that marked the previous stage of development is unfulfilled. At those times we can foster a sense of contrition and renew the desire to introduce "room for true repentance"[18] in what remains of life. Making peace with people that we have mistreated may not be possible, but it is always a good time to reconcile with God. Hence there are no reasons to despair because our Lord is always

---

17 Benedict XVI, *Homily on the celebration of vespers with priests, religious, seminarians and deacons at Fatima*, May 12, 2010.

18 *Roman Missal*, Formula for the Intention of the Mass.

ready to grant us pardon and give us the reward of rejoicing in heaven, even if we come as the laborer of the eleventh hour (cf. Mt 20:1–16).

This approach will lead us to look on the future without apprehension, trusting—on the basis of our divine filiation—that we will receive the reward promised by our Father God: "You are those who have stood by me in my trials; and I confer on you, just as my Father has conferred on me, a kingdom, so that you may eat and drink at my table in my kingdom" (Lk 22:28–30).

WHEN THE END IS NIGH

1. On Death and Dying

How should we approach the news that the time has come? What is the best way to confirm the terminal nature of an illness?

The Swiss psychiatrist Elizabeth Kübler-Ross (1926–2004) is well known for her description of the stages of grief, the psychological process of accepting the news that the end is near. She developed an interest in the topic as a student shortly after the Second World War, when she visited the Madjanek extermination camp in Poland. She was struck by hundreds of images of butterflies along the walls of the barracks. The butterfly would become the symbol of how she understood death—stepping up to a higher life.

She moved to New York in 1958. Initially she was keen on pediatrics, but ended up specializing in psychiatry. Over the following years she was often called upon to help dying patients who were suffering from depression. She listened to them for long hours. She kept them company with words and silence until they peacefully passed away, managing to add a great sense of humanity to her medical expertise. After she had been at the bedside of some 200 patients for the duration of the dying process (she would eventually follow thousands more throughout her career), she wrote her best-known book, *On Death and Dying* (1969).[1]

She describes the five stages her patients went through after they were told of their diagnosis: denial, anger, bargaining, depression and acceptance. Yet she repeatedly cautioned that some stages could overlap, happen in a different order or even be absent altogether, and that their duration could vary depending on the personality of the patients and their personal circumstances. Anger would be more intense for an irritable person, a "born

---

1   E. Kübler-Ross, *On Death and Dying.* Routledge, Abingdon, Oxon, 2009.

fighter" would bargain as much as possible, a pessimist would be more prone to depression, etc.

Kübler-Ross soon realized that the patients' relatives went through the same stages she had described, and that when people were presented with bad news they generally went through the same process. Her ideas can help us understand the suffering of those who grieve, and provide us with tools to help them.

2. First Stage: Denial

"No, not me, it can't be true."

The first reaction of patients when told the bad news is to act as if it had nothing to do with them: "The tests are wrong," or, "They are from another patient," etc. They continue to live as if nothing had happened, and wait for the tests to be done again, or seek a second opinion. Yet, this stage has its use: it gives time to "digest" the news.

According to Kübler-Ross,

> This anxious denial following the presentation of a diagnosis is more typical of the patient who is informed prematurely or abruptly by someone who does not know the patient well, or does it quickly 'to get it over with,' without taking the patient's readiness into consideration.[2]

This opens up to the first step to help someone die peacefully. The right person should break the news at the right time. Those of us who have worked in hospitals have often experienced the following scenario. The doctor informs the relatives, and they work out among themselves who the best person would be to talk to the patient. They often think that it could be the doctor himself ("It's his job!"), or the chaplain who has already started talking with the patient. Although these are legitimate options, the best would be a relative who is closest to the patient, someone who has both moral high ground and enjoys a warm relationship with him or her. It is easier for the patient to share feelings and seek consolation (crying, hugging, etc.) from someone who is closer.

2   *Ibidem*, pp. 31–32

While it does not happen as often as it used to, there are still cases where breaking the news is delayed as long as possible with the excuse—or good intention—to spare the patient a longer period of suffering. People may be tempted to sidestep the difficulty of speaking up. We should keep in mind first of all that patients have the moral (and legal) right to know the state of their health and the results of their diagnostic tests. Even when the results have been given to relatives initially, hiding them from the patient would be an abuse.

Patients can tell when something is wrong. Repeated and more invasive tests, stays in the hospital, being told that "the results are not clear," reading some of the medical paperwork, or a simple search on the internet, will make them suspect that there is something seriously the matter behind all the fuss.

Excessive delays can give rise to silent *pacts*, where both patient and relatives "know that the other knows," but they do not dare to talk about it. The result is that all suffer to avoid making other people suffer. For the sake of saving others from a hard time, they lose out on mutual support and the sharing of emotions that they would do well to express.

Dr. Kübler-Ross recommends that the topic be raised much earlier.

> We are often accused of talking with very sick patients about death when the doctor feels—very rightfully so—that they are not dying. I favor talking about death and dying with patients long before it actually happens if the patient indicates that he wants to. A healthier, stronger individual can deal with it better and is less frightened by the oncoming death when it is still "miles away" than when it "is right at the door," as one of our patients put it so appropriately. It is also easier for the family to discuss such matters in times of relative health and well-being, and arrange for financial security for the children and others while the head of the household is still functioning. To postpone such talks is often not in the service of the patient but serves our own defensiveness.[3]

The last sentence explains why communication can sometimes be lacking. Talking about death is uncomfortable for everyone because it raises

3   *Ibidem*, p. 32.

many specters. It forces us all to face the reality of our own death. This discomfort may be more prevalent now than it was when Kübler-Ross' book was published fifty years ago, when society had a more spiritual outlook towards death. Yet we only need to read the news to realize that death remains a reality. The problem is facing the possibility of *our own death*.

We can look at Leo Tolstoy, one of the classics of literature, to illustrate what we are talking about:

> The example of syllogistic reasoning he had read in Kieswetter's Logic—"Gaius is a man, men are mortal, therefore Gaius is mortal"—had always seemed to him true only in relation to Gaius, not to himself. That it was true of this man Gaius, and of men in general, made absolute sense; but he was no Gaius and was not some man in general. He had always had something unique about him that separated him from others [...]. What to Gaius was the striped leather ball that little Vanya had loved so much? What did Gaius have to do with him kissing his mother's hand, and had Gaius ever heard the silken rustle of his mother's dress? Had he rioted over the pirogies at the law school? Had this Gaius ever fallen in love? And could Gaius ever preside over a courtroom the way he did? So of course, Gaius could be mortal, and it was right for him to die, but for me, little Vanya, for Ivan Ilych, with all my thoughts and emotions— for me it's a different story. It can't possibly be that I have to die. That would be too horrible.[4]

All the above does not mean that we should break the news to the patient in a sudden fashion or rebuke his denial. It is often best to proceed slowly, suggesting the idea, asking open ended questions to find out how he feels, and picking up what the patient wants to hear or is ready to take in. The best way to find out is not only the choice of words he may use, but also his body language and general attitude. In the meantime, it is good (within reason) to let him ask questions and keep up his hope, and request a second opinions or tests.

4   L. Tolstoy, *The Death of Ivan Illich*, VI.

Finding out what is best for the patient, and not for his friends and family, is what really matters. What is best for the person is giving him time and space to prepare himself in all areas. That includes work, family (saying goodbyes, reconciling with estranged loved ones, making a will, etc.), and the spiritual life. Needless to say, the better his actual state of health, the easier it is to handle all the issues.

3. The Second Stage: Anger

"Why me?" "Why not old George?" "It's not fair."

Reality imposes itself, and in the end the wall created by denial in the previous stage crumbles. The terminal patient realizes that things are serious, and he blames his family, his doctor, the healthcare system, society, etc. They did not listen to his initial complaints, they did not carry out diagnostic tests early enough, they did not get the treatment right .... I once saw a tombstone that clearly indicated that the deceased was caught in this stage. It read, "I told you that I was sick."

Sometimes anger is expressed more vaguely by resenting healthy people. They may react with surprise. "Should I be blamed because I am healthy?"

According to Kübler-Ross,

> The tragedy is perhaps that we do not think of the reasons for patients' anger and take it personally, when it has originally nothing or little to do with the people who become the target of the anger. As the staff or family react personally to this anger, however, they respond with increasing anger on their part, only feeding into the patient's hostile behavior.[5]

Indeed, the worst outcome in this case would be "mutual escalation" that puts other people off when they are most needed.

The key at this stage is to show empathy. Note the difference between these two responses: "You're wrong, you're being unfair," and, "I can see you're going through tough times. This must be very hard for you." The idea is to show patients that people respect, care for, and love

---

5   Kübler-Ross, *On Death and Dying*, p. 42.

them, that his feelings are recognized, and that he is not blamed for having them.

When the patient feels emotionally overcome by the illness, he will find some consolation in being part of the decision making, because it gives him a sense of control. For instance, agreeing to how often he should have visitors, or setting a limit to the length of the visits or to medical consultations. In my opinion, a common practice in palliative medicine could also be applied here. I refer to patient-controlled analgesia, which often results in patients taking fewer pain killers.

Anger can also be directed against God: "How could he let me get sick and on top of that leave my family unprotected?" The believer's convictions are tested. He has probably heard hundreds of times that God is good, a Father who provides, that "all things work together for good for those who love God" (Rom 8:28), but he may not have made those beliefs his own, and he rebels against his lot. The response of "defending God" or repeating "the same old advice" may be counterproductive because the patient may interpret them as a standard "ready-made" answer that solves nothing.

Someone with a serious illness is not ready for elaborate reasoning. And it may not be necessary in the long run. It may be better just to let him go on to God—which is the most important thing—with his mistakes. In the Lord's presence the patient will realize how wrong he was. It may be more useful to look for a positive belief that will resonate with his mind and heart: "Despite everything God is your Father, and he loves you," and, "He knows better because he has the perspective of eternity; we are too conditioned by the present moment." We will come back to this at the end of the chapter.

4. Third Stage: Bargaining

"Give me time to see my children's graduation." "I will do anything to get two more years."

This is the reaction of a child, who first demands, and later begs for something, with the promise of a change in behavior. The sick man can try to bargain with the doctor (to donate his body, to develop healthy habits, to stop smoking). More often he tries to strike a deal with God (to go to Sunday Mass, pray, avoid sin…). In return he asks for more time to live or at least to reduce the pain or disability.

Kübler-Ross states, "In our individual interviews without an audience we have been impressed by the number of patients who promise 'a life dedicated to God' or 'a life in the service of the church' in exchange for some additional time."[6] However, she adds with a touch of irony that, "None of our patients have 'kept their promise.'"[7] If they get what they asked for they do not change their behavior and they want more time than what they have already asked for. Doctors and relatives could initially respond, "we will do everything humanly possible," but without committing to what they are not sure of being able to do.

There is another benefit that comes with patience and empathetic listening. We get to know the patient's concerns better. What will happen to his family, remorse for the past, etc. Simply verbalizing his concerns helps remove excessive and irrational fears. For instance, we may say, "You are not going to miss my wedding. If you can't make it in person, you will see it better from heaven," or "Don't worry so much about promises to God if you get out of this. I think that what he wants is for you bear your pain patiently." These conversations have another positive effect—they help the patient to face some of his greatest fears, namely loneliness and being abandoned. "No matter what, I will be with you."

This approach presents us with the opportunity of developing a new way to relate to God, more mature and less selfish. If there's going to be any bargaining with God, it should happen along the following lines: "give me strength to endure my illness and I promise that from now on I will do my best to grow in my love for you and for others." It is the same thing that St. Augustine said many centuries ago. "God therefore does not command impossibilities; but in His command He counsels you both to do what you can for yourself, and to ask His aid in what you cannot do."[8]

5. Fourth Stage: Depression

"I am so depressed ... why should I keep on fighting?"

The illness has followed its natural course and bargaining has failed. God can work miracles but does not always do so. Multiple hospital

6 *Ibidem*, pp. 67–68.
7 *Ibidem*, p. 67.
8 St. Augustine, *On Nature and Grace*, XLIII, 50.

admissions and surgical procedures follow, more strength is lost, and autonomy is ever more limited. The relationship with the body becomes martial. So far, the body had been a faithful companion, but now it wants all of our attention. Weight loss and bodily sensations can even make it difficult for the sick person to recognize it as *his body*.

This is when depression comes in. Kübler-Ross identified two kinds: *reactive* depression and *preparatory* depression. It is important to distinguish them because they have different traits. Health personnel and relatives should approach them differently as well.

Reactive depression is the result of the loss of one's body image, autonomy, social and professional standing, the inability to look after one's family, the awareness of unfinished projects, self-blame for past mistakes, etc. This kind most needs the support of loved ones, who can help the sick person express his fears, see the future (both his and others') more objectively, sort out the causes of his worries as much as possible, be constantly engaged with things and feel as useful and productive as his condition allows.

When the individual falls into severe depression it is hard to keep up a minimum of activity. Other people may have to accompany him in his tasks, or ask for his assistance as a favor (a kind of emotional blackmail). Instead of telling him, "You have to get out," asking for help is more likely to succeed. "I need someone to help me with the shopping, could you come with me?" or "I feel like going for a walk, could you accompany me?"

The role of health professionals (doctors, psychologists, psychiatrists, etc.) is crucial. Even if their job is to look after clinical manifestations of the illness, they cannot neglect its subjective aspects. Medical or psychological intervention will often be required as well.

During this stage, the wish to die as soon as possible is not uncommon. There are even cases of suicidal ideation or requesting euthanasia.[9] The key is to interpret *the real message* that the patient wants to transmit.[10] "I don't want to live anymore," may really mean, "I don't want to live *like this* anymore" (with pain, fear and loneliness). Behind a request "to die with dignity" we may find that they really want

---

9   Along these lines I would recommend H. Hendin, *Seduced by Death. Doctors, Patients, and Assisted Suicide*, W.W. Norton, New York (NY) 1998.

10   I don't refer here, of course, to cases where there is definite clinical depression, which should be managed for what it is: clinical depression.

"to *live* with dignity." These requests are often based on fear of the future more than the present: fear of pain, of being left alone, of being totally dependent on others, of being a burden, etc. There is not much need to fear pain nowadays, thanks to progress of palliative care and pain medication (including sedation). For most, death will not come in the midst of extreme pain. More difficult is the fear of lost autonomy, as we already saw when we looked at old age.

The second kind is what we call *preparatory depression*. It is the result of being aware of the loss of life itself. Unlike the first kind, it is a *silent* depression. There are no complaints or laments, because it is much more difficult to verbalize the problem. According to Kübler-Ross this kind of depression helps prepare people psychologically for imminent death, and helps move them to the final stage, acceptance.

The attitude of health professionals and relatives should change. Words of encouragement are not required, arguments against pessimism or listing all the things that they can still enjoy are not useful. In other words, there is no point in trying to convince them to see things from a different perspective. The cause of this depression comes from an incontrovertible truth: the patient is in fact leaving this life behind.

Much more help can be provided to the terminally ill by allowing them to express their pain and by supporting them in silence, with non-verbal communication. Patients are grateful when people sit by their side, ready to listen, respecting their silence, not insisting that the sick person "cheer up." But sometimes they may want to be left alone. How can we leave them alone but show our love at the same time? How can we assure them that we are close by and available for anything they need? One idea may be short but frequent visits, dropping in to ask or tell them something like, "Do you need anything? I'll sit with you for a little bit."

Another trait highlighted by Kübler-Ross is that the spiritual dimension often comes up because the dying person thinks more about what lies ahead than what he leaves behind. We will return to this aspect in the last section of the chapter.

6. Fifth Stage: Acceptance

"Everything will be all right." "I have no more fight in me, I have to get ready to jump."

According to Kübler-Ross,

> If a patient has had enough time (i.e., not a sudden, unexpected death) and has been given some help in working through the previously described stages, he will reach a stage during which he is neither depressed nor angry about his "fate." He will have been able to express his previous feelings, his envy for the living and the healthy, his anger at those who do not have to face their end so soon. He will have mourned the impending loss of so many meaningful people and places and he will contemplate his coming end with a certain degree of quiet expectation.[11]

The purpose of this whole chapter is to provide relatives and doctors with tools to help patients reach this unique stage as soon as possible. But before we dive in, let's anticipate an easy mistake. "Acceptance" does not mean "returning to normal" and having the patient's mood be the same as it was before the diagnosis.

> Acceptance should not be mistaken for a happy stage. It is almost void of feelings. It is as if the pain had gone, the struggle is over, and there comes a time for 'the final rest before the long journey' as one patient phrased it.[12]

This stage completes what we have described in the previous chapter as "detachment from this life." There may be no depression (there is no sadness, tears or despair) but there remains a degree of apathy or indifference to the outside world. The things the patient was passionate about (hobbies, interests, a favorite sports team, even some family traditions) may no longer have an emotional impact. He sees them as belonging to another world. The fact is that in his own mind he is further and further away from them.

He often wishes to be on his own, and becomes less and less

11 Kübler-Ross, *On Death and Dying*, p. 91.
12 *Ibidem*, p. 92.

communicative, but he still needs and appreciates the closeness of his loved ones.

> The patient may just make a gesture of the hand to invite us to sit down for a while. He may just hold our hand and ask us to sit in silence. Such moments of silence may be the most meaningful communications for people who are not uncomfortable in the presence of a dying person.[13]

Keeping him company will reassure him that many people love him, respect him, and accompany him in his pain, that his life has been meaningful because he has loved and has been loved.

At this stage, the family may be in greater need of help. In the previous stages they had done all they could to support the patient and alleviate his suffering. Now that he is calm and composed, the relatives can settle down and face the situation. In addition to looking after their loved ones they themselves will need to overcome the five stages of grieving. Indeed, we have already stated that Dr. Elizabeth Kübler-Ross applied the same model to the relatives' grieving process, and extended it to coping with all sorts of bad news.

We can finish with a smile by seeing how a wise old professor applied the stages of grieving to his students.

> Whenever I had to fail a student he first *denies* it, assuming that I made a mistake adding the score, or that I have given him someone else's grade; then he becomes *angry* because I asked something which I had not explained with enough detail, or because I have been too severe. Then he asks for a review of the exam and tries to *bargain* for an extra point here or there, and he promises that he will study over the summer break. Then he becomes *depressed* thinking that he will never pass the subject and will have to change degrees or go to another university. But in the end most students *accept* that they need to work harder, put in more hours and just pass the subject without further ado.

13 *Ibidem.*

7. Keeping Company for a Christian Death

Looking at the stages of mourning has helped us to "enter the mind of the patient." Learning about the grieving process in addition to the illness itself will help us be close to him and respect his space and time with warmth and thoughtfulness. So far, we have mentioned little that would offend a non-believing patient. But the Kübler-Ross approach is also open to a transcendence and takes into account our spiritual dimension. In this last section we will go over a few points that can help others *die well* from a Christian perspective.

God's idea for a Christian is based on two premises: God is my Father, and he loves me. These two great truths can never be exhausted, though crisis challenges them. We can all think of unexpected deaths that destroy the survivors' well-being and plans for the future, bringing them pain and uncertainty.

People might benefit from the path proposed by St. Josemaría in *The Way*:

> Stages: to be resigned to the will of God; to conform to the will
> of God; to want the will of God; to love the will of God.[14]

The first two steps (to resign and to conform) seem achievable, but is it possible to want or even *love* God's will when it means losing one's life prematurely? The answer is Yes. We naturally reject death, but for a believer it is the gateway to heaven, a much greater good than any partial evil (loss, pain, suffering, etc.). God is powerful enough to draw good out of evil, and greater goods out of greater evils. This argument provides serenity because it opens the door to the hope of future joy.

However, what is the meaning of the *present* suffering? I recommend reading St. John Paul II's *On the Christian Meaning of Human Suffering*.[15] This letter offers a reflection from both the human and divine perspectives. In the limits of this section I can only provide a few brief brush strokes, but I do so because they fit in quite well with the purpose of the book.

14 St. Josemaría Escrivá, *The Way*, Little Hills Press, St Peters, Australia 1986. n. 774.
15 St. John Paul II, Apostolic Letter *Salvifici doloris*, 11 February 1984.

First of all, pain is an effect of sin. There was no pain in God's original design for us. Pain entered through the disobedience of Adam and Eve (cf. Gen 3 16–19). Pain is part of the punishment that everyone has to assume, though they may not be directly related to our sins. The Book of Job displays this with great drama. Given the extreme misfortune that afflicts him, his three friends insist that he must have done something wrong to deserve it. But Job insists that he has always behaved properly before God. The Lord's actions at the end of the book are a surprise on two counts. Firstly, because he does not explain why we suffer, he simply appeals to his own power and wisdom, and asks Job to trust him and to accept the situation. The second point of interest is that Job recovers both his health and the goods he had lost, and it looks like he goes back to enjoying the reward of his virtue even in this life.

The mystery of pain can only be understood by looking at Jesus Christ, the true just man, who takes up suffering "to the point of death—even death on a cross" (Phil 2:8). He shows how he loves his Father's will (the highest stage proposed by St. Josemaría) and also his love for those he ransomed from sin through his blood (cf. Isa 53:5). Just like in Job's case, the meaning of suffering remains somewhat unclear. But our Lord's passion absolutely confirms that suffering and God's love are compatible. Jesus never doubted his Father's love and never stops loving him.

The gospels point out a dimension of suffering that deserves more consideration. As St. Paul summarized it, "in my flesh I am completing what is lacking in Christ's afflictions for the sake of his body, that is, the church" (Col 1:24). Sharing the mind of the Lord (cf. Phil 2:5) means also sharing—each with his own life—in his Passion, and thus contributing to the salvation of mankind

This overview is too brief to solve every uncertainty about suffering, and is no answer to the mystery. It only offers a little light. If God chose suffering as the instrument to show his love for and save the human race, there must be something to it. As the Second Vatican Council states, "Through Christ and in Christ, the riddles of sorrow and death grow meaningful. Apart from His gospel, they overwhelm us."[16]

16 Vatican Council II, Pastoral Constitution *Gaudium at Spes,* December 7, 1965, n. 22.

Looking at Christ's suffering has more direct consequences for the patient than we might have expected.[17] Jesus himself gave voice to a sort of *bargaining stage* before his Passion. This is how he prayed in the garden of Gethsemane: "My Father, if it is possible, let this cup pass from me; yet not what I want but what you want" (Mt 26:39). He began by appealing to his Father's goodness while trustingly accepting his will. We should not be surprised if we, poor creatures that we are, overstep the bargaining and get angry with God, and proceed to make up and acknowledge that he knows better. When it comes to sickness and pain, freedom often has less to do with doing and more to do with facing up to the inevitable.

What most helps us sanctify sickness and death is placing ourselves— or helping others place themselves—squarely before Christ and reading the gospel, particularly the scenes of the Passion. We can ask Jesus: "How could you put up with all this? Could you help me cope with my suffering?" Having a crucifix on hand will help. Two are even better, one that can be seen from bed, and another to hold tightly in the hand during extreme physical or moral suffering. Lastly, suffering at the foot of the cross puts us in good company—Mary most holy (cf. Jn 19:25) is there too, consoling Jesus, and so is St. John. St. John represents each of the disciples her Son loved.

We may not quite understand why we are in this position. But we need to keep on praying. It is enough to sense and trust God our Father. The best way to help a patient pray is to pray with him and ask him to pray for specific intentions. Then he can feel useful. When a patient is very disabled, simple vocal prayers, like the holy rosary, can fill hours of external inactivity.

Some patients may undergo a crisis at this point. "What if I made a mistake? What if there is no life after this?" It is not usually a real doubt of faith, but a kind of scruple that sneaks in. The solution is to clarify their desire to be with him, to see him face-to-face. Yet sometimes it reveals a faith that is still immature and staggers when put to the test. In neither case is elaborate reasoning appropriate. It is the time for abandoning oneself, humbling the mind if necessary, and return to the simple faith of children. "Let the little children come to me, and do not stop them; for it is to such as these that the kingdom of heaven belongs" (Mt 19:14).

---

17 It is interesting to point out that "patient" comes from the Latin verb *pati*, which means "to suffer." A patient is literally "someone suffering."

Those who have the most direct contact with these patients (relatives, hospital chaplains, volunteers, etc.) should know what materials are appropriate to the occasion—books and brochures, websites, etc. Biographies can be very useful, because rather than explaining they show that it is possible to endure illness with a Christian outlook. They move the mind and the heart to assert, "I would like to die the same way." They provide more meaning to the suffering of the patient. That can mean leaving behind a memory and an example for the loved ones. Kübler-Ross herself explains that for many relatives who have been with their loved ones right down to the acceptance stage the experience is a surprise, "as it will show him that dying is not such a frightening, horrible thing that so many want to avoid."[18]

Victor Frankl wrote that "Man should not ask what the meaning of life is, but rather he must recognize that it is *he* who is asked."[19] Likewise, it will help the sick person to ask himself what God expects of him in his situation and to focus less on what the pain is doing to him but on what he can do with his pain. He can do a lot, both for his own good and for the good of many other people.

All this sounds beautiful, but is it too much for the average person? It may be, and this is the reason why we need outside help. We can trust in the grace of God that comes from the sacraments. Three sacraments are particularly relevant here.

The first is the sacrament of confession. Knowing that no matter how badly we have behaved throughout life, God will forgive us always, is a supreme consolation. It is never too late to reconcile with God, and through him we be at peace with ourselves and with other people.

Second is anointing of the sick. It should be offered to the patient in a timely manner, and not be delayed too long, with the risk that the patient may no longer be conscious. Sometimes the mere mention of the sacrament raises fear, but this fear is similar to breaking the news of the fatal diagnosis. The relatives are more scared than the patient himself.

Finally, holy Communion, which receives a special name when received

18 Kübler-Ross, *On Death and Dying*, p. 92.
19 V. Frankl, *Man's Search for Meaning. An Introduction to Logotherapy*, Hodder and Stoughton, London–Sydney–Auckland–Toronto 1992, p. 111.

by terminal patients: *viaticum*, food for the journey, the last stage of our journey to heaven. That food is nothing other than the very Body of Jesus. I was told some time ago of a conversation between a dying lady and her son at the bedside. He asked her, "Mom, do you think that our Lord will welcome you to heaven right away?" Her answer reflected her great faith: "If I received him every day for so many years, how will he not welcome me today? Yes, he will welcome me."

III. THE CHRISTIAN VIRTUE OF CHASTITY

WHY CHASTITY?

1. Why Can't I Enjoy My Body Anyway I Want to?

I once heard a speaker make the following comment: "If Moses were alive today, he would have written *eleven* commandments. The eleventh would be 'Thou shalt not speed,' because the Decalogue forbids everything we like, and we all love the thrill of going fast, almost as much as sex." He was certainly right about speed. Who doesn't enjoy riding bikes, motorcycles or cars, or going on a roller coaster at an amusement park? Comparing the excitement to sexual pleasure would also be a fair comment.

That said, we could ask ourselves the following question. Did God issue the commandments just to give us a hard time? To answer "Yes" would be like saying that the civil authorities set speed limits for the sake of annoyance. To answer "No" raises another possibility: that there is something innate in us which should lead to a specific attitude towards sexuality. And that would be in reference to our own body and to those of other people. The follow-up question is: is there anything innate to the body that makes it unwise to use it as we please?

In other words, *are things bad because God said so, or did God say so because they are bad?*

Today's prevailing legalistic mentality may lead us to think that we should obey the commandments just because God said so. It is not unusual to find people—even Christians who want to live according to their faith—who do not understand why *it is good for man* to live chastely, in accordance with his state.[1] The truth is that we have forgotten that when we act against our nature, *ipso facto* we damage ourselves.

In this chapter I will offer some answers to the questions without

---

1   We will explain later that "living chastely" is not the same thing as "an absence of sexual intercourse."

exhausting the subject Anyone who wants to delve deeper in this area can look up the references provided in the bibliography. My arguments will be both theological (that is, based on divine revelation), and anthropological (based on human nature). The latter is particularly relevant, because it shows that chastity, like any other virtue, is not "a Catholic thing." Everyone is called to be chaste, just as everyone is called to be sincere, honest, respectful of others, etc. In this way we can set the ground rules to facilitate a conversation between persons of different faiths, backgrounds and value systems. We will look at the theological arguments first.

2. Entering a New Life

Most of St. Paul's letters (Romans, Galatians, Ephesians, Colossians, 1 Thessalonians) have two parts. The first is doctrinal and the second moral, exhortative, or parenetic. There is usually a handful of verses that act as a kind of "hinge." The Apostle encourages Christians to "lead a life worthy of the calling to which you have been called" (Eph 4:1). The second part is a (usually practical) section about morality. It explains what should be done or avoided. There we find long lists of behaviors (sins) that are incompatible with a *new life in Christ.* Occasionally St. Paul clearly states that "those who do such things will not inherit the kingdom of God" (Gal 5:21).

The doctrinal section of these letters deals with the mystery of Christ in one way or another. Jesus Christ has come to the world so that we may share in his relationship as Son towards the Father. We are called to be children of God by grace, like Jesus is a child of God by nature. We come to share in this *divine filiation* through baptism, which implies sharing in Jesus' death and resurrection. This sacrament is usually celebrated by pouring water over the head, which suggests that sin is washed away. Baptism by immersion was used in ancient times. It conveys the idea of entering into a new life, which is the meaning of the sacrament. For the Jews, water was a sign of death (think of the flood, the crossing of the Red Sea, the storm in the lake of Gennesaret). Diving into the water suggested drowning, while coming out of the water was a return to life, like a castaway who manages to reach land. Baptism by immersion is still used in some Christian communities. It clearly portrays what the sacrament does and signifies: dying to sin and rising to new life as a son of God.

A Christian becomes like Christ. It's not about imitating a model, but being transformed from within, to the point of saying with St. Paul: "it is no longer I who live, but it is Christ who lives in me" (Gal 2:20). In the gospels, when Christ's call to "come, follow me" is answered, it reaches down to the core of the human being. This happens through grace. Grace is not like icing on a cake, which decorates and provides flavor but can easily be swiped off and eaten by itself (or not at all). It is more like the Italian dessert *babà*, which is a cake saturated in rum. The rum and the cake cannot be taken apart. And even if we could separate them it would not be *babà* anymore, but only dry cake and a shot of rum. Divine grace enters man and transforms him, but he remains a man. This illustrates the earlier quotation by St. Thomas Aquinas: "Grace does not abolish nature, it perfects it."[2]

This is the meaning of the Ten Commandments that God gave to Moses. They are not a divine whim. They are a guide for man, to bring his ordinary life up to the level of the order of grace. In this way he will attain happiness on earth and in the life to come. "See, I have set before you today life and prosperity, death and adversity [...], blessings and curses. Choose life so that you and your descendants may live" (Dt 30:15, 19).

You may think that we have strayed from the heading of this chapter. It may look like it, but if we are to make sense of the virtue of chastity and its role in the life of a Christian this introduction was needed to put things into perspective.

3. A Temple of the Holy Spirit

Good spiritual accompaniment and catechesis should include conversations about chastity—but only at the right time because it is not the highest priority. The first commandment is to love God, and the second is to love our neighbor (cf. Lk 10:27). We can never insist enough on this point. Then come other aspects of the new life in Christ,

> a whole series of matters that concern ordinary men and women: their father and mother, home, children and so on.

2   St. Thomas Aquinas, *Summa Theologica*, I, q. 1, art. 8, ad 2.

After that, one's job. Only then, in fourth or fifth place, does the sexual impulse come in.[3]

A type of Christian formation that placed the virtue of purity at the forefront would give a false idea of what God expects from people—especially young people—and could overload people's conscience.

Now, in a typical list of sins, the disorderly use of the sexual function is always high up there. Sometimes it even comes first. We see this in St. Paul's letter to the Galatians (5:19–21). In his list, the term *porneia* appears, a word difficult to translate,[4] but he uses others as well, each with their own nuance: "Now the works of the flesh are obvious: fornication (*porneia*), impurity (*akatharsia*), licentiousness (*aselgeia*)" (Gal 5:19). He then continues with twelve other sins of a different nature, and returns to the topic with the last sin: "carousing (*komoi*), and things like these" (Gal 5:21).

Why does he insist so much? One would think that converts from paganism should be encouraged to change their behaviors in other areas first, and gradually be urged to lead a chaste life to complete the process. But that is not how St. Paul saw it. For him, chastity is not the finishing line but the starting point.

In another letter, St, Paul himself gives the reason for his insistence: "Do you not know that you are God's temple and that God's Spirit dwells in you?" (1 Cor 3:16). He is not only referring to the presence of the Paraclete in the *soul*, but lays special emphasis on the body: "Or do you not know that your body is a temple of the Holy Spirit within you, which you have from God, and that you are not your own?" (1 Cor 6:19).

These words can be startling, because many of us have heard from our tender years that the Trinity dwells in the souls of those in the state of grace. So, is God in the soul or in the body? The answer is "in both," but only if we do not mean either in an absolute sense. The Spirit is neither in the body nor in the soul, but in the *person*, the unity constituted by body (*soma*), mind (*psyche*) and spirit (*pneuma*). We discussed this concept at the beginning of the book.

Divisions tend to be artificial and reductive. When we say that "the

3　St. Josemaría Escrivá, *Friends of God*, Scepter, New York 2002[2], n. 179.
4　The LSJ *Greek—English Lexicon* defines it as "fornication, unchastity."

soul will be happy in heaven" we are not describing what really happens. Only the soul united to the body after the resurrection will be fully happy in heaven. St. Augustine even said that after death the soul remains in a sort of state of unrest until it is reunited with the body at the resurrection, at the end of time. Then the person will be able to enjoy the sight of God in heaven fully.[5]

Opposites eventually come together. We see that with regard to materialism and spiritualism. They coincide on one point—what we do with the body makes no difference. The former say that the body is only a handful of clay (in scientific terms, a number of atoms or of cells) and the latter hold that only the soul counts. However, the image of God is also in the body. Fathers and doctors of the Church have put it in different ways, usually when they talk about the Sacred Humanity of Christ. Jesus Christ did not take on "human nature" in the abstract, but a body. That's why the human body possesses great dignity. And to protect that dignity, God, and his Church have warned us time and again about certain sexual behaviors. The words of St. Paul are straightforward: "The body is meant not for fornication but for the Lord, and the Lord for the body" (1 Cor 6:13). And he draws a conclusion: "Therefore glorify God in your body" (1 Cor 6:20). We do it whenever we "pray with the body": a genuflexion before the Blessed Sacrament, kneeling during Mass, bowing our head before an image of our Lady, etc. With that in mind, we see how Paul encourages us to adore God at all times, even in our most basic activities, even when we are not praying in the strictest sense: "So, whether you eat or drink, or whatever you do, do everything for the glory of God" (1 Cor 10:31).

If we are temples of the Holy Spirit, then the inappropriate use of sex, which St. Paul calls *porneia* (sexual immorality, impurity, fornication, etc.) is a profanation of it. The Apostle condemns this with strong words:

> Should I therefore take the members of Christ and make them members of a prostitute? Never! [...] But anyone united to the Lord becomes one spirit with him. Shun fornication! Every sin that a person commit is outside the body; but the fornicator sins against the body itself (1 Cor 6:15–18).

5   Cf. St. Augustine, *Literal Commentary on Genesis*, XII, 35

The connection between fornication and betraying God had special connotations for Christian converts from Judaism. Sexual sin was not just a bodily sin, but spiritual infidelity. Indeed, the Old Testament frequently compares idolatry to fornication. In some cases, the comparison was meant literally because some of the neighboring countries practiced sacred prostitution in the pagan temples. By contrast, the correct practice of sexuality was looked upon as being faithful to God's covenant with his people.

The dignity of the body stems from all that we have mentioned so far. The conclusion is that we need to take care of that dignity in all its dimensions: hygiene, health, and sexuality.

4. Sex Is a Good Thing ... When It Is Lived in An Orderly Fashion

To a great extent we priests are to blame for the present confusion about sex. We do not explain everything clearly, or may give the impression that sex is a bad thing, as if God had given everyone a timebomb that could explode at any moment and jeopardize our salvation.

On the contrary, sex is a wonderful gift that God has given to man. It is the power to share in his creating power. God has given man (and animals) an instinct that enables them to use this power without needing to be taught (animals do not need *sex education*). Furthermore, he has attached great pleasure to it, to make it desirable and pleasant to carry out. But the similarities between man and animals stop there.

"Therefore a man leaves his father and his mother and clings to his wife, and they become one flesh" (Gen 2:24). When love is very strong, man and woman leave their homes to found another one with the beloved and begin a joint adventure. Every culture has protected this union—marriage—by granting it civil recognition according to a specific feature: stability through time. That protects the spouses and the children, who need an environment of affection and security to help them grow up and be raised in a healthy manner.

Jesus Christ raised marriage to the level of a sacrament. For Christians, the dignity of marriage is similar to that of baptism or even of the Eucharist, because the love between the spouses is the image of the love that God has for his Church (cf. Eph 5:21–33). One more reason for this stability through time is that the love of Christ for his Church does not cease despite the defects that we may have. In the words of Pope Francis,

> Holy Matrimony envelops this love in the grace of God; it roots it in God himself. By this gift, and by the certainty of this call, you can go forward with assurance; you have nothing to fear; you can face everything together![6]

This is the right context for the sexual union, which is an act of love (hence the expression "to make love"). Indeed, man and woman not only join their bodies, but they also give themselves to each other spiritually. The spousal relationship is a complete gift, and includes their intimacy, their deepest selves. This completeness includes the reproductive power, the possibility of becoming parents. It is not so much the fact that each union may be fertile—that is not up to the spouses—but the fact that it should not be closed to the *possibility* of becoming parents. Any sexual union that omits this dimension would be missing an essential component. It would mean "I give myself completely, except for my fertility." It would render this relationship incomplete and false.

The Church holds that both dimensions (loving gift of self and fertility) cannot be separated. In other words, they should always be present (or at least not voluntarily separated) in every sexual union. To take either of them on its own would be to use this faculty inappropriately. This is what happens to all the acts that are of themselves closed to procreation (contraceptives, masturbation, same-sex unions) or those that seek reproduction independently of the sexual encounter (*in vitro* fertilization).

5. The Disorder of Concupiscence

When we looked at passions in general we noted that "God saw everything that he had made, and indeed, it was very good" (Gen 1:31). All the dimensions of the human person, sexuality included, have been created by God, and he was very happy with what came out of his hands. Yet, he de-

---

6 Francis, Post-Synodal Apostolic Exhortation *Christus vivit*, March 25, 2019, n. 169.

cided to give man something else: freedom. He gave man the chance to say *yes* or *no*… and then had a problem with the very first couple.

Early in this book we mentioned that as a result of sin, man's passions are in disarray. Significantly, the first sign was that "the eyes of both were opened, and they knew that they were naked" (Gen 3:7), they felt shame in front of each other, and even before God himself (cf. Gen 3:10). They realized that their naked body could be looked at *with evil eyes*: by not appreciating its personal richness, but seeing others *only as a body* that can be *used* to satisfy a whim, a passion, curiosity, the urge to be turned on. However, such a gaze would not respect their dignity, their psyche, their spirit. Adam and Eve become aware of this and protect themselves. First they get dressed—the famous fig tree leaves sewn together (cf. Gen 3:8)—and then they hide from none other than God, who would never look at them in this way.

God's plan for man was not without risk. Man could keep the pleasure for himself and ignore the other person, give of himself only a little, or give of himself completely but only for one night (which means, of course, not giving oneself completely). Such behaviors are like receiving a present and throwing the wrapping away, or opening a letter and discarding the envelope. This is the reason why some behaviors are never rightful although apparently *no one gets hurt*. Whether it is done with the other's consent or with one's own body makes no difference. They are harmful to the very persons who commit them, even though they may not be aware of it. Their dignity suffers and is ignored, and the other person is reduced to a body for the sake of arousal and pleasure.

I would like to share a real-life case. A group of college students was talking between class. Suddenly a girl glared at one of the fellows and said angrily, "Stop staring at my breasts." You could have cut the silence with a knife. Everyone was embarrassed, and no one could look at the two persons involved, who were both flushed, one with anger and the other with shame. What was the offended woman's message? That there was a person standing in front of the guy, yet she felt she was being looked upon as a sex object.

One more feature from the story: the wickedness in his gaze would have been the same even if she had not noticed it. Our actions have an impact on ourselves first of all. When someone steals, he does not harm the person robbed as much as he harms himself, by becoming a thief. Whoever tells a lie becomes a liar and whoever has a wrongful sexual experience becomes lustful, or even perverse. This is the root of the evil of internal sins, of those committed with oneself and of the impure looks at others. Let us consider them in greater detail.

Popular wisdom holds that *the eyes are the mirror of the soul.* A clean gaze indicates a clean soul. But what is a clean gaze? Jesus himself tells us. "Everyone who looks at a woman with lust has already committed adultery with her in his heart" (Mt 5:28). What we look at and how we look at it are not indifferent. Jesus follows up with some stern advice: "If your eye causes you to stumble, tear it out and throw it away; it is better for you to enter life with one eye than to have two eyes and to be thrown into the hell of fire" (Mt 18:9).

The stakes are high when it comes to our eyes and our gaze—beholding God for all eternity. We are not called to contemplate God with mystical "eyes of the soul" (which do not exist), but with our bodily eyes, the same ones you are reading this page with. "And after my skin has been thus destroyed, then in my flesh I shall see God, whom I shall see on my side, and my eyes shall behold, and not another. My heart faints within me!" (Job 19:26–27).

The eyes *become dirty* when they look at others in an obscene manner, that is, making other people a sexual object. Obviously, that is only a manner of speaking because the person who gets dirty is the person who is looking. One clear example of this is pornography, which we will discuss in the next chapter. Whoever looks at bad images only seeks arousal and gives nothing in return. There is no personal encounter and no thought spared for the man or woman being looked at, who happens to be another person, with a life, feelings, family, even financial needs that force them to expose their bodies, and reduce them to a thing for the sake of pleasure.

Waiting for marriage to engage in sexual intercourse protects people from being used as an object of pleasure without commitment and without the other person giving him or herself totally, body and soul. Hence, we have another reason for marriage requiring exclusivity and stability over time. It is not possible to give oneself *totally* to one person, later to a different person, and to others later down the track, etc.

The term *pre-marital sex* is misleading. It would be better be called *un-marital sex* because frequently it happens without any reference to a future marriage. And even when there is an established relationship or engagement, one crucial component is still missing: the solemn promises of the wedding ceremony. This flies in the face of the common view that the wedding is a purely social occasion, as if it simply confirms before friends and relatives (or even the Church) what was already clear to everyone.

On the contrary, marriage transforms the spouses. The very words signify transformation. Until the very moment of the celebration they are fiancées, and are free to go back on whatever promises they have made and find someone else to build a common life project with. After the wedding celebration they become spouses, husband and wife, and this gives them new rights and duties. To skip a step and have sexual relationships early would be to assume rights to which they are not yet entitled.

Nowadays marriage is often delayed, sometimes for reasons outside the couple's control. It can make it difficult to wait, or it can also lead to a "verbal commitment of stability" until life allows the wedding to happen. Even in a stable relationship of that kind, the gift of self would not be complete (exclusive and forever), because the commitment would not be sealed. Indeed, both the Church and state allow for such a verbal pact to be broken. The difficulties that the couple may encounter are real, but waiting until marriage is a chance for the couple to display their trust and the love.

Having said that, it is possible to take advantage of the other person as an object of pleasure even within marriage. Unfortunately, we read many cases of this in the news. However, there is a clear difference between this situation and that of the unmarried: the *objective* framework of the marriage commitment protects both spouses.

In short, sins against the virtue of chastity are committed with the body, but they harm the soul as well because the two cannot be separated. They mess up the inner world of the sinner and distort one's self-understanding and vision of other people. They produce distress, sadness, and the feeling of dirtiness either in one's self or in one's relationships with others. Indeed, they sully the temple that should be God's abode and damage one's dignity and the dignity of the other person. Both are reduced to being *a thing* that generates pleasure, rather than *someone* who gives and receives within the framework of total self-giving. Finally, these sins destroy God's plan, who gave man the ability to share in his creative power, and sees it reduced to a mere source of pleasure, the result of selfishness.

Love, self-giving, marriage, dignity, and respect are all universal realities regardless of one's religion and value systems. This book has been written for people who want to lead a Christian life. However, most of the thoughts contained in it are applicable to anyone. Everybody has the same dignity, body and soul, and all are called to respect it in themselves and in the others.

6. The Virtue of Chastity

At this stage it is worth repeating that sex and everything that goes with it—attraction, pleasure, etc.—did not become evil with the fall. They became *disordered*, or out-of-place with regards to the hierarchy of values. Passions tend to their satisfaction, with no regard for the other aspects of man, for his dignity and call to transcend the material world. God considers sex to be a good thing, provided that it is practiced according to its own rules. These rules were not made arbitrarily or just to annoy us, as the speaker cited at the beginning of this chapter suggested. They are the conditions necessary to respect the welfare and the dignity of men and women. These rules are expressions of the virtue of chastity.

The *Catechism of the Catholic Church* states that

> Chastity means the successful integration of sexuality within the person and thus the inner unity of man in his bodily and spiritual being. Sexuality, in which man's belonging to the bodily and biological world is expressed, becomes personal and truly human when it is integrated into the relationship of one person to another, in the complete and lifelong mutual gift of a man and a woman.[7]

The Catechism uses the word *integration*, which I find particularly well chosen. What does *integration of sexuality* mean? The following example may be silly, but it illustrates the point. A friend of mine once told me, "My glasses are so much a part of who I am that I sometimes walk into the shower with them without realizing it." Man's sexuality includes reference

7   *Catechism of the Catholic Church*, n. 2337.

to the corporal, psychological, and spiritual parts of his being. They need to be put in the right order and balance—*integrated*—to achieve the overall good, like everything else in life. Just like my friend and his glasses, we carry our integrated sexuality with us wherever we go: in our dealings with God and our neighbor, in our relationships and our friendships, when we watch TV or surf the internet, in marriage or celibacy, all the while respecting the two essential elements of the sexual act, total gift and openness to life.

Like any other virtue, chastity is much more than a prohibition of specific actions. Yes, the commandments set a line below which we cannot claim to love God or men. But above this line there is room for infinite growth. For example, the fifth commandment tells us, "Thou shalt not kill," but that's a low bar for governing social harmony. The commandment is a call to grow in charity, to love others and so not even wish to harm others, let alone kill them. Therefore, the virtue of chastity, or purity—some authors call it *holy purity*, to highlight its positive, cheerful nature—is the positive side of the sixth and ninth commandments.

We should not look at virtues as watertight compartments, but as the framework that holds a person together. Charity is the cornerstone, and chastity is a form of charity: God's love (seen in his act of creation), love for others and love for one's self. St. Augustine wrote,

> Temperance is love surrendering itself wholly to him who is its object; courage is love bearing all things gladly for the sake of him who is its object [...] keeping itself entire and incorrupt for God.[8]

Chastity, a sub-virtue of temperance, is about loving with the body, acknowledging and respecting its dignity as God's image and temple. The first commandment the Lord proposes to his followers could have an addendum: love God with all your heart, with all your soul ... and with all your body.

Likewise, chastity means to love oneself and others (one's boyfriend, girlfriend, friends, spouse) with the body. It is much more than the absence of sexual relations. It should be lived within marriage, albeit in different

8   St. Augustine, *On the Morals of the Catholic Church*, XV, 25.

ways. Respect for others and for the nature of the sexual act is the best culture for growing in conjugal love. Children—as many as God sends, together with the responsible decision of the couple—will be a display of that love.

If chastity were limited to a collection of prohibitions (do not do this, do not look there) the best we could aspire to would be *continence*. The continent behaves—exteriorly—like the chaste, but with a big difference. They put no heart into it. Love is not the origin and end of their actions. On the contrary, charity creates virtuous people who are able to love *with all their heart*.

Living a chaste life before marriage may be hard, but it is neither impossible nor for a select group. It is worthwhile to remind ourselves of St. Paul's inner battle, which we mentioned when we considered the passions in general: "I can will what is right, but I cannot do it. For I do not do the good I want, but the evil I do not want is what I do" (Rom 7:18–19), and his sorrowful cry: "Wretched man that I am! Who will rescue me from this body of death?" (Rom 7:24). Some people have claimed that this lament refers to a physical defect or hardship—possibly a stutter—that he mentions in other letters. But I am not convinced. I have met many stutterers, and while they regret their speech defect, none has expressed their anguish so dramatically as St. Paul does. I have also come across many good people, men and women, who at times find it hard to live chastity, and their cry is closer to St. Paul's. I may be wrong, in which case the apostle will have to forgive me, but it seems like he also had to struggle, something that encourages many people who read his words. We should also take heart from the encouragement that our Lord gives St. Paul: "My grace is sufficient for you, for power[a] is made perfect in weakness" (2 Cor 12:9).

In addition to grace, chastity requires man's struggle to control himself. Self-mastery is not a shackle. It liberates us and opens the door to self-giving. You can't give what you don't have. Indeed, "people are slaves to whatever masters them" (2 Pet 2:19). Whoever manages to overcome his passions can enjoy a life that is authentic and attractive, and he makes himself able to love and be loved.

Chastity does not take anything away from a person, it brings back what had been lost through sin, original and possibly any personal sins that may have been committed. It allows us to come before God in the condition he wanted us to be in, to reorder our disorderly passions which led us to do what we did not want to do. As a matter of fact, the more we grow in this virtue the more attracted we are to order and beauty in general, rather than the confusion born from a unidimensional view of the person.

7. The Traditional Means

Given that chastity is a positive virtue that has a lot to do with love—for God and for others—the way to grow in chastity can be summed up as "growing in love." We have already mentioned the words of St. Josemaría:

> I would remind you that for Christians (for you and me) our life is a life of Love. This heart of ours was born to love. But when it is not given something pure, clean and noble to love, it takes revenge and fills itself with squalor.[9]

In this section we will briefly cover some of the methods that Christian tradition has developed to help this love to take root in the human heart, so that the heart can open itself to receive the grace of God in an environment that is *in tune* with him (Table 12). Then it will be easier to say *YES* to whatever brings us closer to him and *NO* to what threatens to distance us from God.

To know what we should do and the reason why.
A life of prayer.
Knowing that God loves us.
Frequenting the sacraments (confession and the Eucharist).
Mortification.
Deeds of service towards others.
Modesty.
Good use of time.
Fleeing occasions of sin.
Spiritual direction.
Devotion to Our Lady.

Table 12. Traditional means to preserve chastity.

9 St. Josemaría Escrivá, *Friends of God*, n. 183.

It may sound obvious, but to begin with we need to understand what chastity is all about: *what I should do and the reason why*. Getting there may require repeated reading, reflection and prayer.

Next I would suggest a *life of prayer*. If we are to love God, we need to spend time with him. That doesn't mean just saying a few prayers (the rosary, a few minutes of recollection before the Blessed Sacrament or in our room, etc.). That's necessary, but not enough. Our whole lives should be a dialogue with him. How can we achieve that? First of all, by living in the *presence of God*. Being aware that our Father God is constantly looking at us and is in our midst, addressing him from time to time to tell him that we love him and that we want to do everything for his glory.[10] Of course, we cannot speak with God all the time, because our mind is engaged in activities that require our undivided attention: study, work, reading, talking with others. All of these things can be turned into *prayer* when they are carried out with the desire to do his will and give him glory. Thus, it will be easier to seek him in the good times and the bad, and also when temptation arrives.

Then we are in a position to grow in the love of God and we can make a new discovery: God loves us. It is easy to say, but it is amazing how life can change when we truly realize that it is so: that *we feel that God loves us*. That awareness led many sinners to change when they met our Lord: Mary Magdalen, Zacchaeus, Dismas the good thief. It is the main source of a healthy self-love and it fills our heart to the full. Other affections can also fill the heart, but only to a point, because they are limited and on occasions disappointing. On the other hand, God never lets us down.

The *sacraments* are closely related to prayer: receiving the Eucharist and going to confession frequently. Jesus himself promised it: "I am the bread of life. [...] Whoever eats of this bread will live forever" (Jn 6:48–51). Receiving holy Communion at Sunday Mass—and more often if possible—is the food that strengthens us to do good and avoid sin.

---

10 "Now, since the performance of actions enjoined by virtue or by the commandments is also a constituent part of prayer, he prays without ceasing who combines prayer with right actions, and becoming actions with prayer. For the saying 'pray without ceasing' can only be accepted by us as a possibility if we may speak of the whole life of a saint as one great continuous prayer" (Origen, *The Prayer*, XII, 2).

However, the Bible tells us that "For all who eat and drink without discerning the body, eat and drink judgment against themselves" (1 Cor 11:29). Indeed, the soul needs to be in the state of grace to receive the Lord. That means not being aware of having committed a mortal sin. But Jesus also said: "I have come to call not the righteous but sinners" (Macc 2:17). How can we make these two statements compatible? Through the sacrament of penance, which reconciles us with God and wins back the life of grace. God loves us as we are, with our defects and our sins. This is the reason why he forgives us, and says: "Neither do I condemn you. Go your way, and from now on do not sin again" (Jn 8:11). Confession restores our friendship with God, and so it is called *the sacrament of reconciliation* and *the sacrament of joy*. The best way to thank him for it is to receive it as often as needed, and as soon as possible when we need it. It may be tempting to receive Communion anyway out of embarrassment of what other people will say, but that would mean not treating the Lord as he deserves, and it would also hurt our souls.

Chastity is affirmation, but when temptations come it requires having a definite *NO* ready. Hence it is important to strengthen the will in little skirmishes throughout the day. That means not only renouncing evil things, but also depriving ourselves of good things that we can either delay or pass by, which may entail a little discomfort. We call this *mortification*. It is not simply about self-mastery. We saw this when we talked about the meaning of sorrow. Our sacrifices are one way of uniting ourselves to the Lord's Passion. In other words, they are a way to atone for the sins of all men, and our own in the first place. Atoning with the body makes sense if we have offended God with our body.

So far, we have talked about growing in the love of God. Let us now talk about growing in our love for others. If chastity is about respecting others, and sins against it are about *using others*, there is nothing better than selfless service to repair the damage. On the other hand, mixing with all kinds of people and particularly within a framework of friendship will help us to see others as *subjects*, never as objects, let alone *sexual objects*. It is worthwhile pointing out that social media has made the world smaller, and given us the chance to have closer contact with other people thousands of miles away. But they have not changed one thing: meeting face to face, without screens, remains the best by far.

On a personal level, the way to protect chastity is *modesty*.[11] This virtue involves both physical, psychological and spiritual aspects, because it is about hiding one's intimacy from unwanted outside interference. We all have matters that we regard as private. Airing them indiscriminately would be an embarrassment. Only those who we know will respect them should be allowed in. Some of these matters are deep convictions and affections, as well as the more intimate, sexual parts of the body. Sexual modesty is that which is manifested with respect to the parts and organs that determine sex. It seeks to prevent the other from confusing what he sees with what I am: "my body is more than my body" is the motto of modesty. It is a form of self-defense. How we talk, act and dress ought to portray clearly what we are about, and give no opportunity for misunderstandings.

A father once told me that when his teenage daughter bought some immodest clothing, he never entered into arguments with her. He used to tell her to wear them and do the "central plaza test." He explained that their home faced the central plaza of their town. On most afternoons a bunch of hooligans would gather there and talk about passers-by. The test consisted in her walking nearby and listen to their comments. She often returned home very angry, and threw away the recent purchase.

Sadly, it is not uncommon to experience temptations at times of idleness, *whittling away the hours* surfing the internet with no end in mind, or looking for "what's going on" on social media. It also happens when we do not put our mind to the task at hand (study, work, housework, etc.) or when we let the imagination wander. In other words, temptation comes with laziness. At those moments it is difficult to resist evil thoughts or desires. On the contrary, *good use of time* helps to reduce temptations and helps us gain in self-mastery. A schedule is useful (even on holidays and weekends) for allocating time for work, sports, reading, socializing, catching up on the news, resting, etc. St. Jerome recommended: "Engage in some occupation, so that the devil may always find you busy."[12] It is not just *occupational therapy*, nor being frantically active all the time. On the contrary, it is a matter of carrying out what God wants of us at any given time, *here*

---

11 Cf. W. Shalit, *A Return to Modesty: Discovering the Lost Virtue*, Free Press, New York (NY) 1999.
12 St. Jerome, *Letter CXXV*, 11.

and now. Sometimes it will mean work, at other times rest, but always with the awareness that he is present.

St. Josemaría had this piece of advice: "Don't show the cowardice of being 'brave': take to your heels!"[13] Everyone has weak points, and we may be more or less conscious of them. The devil usually knows them, and uses them to attack. When the attack comes it is best not to fight, but flee: to stop reading, leave the movie theater or change the channel, change the topic in a conversation that arouses us, etc. On these occasions the means we just listed come in handy. Someone who prays and is aware of the presence of God realizes that something is not right, and has the willpower to sever the temptation. Someone with the fortitude that the holy Eucharist and mortification provide will manage to change course and get back to where God is: work, service to others, etc.

"If they fall, one will lift up the other; but woe to one who is alone and falls and does not have another to help" (Eccl 4:10). The Church has always recommended *spiritual direction* or *accompaniment* to progress in one's Christian life. Many saints have taken advantage of this, beginning with St. Paul from the moment of his conversion (cf. Acts 5:9–18). A priest (even within the sacrament of confession itself) can do it, or a lay person who is adequately trained, as Pope Francis has reminded us recently.[14] These regular conversations cover progress and difficulties in the interior life, and the director suggests points of struggle and strategies for improving. This is not something exclusive to Christianity. Coaching, mentoring and tutoring are names used in other areas of high endeavor. The reason behind the practice is always the same. It is easier to see things from the outside, and the experience of the coach, mentor or counsellor contributes to solving problems that appeared to be difficult to overcome.

A point of caution. Spiritual direction will only work if there is freedom. Freedom to choose the person with whom to talk, freedom to tell the counsellor what the individual considers appropriate, and freedom either to follow the advice or not. There is no obligation to raise any particular topic, but it is in one's best interest to talk about whatever difficulties are encountered in the struggle to lead a Christian life. This is particularly

13 St. Josemaría Escrivá, *The Way*, Scepter, New York, 1992, n. 132.
14 Cf. Francis, *Christus vivit*, nn. 242, 247.

important in matters related to the virtue of chastity. Sexuality is a very private area, and there is obvious resistance in opening up. Moreover, the problems encountered in living this virtue can be embarrassing and even humiliating. It is necessary to bring these sins up in confession in order to regain the state of grace. It is also a good idea to bring up these struggles in spiritual direction, so that the director can have a realistic idea of the state of the soul. It would make little sense to set lofty goals of prayer and self-giving to God when more basic aspects of a Christian life need to be worked on. It would be like recommending an off-the-shelf suit that was several sizes too big or too small. Ultimately it would not be in the best interest of the individual concerned.

In addition, being sincere in spiritual direction helps us grow in the virtue of humility. By opening up we acknowledge what we are really like and we seek assistance, well aware that on our own it would be much more difficult to move forward. It is an attitude that makes the soul ready to receive the grace of God, for, "Holy purity is given by God when it is asked for with humility."[15]

Last but not least, I would mention devotion to our Lady. I left it for the end not as a last resort, but rather as the crowning of all the means mentioned above, and possibly one of the most traditional means of Christian asceticism. Holy Mary is the model of all virtues. The fact that she is immaculate and ever-virgin makes her the best model of purity. Therefore, seeking her out in a filial, trusting way is a principal resource to attain this virtue. "All the sins of your life seem to rise up against you. Don't lose confidence. Rather, call on your holy Mother Mary, with the faith and abandonment of a child. She will bring peace to your soul."[16] If we keep going to her, even in times of difficulty and defeat, she will make sure we are ready at the most important moment of our lives, when we give our souls to God.

8. Affectivity and Chastity

Let us return to the psychological aspect of chastity, in line with the main features of this book. We saw earlier that the purpose of forming affectivity

15 St. Josemaría Escrivá, *The Way*, n. 118.
16 *Ibidem*, n. 498.

is to help the intellect and the will to manage emotions, affections, feelings and passions. Ordered affectivity knows what the good is, wants to reach it and is capable of using the appropriate means to attain and enjoy it. It is also aware that it may mean giving up other things, pleasant in themselves, but which are lower in the value scale. Using the same word as the Catechism, we may say that *integrating* sexuality in the whole of the person is an important element in the training of affectivity, which of course encompasses many other components.

The sexual dimension of the person is a meeting point for the corporal, psychological, and spiritual dimensions. It is not surprising that many sexual disorders—whether they entail moral repercussions or not—derive from these three areas. In other words, an attempt to approach a sexual problem—loss of libido, unsatisfactory sexual life, masturbation, pornography—from a single angle while neglecting the other two areas would be too simplistic. These difficulties are often the tip of the iceberg, and point to deeper problems that need to be uncovered and sorted out. They are the tell-tale signs that something is not right in other domains of the person's life.

If there is improper use of this faculty from a moral point of view, formators (parents, spiritual directors, confessors, mentors, etc.) need to be trained and familiar with the underlying psychological aspects of the issue. This will help them not to rely exclusively or repeatedly on ascetical measures such as those we have looked at. They should look at the whole of the person: problems in the family or workplace, lack of sleep or rest, general unhappiness with one's present lifestyle, relationship problems, past hurts, etc.

Not everyone can access this type of training, at least not in much depth, and there are sometimes complex problems that should be referred to a specialist, either a psychologist or a medical doctor. We will deal with this in greater detail when we look at pornography addiction.

At the other end of the spectrum, it would be a mistake to *psychologize* all chastity related problems, because the *traditional* ascetical means will be enough to grow in the virtue for most cases. Those who have fairly set habits, or who have only recently decided to lead a Christian life will need to be taken slowly up an inclined plane. The emphasis should be on hope and trust in the grace of God. It is also important to train the mind, that is, explain what a good thing it is to live chastely, employing terminology appropriate to the audience's age and mentality.

How can we juggle both extremes? This shows clearly that a spiritual director needs knowledge and experience. It is no surprise that St. Gregory the Great wrote that "the government of souls is the art of arts!"[17]

We will be exposed to concupiscence from birth and up to the day we die. Therefore, a perfect balance cannot be achieved in our lifetime. I would even dare to say that we do not need to achieve that balance. We can always make progress. It is not only a matter of avoiding certain behaviors or impulses, we also need to purify the heart and our affections.

To suggest that it is impossible to live the virtue of chastity in this day and age would be false. There is no doubt that the environment is aggressively sexualized, and pornography is only two clicks away on the computer screen. However, I insist that it is possible to live this virtue. I have met many people of all ages and backgrounds who manage to live it. All of them have to struggle, some with occasional stumbles, others have developed stable habits with a lot of effort, and all of them with the assistance of God's grace. Not only are they normal people, but they are also outstanding individuals, both human and supernaturally, generous and capable of loving a great deal. They are able to give themselves to others, and some of them have dared to give themselves to God.

---

17 St. Gregory the Great, *Pastoral Rule*, I, 1.

THE ADDICTION OF THE
TWENTY-FIRST CENTURY

1. The Virtual World

The twenty-first-century world would not be the same without the internet. Communications, information, shopping, study, work, entertainment and leisure are all linked to it. Few inventions have been of more service. Yet, there is a dark side to it.

Everything is on the internet, what we are looking for and what we would rather not see. There are websites that help us unwind and others that ensnare us, resources that can bring us closer to God and others that separate us from him. There are sites that we know we should avoid, and others that we seek in moments of frailty. The problem is that they are all jumbled together. We have all experienced what the internet has given us, but also what it has taken away from us: time, relationships, work performance, reading, hobbies, etc.

In this chapter we will look at one of the most negative elements that the internet has brought into our homes and our wallets: pornography. We will define it as the display of explicit sexual images (drawings, photos, or videos) with the sole purpose of sexually arousing the viewer.

2. Is It a Vice or an Addiction?

For many years I have helped prepare candidates for the priesthood. The following experience is relatively common. Many new priests come across young—and not so young—penitents who confess that they have looked at pornographic images on the internet, after which they masturbated. These new priests had been aware that such situations were common, but they were surprised by how frequently it now happens. Often the penitents are people who want to lead a Christian life, they pray every day and attend holy Mass at least every Sunday. In addition, they try to live out the traditional methods to live chastely, and this is the reason they go to confession. The newly ordained priests ask themselves—and have asked me—is God's grace not enough, contrary to St. Paul's experience? Or are people no longer able to control themselves? In other words, are we facing an old vice, now more difficult to get rid of, or are we seeing a new type of addiction?

In this chapter I will look at the answer to the last question in some detail, and I will suggest a few strategies for those who hold a position of formation, whether they are priests or other.

The first point that we should consider is that the choice between a vice or an addiction is not the right way to look at the problem. What is a vice? Philosophical ethics provides a starting point—it is the opposite of a virtue, a habit of bad behavior. In the *broad* sense they do not necessarily imply a moral failing. We saw this in the case of a child's confused confession: "I pulled my sister's hair, I poked my nose, and I bit my fingernails." All of the above actions are low on the malice scale, and the last two are not sins at all, yet they could be classed as a vice, which is a bad habit or a lack of manners.

In the *strict* sense a vice does have an ethical component. That is obvious if we want to make vice the opposite of virtue. Vices are actions that make a person worse. They are not just a tendency to act inappropriately, because they have more serious effects. They change the person from within (someone who steals becomes a thief, telling a lie makes someone a liar, etc.). This implies that the subject will be les attracted to behaving properly, and it will be harder to act uprightly even when he wants to (because the will has weakened), and doing good will not produce the same level of satisfaction. A deep-rooted vice can obscure the intellect, and the subject ends up confusing good and evil: "we either live as we think, or we end up thinking the way we live."

On the other hand, *addiction* is a medical or psychological term.

> Addiction is a primary, chronic disease of brain reward, motivation, memory and related circuitry. Dysfunction in these circuits leads to characteristic biological, psychological, social and spiritual manifestations. This is reflected in an individual

pathologically pursuing reward and/or relief by substance use and other behaviors.[1]

There is no mention of ethical issues or about following human or divine guidelines. We have moved to the domain of human health, mental health to be precise. And the same thing we said about vices can be applied to addictions. Some addictions are not sins as such, like smoking (historically the traditional position, although some authors think otherwise). But in most cases—including smoking—letting oneself fall into an addiction has negative moral implications because it amounts to consenting willingly to a behavior that leads to a loss of freedom and involves personal physical or psychological harm.

3. Addiction and the Internet

If we go back to our subject, whether the consumption of sexual images on the net is followed by masturbation or not, it could be a "once only" episode—which needs to be subject to moral assessment, but which does not appear to result in psychological harm; but it could also lead to a vice or an addiction. Where should the boundary be? First, we should look at the idea of addiction.

What can trigger addiction? The first category we can think about is *substance abuse*, among which there are drugs and alcohol. However, some *behaviors* can also be addicting, like gambling and betting. In short, any circumstance (broadly speaking) that produces pleasure (physical or psychological) or helps relieve stress can give rise to addiction. Indeed, addiction cases have been reported that were triggered by a variety of causes, like coffee, sports, video games, chatrooms, high risk activities, and of course pornography. It is worth noting that all these activate the same neuron circuits in the brain, and all of them involve dopamine,[2] a well-known neurotransmitter (it transmits information from one neuron to another).

1   Cf. American Society of Addiction Medicine, *Public Policy Statement: Definition of Addiction*, 12 April 2011, in: https://www.asam.org/docs/default-source/public-policy-statements/1definition_of_addiction_long_4-11.pdf?sfvrsn=a8f64512_4 (accessed: January 1, 2020).
2   The neurobiological aspects of pornography are mainly related to reward me-

Obviously, not all these activities have the same capacity to trigger addiction (*addictive capacity* is the technical term). It depends mainly on two parameters: the *proximity* to the consumption of the substance (or to the execution of the behavior) to the pleasure it produces, and the *intensity of the pleasure* or stress relief. Many behaviors even allow us to play with the *range of pleasure*: increasing the stress will result in greater pleasure, so that when engaging in that particular behavior the release (of dopamine) is greater and the sensation of well-being and relaxation is enhanced. This is the aim of putting oneself in extreme or risky situations.

Sex meets both conditions: it produces the most intense physical pleasure that can be achieved by natural means (meaning without drugs), and the pleasure takes place immediately (stimulation with images, masturbation, physical acts with another person, etc.).

If we take one further step further along this line of thought, we see that the mix of internet and sex becomes explosive, because the internet brings in three key factors that Dr. Al Cooper of Stanford University highlighted already back in 1998. They are known as the *Triple A Engine*[3]:

Access: Cooper based his observations on the phenomenon of personal computers, which can be connected from home, school, or work at any time of the day. Nowadays it is even easier, because the internet can be accessed through smart phones, which are almost always in our pockets.

Affordability: it is easy to find free content online, and it represents no extra charge on a plan.

Anonymity: the belief that one is unknown, and can "look without being seen" makes it easier to engage in behaviors that would never be undertaken in the presence of others. It also reduces the subjective consciousness of responsibility.

chanisms and have been researched at length. Among others, J.D. Stoehr, *The Neurobiology of Addiction*, Chelsea House, Philadelphia (PA) 2006; W. Struthers, *Wired for Intimacy: How Pornography Hijacks the Male Brain*, InterVarsity Press, Downers Grove (IL) 2009; C.M. Kuhn, G.F. Koob, *Advances in the Neuroscience of Addiction*, CRC Press, Boca Raton (FL) 2010; G. Wilson, *Your Brain on Porn: Internet Pornography and the Emerging Science of Addiction*, Commonwealth Publishing, London 2014.

3   A. Cooper, "Sexuality and the Internet: Surfing into the New Millennium," *Cyberpsychology & Behavior* 1 (1998) 187–193.

How do we know that the threshold of addiction has been reached? There are two typical symptoms. This first is *dependence*. It ordinarily presents as *abstinence syndrome*, otherwise known as *craving*, that appears after a period of no consumption. It is an intense desire, associated with anxiety, restlessness, and autonomic symptoms (sweating, palpitations, tremors, etc.). You can see it in smokers when they do not have a cigarette handy: they fret about looking for one, ask around, trying to do other activities, but they only settle down when they get a cigarette.

The second symptom is *tolerance*. It is a need to increase the dose (either more often or in larger amounts) to achieve the same effect, or just to settle the restlessness: more alcohol, stronger drinks, or in the case of pornography, hard core images. In the *Divine Comedy*, Dante uses the example of the she-wolf as the symbol of concupiscence, and describes it as an insatiable beast, who "never sates her greedy appetite, and after food is hungrier than before."[4] Consumption is not a pleasurable experience anymore. It becomes a chain, a toll that has to be paid for the body to be able to function and the body always asks for more of it, because "one never has enough of that which he does not really want."[5]

Tolerance is the reason why many people cross the *red lines* that they never intended to cross: expenditure, moving from virtual relationships to real ones, watching increasingly violent images, or images involving children, etc. In short, it opens the gate to behaviors that are both pathological and often illegal. They are now much more accessible (the first A of the *Triple A Engine*).

The problem here is surely on a different level than what we saw in the previous chapter. It is not a matter of having temptations (evil thoughts or evil desires that are difficult to stem), or that curiosity has been aroused by imprudent use of internet. Here *the body is unwell*, restless, and it needs a *dose* (a fix) to settle the anxiety. It is not easy to be certain of where a particular subject is at because there is a *grey area* that complicates matters.

New lifestyles can give rise to new pathologies, or new symptoms of previously known illnesses. The internet is one of these lifestyles (as are, in a

---

4   Dante, *The Divine Comedy*, Inferno, Canto I, 99.
5   M. Shea, "Catholics and the Cult of Fun," in: http://www.mark-shea.com/fun.html. (Accessed: January 28, 2001)

broaderer sense, all the new "information and communication technologies") that have created new addictions. It is not just that they are more prevalent than they were in the past; the environment itself facilitates their emergence.

4. A Medical Issue

We have already spoken of the widespread view in society that the body—and therefore sex—exists to be enjoyed. Those who think this way only object to restrictions in sexual behavior when they harm the other person (sex with minors, blackmail, humiliation, lack of consent, etc.) or because of religious and moral principles. Any behavior that does not harm the other person is therefore acceptable and healthy. What does medical science have to say about this? Can we say from an impartial, objective perspective that some sexual behaviors are normal and healthy, whereas others are pathological?

The answer to the last question is a definite YES. Psychiatry textbooks have traditionally held that some sexual behaviors are abnormal. Like in other fields of medicine, the word *disorder* is preferred to the word disease (for reasons that are not relevant here). Paraphilia would be an example. In the past they were called sexual perversions, but the obvious moral connotations of the word have rendered it virtually obsolete. Exhibitionism, fetishism, pedophilia, etc., are all considered to be unhealthy ways to achieve arousal. Could the same be said of internet pornography?

There are two main disease classifications. The WHO *International Classification of Diseases* (ICD-11), now on its eleventh edition, is one, and the *Diagnostic and Statistical Manual of Mental Disorders* (DSM-5) of the American Psychiatric Association, now on its fifth edition, is the other. Clinicians and researchers have made submissions to both organizations to include the situation described in the previous paragraph as a specific category. By way of example, the Journal of Sexual Addiction & Compulsivity was first published back in 1994 (the internet was in its infancy): four quarterly issues a year, with 8 to 10 papers per issue. The authors were psychiatrists, psychologists, sexologists, social workers, family therapists, pastoral counsellors and members of the legal field. Thousands of articles, books, and websites have appeared before and after that date. They approach the problem from various angles, and not necessarily from a moral or religious perspective.

All these publications have a common trait: they seek evidence of individuals who lose control of their sexual activity and become dysfunctional or distressed in their family, social, legal, professional, and financial lives. These individuals want to change but they are unable to resist the urge. Many names have been proposed to categorize this state of affairs: internet addiction disorder, hypersexual disorder, pornography or sex addiction, etc. However, the medical community has not reached an agreement to accept any of these clinical presentations. Various arguments have been raised, which range from the lack of clinical evidence to the accusation that religious or moral considerations were an attempt to *pathologize* sexual behaviors. In other words, anyone wanting to live according to his faith or value system should visit a spiritual director or a coach, not a medical doctor.

Finally, the ICD-11 version was approved in the Seventy-Second General Assembly of the World Health Organization and came into effect on 1 January 2022. The petitions made in this respect were accepted and included in the term *compulsive sexual behavior disorder*. Its prevalence has been calculated to run between 1% and 6% of adults.[6] Table 13 below lists the symptoms of the disorder, which is classified as 6C72 in ICD-11.

Persistent pattern of failure to control intense, repetitive sexual impulses
Repetitive sexual activities becoming a central focus of the person's life
Neglect of health and personal care or other interests, activities and responsibilities
Numerous unsuccessful efforts to significantly reduce repetitive sexual behavior
Continued repetitive sexual behavior despite adverse consequences or deriving little or no satisfaction from it
Manifested over an extended period of time (e.g., 6 months or more)
Marked distress or significant impairment in personal, family, social, educational, occupational, or other important areas of functioning
Distress that is entirely related to moral judgments and disapproval about sexual impulses, urges or behaviors is not sufficient to meet this requirement

Table 13. Features of Compulsive Sexual Behavior Disorder.[7]

6   Cf. S.W. Kraus, R.B. Krueger, P. Briken, M.B. First, D.J. Stein, M.S. Kaplan, V. Voon, C.H.N. Abdo, J.E. Grant, E. Atalla, G.M. Reed, "Compulsive Sexual Behaviour Disorder in the ICD-11," *World Psychiatry* 17 (2018) 109–110.

7   Cf. https://icd.who.int/browse11/l-m/es#/http://id.who.int/icd/entity /1630268048. (Accessed: May 10, 2021)

The WHO's description of the clinical picture is not that of addiction, as we have described in the previous section, although there were proposals to that effect. It has not been excluded, but there is hope that further evidence from clinical experience and research studies will facilitate it. On the other hand, it considers that the key symptom is the inability to restrain an *impulse*, like kleptomania (impulse to steal), pyromania (light fires), trichotillomania (pulling one's hair), or onychophagia (biting one's fingernails). Technically an impulse is the repetition of an action acknowledged to be absurd, even harmful, that the subject would like to avoid, but cannot.

I think that many people who would like to quit the consumption of pornography will acknowledge their Compulsive Sexual Behavior Disorder. The last feature in the above table reflects the concerns of those who claim that sexual behaviors are *pathologized* because of religious or moral motives.

5. A Social Problem

Internet pornography is not just a moral or a health problem; it is a far more serious challenge for the whole of society. In this section we will outline some of its negative effects in different areas (Table 14).[8]

First, pornography *alters the perspective of sexuality*. The images offered are filmed by professionals. The purpose is to trigger arousal. This means that sex acts are unnatural: behaviors are extreme, they are performed to give the spectator a clearer view, what the actors experience is not shown, etc. They can be compared to films that seek to move, to thrill, or to arouse other passions, but real life is not intense in that way. Consider the following example. A fan of action films may come to believe that driving a car is like a car chase in a James Bond movie. When he takes the wheel of a car he will either be disappointed, or will crash at the first turn if he tries to imitate the movie. Both possibilities reflect what happens with pornography; it is not

8 Cf. G. Dines, *Pornland: How Porn Has Hijacked Our Sexuality*, Beacon Press, Boston (MA) 2010; J.R. Stoner, D.M. Hughes (eds.), *The social costs of pornography: A collection of papers*, Witherspoon Institute, Princeton (NJ) 2010; G. Wilson, *Your Brain on Porn: Internet Pornography and the Emerging Science of Addiction*. Commonwealth Publishing, 2014.

about showing images to be viewed and enjoyed as a simple spectator, but about enticing the viewer to become a participant and to try it for himself. And when an amateur tries to copy a professional, the results are likely to be disastrous.

Altered perspective of sexuality
High expectations of sex that in the end become disappointing
Spouse reduced to an object of pleasure
Problems in the life of a couple
Marital infidelity
Prostitution
Divorce
Premature sexualization or hyper sexualization of children
Ability to struggle, to wait, and to seek arduous goods is restricted
Tendency to isolation
Rise of the excitability threshold (seeking violent, illegal images, etc.)
Sexual identity disorders
Violence in real life
Legal problems
Financial problems
Sexually transmitted diseases (STD)
Emotional wounds
Depression
Future problems

Table 14. Social consequences of pornography.

Pornography *generates high expectations from sex that in the end become disappointing*. A spouse cannot match a professional actor. Neither can oneself. There are repercussions in the life of a couple. It does not satisfy, or there is background stress because the individual cannot fulfill the expectations of the other spouse. In other words, men feel that they are not manly enough, and women feel that they are not feminine enough. Unsurprisingly, there is evidence of the link between pornography and several sexual dysfunctions, and with lower levels of satisfaction in marital sexual relations. The attempts to imitate what is seen in pornographic material fare even worse. The spouse—particularly the wife—can feel that she is being *reduced to a sex object* to provide pleasure because she is asked to act in ways that are neither natural nor spontaneous. On the contrary, tenderness, cuddles, dialogue, waiting, respecting vital rhythms, leaving it until tomorrow, etc., rarely figure in the images we are talking about. Furthermore, such behaviors are not always suggested, but physically or psychologically demanded. It constitutes an authentic abuse, even within a marriage relationship. Pornography promotes the great danger that was pointed out in the previous chapter: the *reification of the spouse*, especially the woman.

The combination of the two factors is a source of major *problems in the life as a couple*. Some people who have a deeply ingrained habit admit that spousal sex does not satisfy them anymore: what really turns them on is pornography, and they therefore prefer to watch it on their own, and leave the other out of it. On the other hand, when they realize that it does not fulfill them, they open the door to looking for arousal with someone else, whether an acquaintance or a sex worker. Thus, pornography encourages *marital infidelity* and *prostitution*. There is also published evidence that links pornography use by one of the spouses to *divorce*.

Children and teenagers are more sensitive than adults. Recent studies in Spain and the USA found that boys began to watch pornography at the age of fourteen on average, and girls at the age of sixteen. However, there is evidence that one in four boys has accessed pornography before the age of thirteen, and the youngest age recorded is before the eighth birthday. What can a teenager understand—let alone a child—of the wealth of sexuality as a gift of self that includes the spiritual dimension, when they only see the encounter of two bodies? The result is *premature sexualization,* or *hyper sexualization*, that has been compared to child abuse.

Regardless of age (though the younger the age of first contact, the greater the impact), the ease and immediacy of the pleasure provided by pornography restricts the development of the *capacity to struggle, to wait, to seek arduous goods*. It also impacts negatively on their self-confidence and social integration. It is easier to remain in front of the screen than to contact real people who might reject you. This in turn leads to a *tendency to isolation*.

The *excitability threshold rises* with the consumption of pornographic images, through neurological and psychological pathways similar to those produced by addiction. The brain becomes accustomed to the images, and needs stronger, cruder, *harder* images to produce the same intensity of arousal. The effects on the life of a couple have already been mentioned. There are also repercussions on how the web is used: searches for increasingly violent or illegal images (non-consensual or involving children), or homosexual ones, etc. I make a point of the latter because I have encountered some individuals who followed a heterosexual trajectory well into their late teens, who went down a different path when heterosexual pornography no longer aroused them and when they lost the attraction to persons of the opposite sex in real life. No doubt there were other factors involved, but the fact is that problems of sexual identity arose several years later than usual, and were clearly related to these images.

We have already mentioned that the consumer tends to imitate in real life what he sees on the screen. The consumption of violent images, coupled with the loss of the ability to wait leads directly to *increased violence* (of any kind, but particularly sexual) and abuse. There is good evidence that pornography use is greater among abusers, rapists, individuals with behavioral problems (theft, violence, crime), etc., than in the average population. As a result, these pornography users have more *legal problems* than the general population.

These behaviors can lead to serious *financial problems*. Have we not said that the web is *accessible* and virtually free? Not quite. Many web sites that offer these *services* take advantage of the tendency to surf for more exciting sites, and highlight links to pay-per-view sites, often through the *dark web*, that is made up of sites not accessible through ordinary search engines, and are therefore harder for the authorities to track down. They are the ideal method to upload illegal content. The expenses involved in online material are not the only ones. Often there is associated expenditure to satisfy the need for arousal in the real world, notably through prostitution.

We should not forget that in the opinion of many, pornography is one of the net's more lucrative domains. It is difficult to find reliable data because many ventures are illegal, but online pornography moves around one hundred billion dollars a year.[9] Someone must be paying. Such amounts are not surprising if we consider that in 2017, 25% of Google searches,

9   Cf. J. Stringer, *Unwanted: How Sexual Brokenness Reveals Our Way to Healing*, NavPress, Colorado Springs (CO) 2018.

35% of downloads, and 12% of websites (close to 25 million) are related to pornography. There is no need to be a conspiracy theorist to suspect that there are unscrupulous individuals who will try to get as many users as possible—whether by direct payment or indirectly from advertising—regardless of people's ages, or the fact that they promote addictions, or unhealthy or illegal behaviors.

We have spoken of addiction as a medical condition, but there are so many problems caused by pornography that we can talk about a social and public health problem. First of all, the increased prevalence of *sexually transmitted diseases*, as a result of the sexual promiscuity caused by these sites. That's not all—it causes a deep *emotional wound* in the individual, because the unity of body-psyche-soul is broken; it produces a loss of self-esteem, insecurity, difficulty in establishing emotional bonds with other people, clinical *depression* (including suicide attempts), and a long list of other issues.

We should also mention the area of *future problems*, if Cooper's third A, Anonymity, comes under scrutiny. The web leaves a trace, both in the search history of cell phone, laptop, family home, or work computer, and in the register of search engines. It is a well-known fact that requests by individuals to remove a search history result in removal from public access, but the company keeps the record for a period of time. A purpose-directed search, or casual findings, can make many honest citizens blush. In addition, links or messages sent, with or without knowledge of the individual, can fall into unscrupulous hands, and compromise anyone years after an episode that was intended to be a dirty joke for a trusted friend.

I want to end this unpleasant section. It is not a matter of overstating the problem, or of scaremongering. However, the data is available to anyone who wants to find it. It is an unpleasant reality, and simply looking away is not an option. Formators—parents to begin with—should be familiar with it, so that they can help prevent their dependents from falling prey to the darker areas of the internet, and help them come out should they fall into it.

Having said that, the problem is even greater, and it requires a more comprehensive approach. If pornography is a social problem, it is up to the whole of society to find the right safeguarding measures and act on them, and for authorities to establish the appropriate means to protect their citizens. What about restricting the possibilities of offering and viewing sexual content on the net? Would it amount to curtailing freedom? The answer is no, and indeed it is already happening and readily accepted, although the measures are not always obeyed. All governments have enacted legislation to regulate the internet in general (illegal sales, cyberattacks, hacking, *fake news*, etc.), and pornography in particular. Usually, explicit images cannot be shown publicly, even in the shop windows of establishments that sell this material because it is deemed to be a crime against public morality. Yet, there is still a legal vacuum in the interaction between the internet and pornography. It is taken for granted that a pornographic image on a shop front is damaging to a minor, but there is no consideration of the fact that the same minor has access to the same material on his cell phone or on any gadget with an internet connection.

Those who object to restrictive measures say that the internet should regulate itself. We cannot be naïve: in most fields, self-regulation is impossible. Interest groups (journalists, doctors, lawyers) are intent on retaining as much independence as possible. Similarly, there are many vested interests in the internet, both of a financial and/or of an ideological nature: communication and information technologies are looked upon as *key areas* where freedom of expression and access to information cannot be challenged. But the state has the obligation to defend its citizens here just as it does with regard to other potentially dangerous behaviors: informing its citizens of the risks involved, and limiting or forbidding access to potentially harmful items. This is what happens with tobacco, alcohol (drunk driving), and gambling, which represent other instances of great dependency.

6. The More Vulnerable Individuals

Let's think about the "net" in inter*net*. It can be compared to a spider's net, which catches anyone who falls into it. But are there people who are more easily caught? Can we outline specific risk factors, identifying which groups in society need greater protection? We should begin by saying that *anyone* can fall into it, young and old, men and women, married and single, practicing Catholics and avowed atheists. Anyone can access this material, whether intentionally or by chance, and be dazzled by how easy it is to obtain pleasure; it is only when they try to get out of it that they find out that it is not so easy to say no as it was the first time. Table 15 outlines some risk factors, which are discussed below.[10]

Any psychiatric disorder
Affective disorders: depression and anxiety
Excessive stress, chronic tiredness
Impulse control disorders
Addictive personality
Disordered or ill-trained affectivity
Personal factors (insecure attachment, marginalization, social rejection, abuse)
Early exposure to pornography
Certain educational styles
Lack of affective-sexual formation
Voluntarism within Christian asceticism
Difficulties in social interactions

Table 15. Pornography addiction predisposing factors.

Broadly speaking, *any psychiatric disorder* predisposes one to these behaviors to a greater or lesser extent. These will be covered in the last two chapters of this book. For the moment we only need to mention that it has a direct relationship with the present topic.

Let us begin with *affective disorders*. *Depression* is a predisposing factor of the highest order. It is marked by low mood (sadness, lack of motivation to do anything, even activities that had been enjoyable). A depressed individual feels weak-willed, and may think that the only way to feel better and forget his suffering is to engage in a particular behavior or abuse certain substances. However, in the medium and long term, these only make things worse, because the two evils reinforce each other, thus creating a vicious circle, like the episode of the little prince with the tippler:

10 Cf. C. Chiclana, "A Comprehensive Approach to Out-Of-Control Sexual Behavior," in F. Insa, D. Parker (eds.), *Loving and Teaching Others to Love. The Formation of Affectivity in Priestly Life*, Independently Published, 2021, pp. 109–139.

"What are you doing there?" he said to the tippler, whom he found settled down in silence before a collection of empty bottles and also a collection of full bottles.

"I am drinking," replied the tippler, with a lugubrious air.
"Why are you drinking?" demanded the little prince.
"So that I may forget," replied the tippler.
"Forget what?" inquired the little prince, who already was sorry for him.
"Forget that I am ashamed," the tippler confessed, hanging his head.
"Ashamed of what?" insisted the little prince, who wanted to help him.
"Ashamed of drinking!" The tippler brought his speech to an end, and shut himself up in an impregnable silence.[11]

Anxiety can trigger addictions of any kind. A nervous person needs periods of peace and may reach a certain calm by a substance or a behavior that eventually creates dependence. The problem here lies in the fact that an "easy" solution leads to forgetting about other ways to settle down. These alternatives may not work as quickly, but they certainly are healthier and longer lasting.

Excessive stress or *chronic tiredness* in daily life are not diseases, but they are predisposing factors, because they can activate the same mechanisms that anxiety and depression do.

Compulsive sexual behavior disorder is one of several *impulse control disorders* listed in ICD-11. It is also a predisposing factor. It makes sense because the will is a single entity. If the individual is not able to restrain himself in one area (outbursts of anger, pulling one's hair, biting fingernails, etc.), he will find it difficult to control himself in other areas. For this reason, we have included *attention deficit hyperactivity disorder (ADHD)*, both in children and in adults, because impulsiveness is one of its typical features.

Moving on to personality disorders (they will be addressed later on), some researchers speak of an *addictive personality* pattern, which borrows

11 A. de Saint-Exupéry, *The Little Prince*, XII.

features of several recognized kinds. We are speaking of individuals who are anxious, insecure, who have unstable moods, low self-esteem, poor social skills, poor handling of their impulsiveness, inability to delay reward, etc.

There are other psychological factors outside the field of pathological behavior that cmay predispose someone to the development of addictions. Broadly speaking we could talk of *disordered or ill-trained affectivity*. It is a lack of balance between passions, feelings and affections. While it may not be an illness as such, it makes individuals dependent on their moods, with little wherewithal to control them and to control themselves.

In this cases immaturity is usually related to *biographical factors* from one's personal history which have interfered with the development of the individual's personality. Sometimes the parents have not been around, or they have not been able to help the child develop *secure attachments*, or the family suffered *marginalization, social rejection*, etc. Of course, having experienced abuse of any kind is factor of the highest order because the individual's living experience of his own corporeality and that of others has been dramatically altered. In cases of sexual abuse the internalization of one's sexuality is severely warped. How can you make a child understand that sex is good, a complete, free self-giving to another with one's body and emotions, when his first experience was *being used* for the sake of someone else's pleasure? We have already seen how *early exposure to pornography* can lead to a similar deformity, albeit to a lesser extent.

Some *educational styles*—at home, at school or wherever the child receives Christian formation—can contribute to the advent of these disorders. We are mainly talking about rigid approaches to education based on rules, with little regard for the reasons behind them, with scarce attention paid to the subjective dimension generally, and to emotional dimension specifically. Within the area of sexuality, education based on taboos and evasive responses to questions raised by childlike inquisitiveness, or severe reprimands for behaviors that the child is not able to gauge from a moral point of view, are particularly harmful. Absence of appropriate *affective-sexual formation* (not simply *in*formation) can lead them to pornography so as to find out for themselves the answers that they have not been given, or have not dared to ask. We should not ignore the natural fascination people have with evil and forbidden things, and the excitement that the feeling of rebelliousness can produce in a teenager when he breaks external limits that he has not been able to internalize. On the other hand, the view that sex is something bad or should not be mentioned will lead to stress when confronting it, both before and after getting married. All these attitudes make *integration* (a key concept) of the sexual dimension within the whole of the person difficult.

The process of Christian upbringing is not immune to all this. A *voluntarist approach to the ascetical life* would encapsulate the same problems outlined above. Such an approach would focus on actions forbidden by the commandments, the seriousness of indulging in these actions (mortal or venial sins) and the punishment they attract. The harm done to a child who begins to form his conscience is huge when the emphasis is placed on the possibility of eternal damnation, instead of highlighting God's merciful goodness, his love for men and his desire that men love and respect each other. It would be like trying to build a house from the rooftop, with the obvious risk of collapse because there was no foundation.

Such an approach to formation can hardly produce Christians who calmly try to practice virtues. If the child has an obsessive bent, he can easily develop scruples that will torment him for the rest of his life. If, on the contrary, he has reduced everything to a dry balance between the fulfillment of a norm and divine forgiveness, he will discount any falls in this area. He'll see going to confession as a sort of routine process, like getting a car wash, and while it is great for him to confess his sins and return to the state of grace, he may ignore how his behavior impacts other areas of his life. We have already stated it: it's not just about sin. Finally, anyone raised along these lines may find difficult the gift of self, whether in marriage or in celibacy.

Lastly, *difficulties in social interactions*. A lack of personal skills in relating to others can lead one to settle for online contacts. These are not bad as such, but overusing them is dangerous on two counts. Spending a lot of time before the screen increases the chances of coming across inappropriate sites and entering them. Secondly, the proportion of individuals who access pornographic sites and encourage others to do the same is higher among the frequent internet surfers. At the risk of repeating myself, I insist on the need to promote face to face interaction with others.

In summary, out-of-control sexual behaviors often hide a cry for help about deeper problems. The existence of risk factors should help people decide whether these problems should be addressed in a professional setting, in order to reach a true and long-lasting recovery.

A holistic approach is necessary, even within a medical context. I recall a clinical session during the years I worked as a psychiatrist that involved a patient in his thirties who was being treated for addiction to soft drugs. After a long time in therapy he managed to stop abusing them, but soon after he started taking tranquilizers, followed by a coffee addiction. He drank up to thirty cups a day. Everything we have said in this chapter became obvious. He needed to be looked at in a holistic way. Only then did he overcome all his addictions.

HELPING OTHERS TO LIVE CHASTITY

1. New Problems, New Strategies

No one is born addicted to the internet, or to anything else for that matter. People usually become addicted gradually. They just do what helps them feeling good—without even realizing that it is becoming a trap—while they neglect other ways of improving their mood. Once they have fallen into the vice, their recovery will require long and steady struggle on several fronts.

Some illnesses are not cured by pills alone. We can just think of someone with high cholesterol. People often need a *change in lifestyle* to overcome the problem, by adopting healthier habits. That means physical exercise, keeping one's weight down, improving one's diet, finding a better balance between work and play, etc. It may be hard, but in the long run it is healthier and more effective than just taking drugs. In my opinion, problems in chastity call for a similar approach.

In the following pages we will look at resources for formators to help people trying to lead a clean life. We will go back to some ideas from the previous chapter, as we will focus in on the area of pornography. In fact, in most cases problems with unchastity are related—either preceded or followed—to the consumption of pornographic images. Anyway, many of the strategies we will talk about are applicable to other difficulties in living chastely.

I will not repeat the suggestions made in earlier chapters, except to insist that they are crucial for growing in this particular virtue. In fact, whoever regularly uses the *traditional means* is well ahead of the curve. The ideas mentioned in the chapter *Developing affectivity from the theological virtues* are particularly important here. Fostering interests beyond the purely material is key, as are the dynamics of delayed gratification and loving and feeling loved.

Yet, some people who use these traditional means—no doubt they could practice them better and more regularly—continue to have serious difficulties and frequent falls in the area of chastity. Many formators feel that they have few instruments to help people who want to lead a Christian life but are *stuck* in impurity.[1] They are even more confused when they meet with severe cases that are clearly pathological.

2. Using the Internet Wisely

"Treat the internet the way you would treat an unpleasant neighbor." Such was the advice that one catechism instructor gave to his students. The idea is to spend as little time as possible on the internet, to get in, do what you have to do, and get out. I personally think that this is excessive. The advice may result in some undue stress, and is not entirely applicable to the internet, which is a necessary tool for work and useful for leisure. We need to learn to live with it.

Ultimately it is a matter of common sense. When we buy a cell phone, household appliances, or a car, we are given an instruction manual. Maybe we won't read it—most people don't—because there's a certain pleasure in figuring it out for oneself. Yet delicate appliances can break down if the instructions are not followed, or we can come to grief if we do not use the purchased item in the right way. The manufacturer cannot be blamed because we didn't follow the instructions. The fact is that most people begin to use the internet before they learn how to use it, and we ourselves may even have fallen into this trap.

1 There is extensive bibliography on this subject, that covers various aspects.: R.J. Molenkamp, L.M. Saffiotti, "Dipendenza da cybersesso," *Tredimensioni* 3 (2006) 188-195; M.A. Fuentes, *La trampa rota*, Ediciones Verbo Encarnado, San Rafael (Mendoza, Argentina) 2008; C. Chiclana Actis, *Atrapados en el sexo. Cómo liberarte del amargo placer de la hipersexualidad*, Almuzara, Córdoba 2013; G. Wilson, *Your Brain on Porn: Internet Pornography and the Emerging Science of Addiction*, Commonwealth Publishing, London 2014. In addition, there are many web pages in many different languages that provide information and assistance, such as: saa-recovery.org, fightthenewdrug.org, covenanteyes.com, purityispossible.com, yourbrainonporn.com, chastity.com, and countless others.

I will now offer several ideas that can help us avoid certain problems with the internet (Table 16). Parents should be the first to become familiar with them so that they can put them into practice in the family setting in a natural way. This is the best way for the children to do the same from an early age.

Have a clear purpose.

Set a time limit.

Use apps rather than browsers.

Don't go online when we are bored, or in a bad mood, etc.

Don't surf the web before going to bed.

Use the *safe mode* option.

Use filters.

Set offline times during the day.

Organize long lasting activities that don't require a cell phone.

Foster offline activities and rest.

Get rid of social media, leave unnecessary text groups, etc.

Beware of virtual relationships.

Carefully read our emails and texts before we send them.

Prioritize in-person relationships over virtual ones.

Leave the cell phone outside one's room at night.

Install app blockers.

Look into accountability programs or strategies.

Table 16. Healthy habits for internet use.

Have a clear purpose. The expression "surf the web" is very appropriate. No one would think of going surfing without any knowledge of the local conditions: the currents, when the tides are, what the weather will be like, etc. Otherwise, there is a risk of getting swept away, getting stuck in a current, or even drowning. Similarly, the internet is a sea of information and images. If you do not want to get swept away you need to be clear about what you're there for: to catch up on the news, check the highlights of your favorite team, or watch a movie trailer, etc.

Set a time limit. Of course, one needs to be flexible, but when the time limit is reached, it is time to disconnect. This is also a good way not to waste time—

it is so easy to jump from link to link. What's more, time limits are a good way to develop self-mastery. Whoever learns to stop when the time has come to disconnect will find it easier to do so when faced with inappropriate content.

Use *apps rather than browsers*. Email, news, and social media apps are more convenient than their browser equivalents, and exactly correspond to what we are looking for. There may still be links to other content, but leaving the app will already be a warning that we are past the reason we connected to the internet in the first place.

Don't go online when we are bored, or in a bad mood, etc., because then you are at your most vulnerable. There are more effective ways to improve our mood, rest, or lighten the atmosphere, both in the short and long term. How often have we ended a long session on the internet, maybe for hours, certainly much longer than we originally planned, all with the unpleasant feeling of having wasted an afternoon or lost precious hours of sleep! Lost sleep is certainly not the way to overcome a period of feeling down.

Don't surf the web before going to bed. We are usually tired at the end of the day, and our defenses are low. There is no reason to play with fire. It is much better to spend the last hours of the day chatting, playing a game or watching a clean series with the rest of the family. What happens if we cannot come to an agreement on what to watch? That's the risk of modern technology, and the ability to plan our entertainment on our own is a temptation to isolate ourselves from other people. It is better to give up our personal preferences to spend more time with the rest of the family than lock ourselves up in our room to watch our favorite show on the computer. Furthermore, computer screens can keep us awake. The light directly stimulates the retina and tricks the brain into going into "day mode."

Use the safe mode option. Most search engines, including Google and YouTube, provide options to block inappropriate material (violence, nudity, sexual images, etc.). They are easy to set up (and also to remove). They are not 100% reliable, but certainly help.

Use filters. Their role is similar to *safe mode* options but are more reliable. Subscription-based filters are the best, and the expense is a worthwhile investment for the family computer, in schools, etc.[2]

---

2   The *premium* version of *qustodio.com* appears to be among the best in the field of education.

Set offline times during the day. It is sad to enter a room or a restaurant, where friends and family members are all looking at their phones, *disconnected* from each other. Certain moments like meals, classes, study/work, or times of prayer are best lived in airplane mode, or at least disconnected from data or wi-fi. If any urgent matter comes up, people can always call us. And finding no important notifications when we reconnect is a pleasant disappointment. It also reinforces the idea that it *is* possible to disconnect at times, and check news and emails only at certain moments during the day. I also recommend going offline at night when going to bed. Going on the internet at night should already be a warning. Some friends have told me that they find it useful to leave the computer in a different room and switch it off rather than leaving it on "sleep" mode, or leave the laptop in a closet rather than on the desk. In this way they manage to isolate work, leisure, and rest.

Organize long lasting phone-free *activities.* This is a simple extension of the previous piece of advice. We can do this on many occasions: family trips, camps, excursions, workshops or study weekends—it's surprising how much study can be fit in! If curiosity comes up the device would not be so easy to reach. And at the end everyone rushes to reconnect—you see this when a plane lands and everyone's allowed to reconnect. Usually nothing important has happened, and this reinforces the idea that it is possible to be offline for prolonged periods and the world does not come to a standstill. If the practice is to be really helpful (and help us grow in virtue), everyone in the group has to agree to do it. These things cannot be imposed from the outside.

Foster offline activities and rest, especially creative activities and those that involve close contact with nature. Most people use any free moment they have to check for notifications on their phone. Sometimes we do the same to fill in longer periods of time. We forget that in ten or twenty minutes it is possible to do many pleasant and useful activities: going for a walk, playing a musical instrument, listening to music, reading, etc.

Get rid of social media, leave unnecessary text groups, etc. Have no fear here. If something takes more than it gives, there is no reason to keep it. If people ask, give a simple explanation: "It was taking too much of my time." For many people this is the litmus test of their convictions.

Beware of virtual relationships. We all know, or have even experienced, how easy it is to create a false profile and how difficult it is to know who the person on the other screen is. *Sexting* is a dangerous world to enter. For some it is exciting, but for many it is the sad domain of those who do not dare to get out for fear of rejection. (They may have been rejected for good reason.) There are people with evil intentions out there. Beware, because they may be looking for something more than a simple chat.

Carefully read our emails and texts before we send them. If you do not want something to become public, don't send it. That's even truer when it comes to photos or videos that we do not want to make available to everyone. An angry comment, a bad joke, or the simple mistake of sending something to the wrong person can go viral and reach anyone: friends, relatives, colleagues, bosses, clients, the media, or anyone who happens to see it.

Prioritize in-person relationships over virtual ones. People are better face to face. Besides, they can help you improve, because they give you the chance to get out of yourself, serve others, develop friendships, and have conversations. Pope Francis has said that human relationships need "physical gestures, facial expressions, moments of silence, body language and even the smells, the trembling of hands, the blushes and perspiration that speak to us and are a part of human communication."[3]

So far, we have covered general advice on being more detached from the internet. Next we will look at more specific strategies. People with problems related to the internet need a trustworthy person—a mentor—who is prepared to help them. Going to a mentor (even to a "virtual mentor") may sound extreme or difficult to keep up in the long term, but mentors are useful for short term abstinence. The only problem is that the "brake" comes from the outside, so it will only work if the person is really committed and open to new strategies. Otherwise it will be easy to cheat and make excuses (which will be more or less credible), and the individual will either drop out as soon as possible or access the sites with another gadget.

Leave the cell phone outside one's room. Many consumers of pornography have established patterns. They use their cell phones in their rooms at the end of the day, when they have done everything they had to do. If the phone is left in a different room, the mere fact of walking to it is already a warning signal. Another strategy is to leave the phone with another member of the family, and ask for it if needed.

3   Francis, Encyclical letter *Fratelli tutti*, October 3, 2020, n. 43.

Install app blockers. They are apps that prevent other apps from working (usually the browser and the app store). In other words, they restrict the phone to a limited number of "safe" apps. The mentor (or the people chosen) creates the password and is the only one who knows it. If the owner needs to use the blocked app, he asks for the password, uses the app, and then the password is changed.

Install website blockers. This consists of an app that blocks access to certain web addresses that it judges to fall within this category.[4] The user can add other sites, so that if he discovered a website in a "bad moment" he can block it for the future.

Look into accountability programs or strategies. There are applications that will warn someone (like a mentor, spouse, friend, self-help group, spiritual director, etc.) when a suspicious site is accessed. *Covenanteyes.com* is the best I know of. The idea is to eliminate anonymity, and this is a strong incentive "not to go there," because the person will think "I'll be ashamed if they find out," "he will really have something to say," etc. But when he is calm he will think to himself, "I'm not alone in this struggle; people who love me are helping me." In some families it is a precondition for buying a cell phone for their children. Others go so far as to install it into the phone of everyone who lives in the household—parents included.[5]

3. Finding a Personal Solution for Each Individual

"Know thyself" were the words written on the front of Apollo's temple in Delphi. Knowing one's strengths and weaknesses will help us to find a practical solution for each particular person and problem (Table 17).

Identify triggers.
Prepare behavior inhibitors.
Have an escape plan ready.
Use self-instructions.
Establish the cost of response.
Set positive reinforcement.

Table 17. Finding a personal solution.

4   I have heard very good things about *Blocker* (by *Blocking sites*), which is a pay app.
5   Other useful Apps for accountability are *AntiFappi* and *Fortify*.

Identify triggers. It is necessary to understand the patterns that lead to problems, if there are any: days of the week, times of the day, moods, activities, circumstances, etc. It is not the same thing to have problems after dinner or on Sunday afternoon, or during final exams or on vacation, in a state of boredom or stress, after spending time with a fiancée or with friends, or after a slow afternoon at home. Examining the situation can point out whether there was something that sticks out in the behavior we want to avoid, and will give an idea of what needs to be done in other areas, so that the sexual dimension may return to normal.

A short examination of this sort will help us discover the circumstances that stir one's curiosity or produce sexual arousal. They could be apparently benign, such as certain types of music, particular films, specific environments or friends, the way we interact with a significant other, heavy meals, excessive drinking, lack of sleep, etc.

Prepare behavior inhibitors. We are talking about things that will be in the field of vision when looking at the screen. They could be a reminder of why these particular sites should not be visited, such as a family photo, a crucifix or an image of our Lady, the bill from the last "mistake," etc.

Have an escape plan ready. The wrong time to strategize is when arousal begins to cloud the mind. Plans must be made in advance, preferably in writing, with different strategies for different situations (alone in the bedroom, at work, in the middle of the night, etc.). They could be things like calling someone (a mentor, relative, friend, or spiritual director), or reading a book (a hard copy), listening to calming music, praying the rosary, etc. The alternative activity must be pleasant. It is not enough to say, "If a temptation comes I will start working," unless the particular job is very gratifying.

Use self-instructions. Talking to oneself, out loud if possible and when alone, and reminding oneself of the reasons for avoiding these behaviors, and the strategies to follow in each case.

Establish the cost of response. Set a price on every fall. It could be reducing the time spent on something enjoyable, an act of self-denial (we talked about those in a previous chapter) such as walking to work instead of driving, skipping a snack, or having no dessert or a favorite drink, or a financial hit (not buying something, making a charitable donation larger than what we had planned on), etc. They are most effective when directly related to personal behavior, such as not using the phone or computer for a specific period of time.

Set positive reinforcement: positive reinforcement is usually more effective than the negative, and contributes to one's self-esteem. The greatest delight is being free from these behaviors for a while. It is worthwhile to go over what we said in the first chapter about the *internal locus of control*: the first person to be congratulated is oneself. It is also helpful to establish special rewards to celebrate that "nothing has happened" throughout a pre-established period. That may mean going to the movies, dinner at a restaurant, indulging in a purchase, etc.

4. Catechesis, Spiritual Accompaniment and Confession

The relevance of *affective-sexual formation* has been highlighted several times. I will now raise other aspects of the problem that have not been mentioned previously. They are related to catechesis (it is important to point out that it begins within the family), spiritual accompaniment and the sacrament of penance. They all require patience and refinement and should be age appropriate, bearing in mind the formation that the individual has received and the personal circumstances of the individual, which may make it advisable to emphasize specific areas.

First of all, it is crucial to *explain why sexuality is so important* for the human person as a whole, and clarify the reasons why everyone, married and unmarried, should live the virtue of chastity. The explanation should consider human nature and Christian revelation. In the Apostolic Exhortation *Amoris Laetitia*, Pope Francis dedicates a whole chapter to formation in this area, entitled *The Need for Sex Education*. He proposes beginning in early childhood, with a positive and gradual approach that uses age-appropriate terms. He mentions many of the ideas that have been raised throughout this book, such as love, decency, interiority, respect for the other that leads to not using him/her as an object, the procreative purpose of sexuality, commitment, tenderness, communication, gift of self, the language of the body, self-mastery, respect, the different roles of men and women across times and cultures, etc.[6] Often children and teenagers unconsciously learn

6   Cf. Francis, Post-Synodal Apostolic Exhortation *Amoris laetitia*, March 19, 2016, nn. 280–286.

about these matters in the family environment and then they become second nature.

Those who remain celibate need to understand the reasons behind celibacy from the beginning of their vocational path (whether they find it difficult or not), and the fact that renouncing the use of their generative power does not mean forgetting about their sexuality, because sexuality cannot be renounced. Of course, if there are issues in this area they should be considered when one discerns a vocational call. The next chapter will deal with apostolic celibacy more in depth.

Sins in this area *should be given due relevance.* We have already seen that focusing too much on them is counterproductive because they can cause distress and scruples. It is better to insist on the dignity of the human body—both one's own and everyone else's—patiently and in a positive manner, and on the love and self-giving that sexuality entails, and on the merciful love of God, who gives his grace to overcome temptations and who forgives as often as necessary.

Having said that, a struggle focused mainly on this problem rarely works out well. It is often preferable to solve it in an indirect way. Leo Tolstoy, the Russian novelist, recounts the test he had to pass in order to hang out with his older brother's friends. On the surface it was simple enough. He had to sit on an armchair until he stopped thinking of a polar bear. He tried for hours to no avail. The harder he tried to remove images of polar bears from his mind the more they returned with greater force. When he shouted, "I finally stopped thinking of the damn animal," the very fact that he mentioned the animal made it come back to his mind. This is how he finished the account of his experience: "Try to set yourself the task of not thinking of a polar bear and you will see the bloody beast every passing minute."

The best way to stop thinking of something is to think of something else. It could be a supernatural thought, time spent in mental or vocal prayer (for instance, the holy rosary can be said walking down the street or laying in bed), or meeting with someone, reading a book, watching an entertaining video, or starting any activity that involves the mind. Everyone knows what activity can capture the imagination.

At the other end of the spectrum formators will reject a misplaced worldview that ignores how important these problems may be, or fall into anthropological pessimism such as "it is normal for teenagers to fail in this area," "the digital world is hard to handle," or fall into a mistaken idea of the individual's psychosexual development.

It is important to realize that *numbers matter*. We find in pastoral work that for some people who make a definite effort to live the virtue, when they happen to stumble, they only go to confession after several episodes. This is partly due to discouragement, shame, difficulty in accessing the sacrament or for other reasons. Without being really conscious of it, people might think "in for a penny, in for a pound." Once they have made a mistake they don't care how many more they make, because absolution and probably the penance that will be given to them will be the same. It is just as easy to forgive one sin as five. This is often the tell-tale sign of a lukewarm attitude that only thinks of fulfilling duties, but with little love of God. We can all offend someone we love in a moment of weakness, but there is no reason to do it three times.

Anyone with this kind of attitude needs help in thinking seriously about the meaning of sin: the offense against God and the harm caused by each action on the person who commits them. Often the origin of addictions and compulsive behavior in people who appeared to be able to lead a chaste life lies in allowing a fall to become several. This leads to the development of a bad habit or vice, and finally an addiction.

Teaching these people *to make a good confession* will help them a great deal. The Church's teaching is that a good confession must specify the number (that is, the number of times that the person remembers having committed the sin, or the approximate number if he is not sure), and the species (that is, the specific type of sin committed). Regarding the second aspect, confessors can help the penitent be more sincere by teaching him to be more refined in the use of words; for instance, "I accuse myself of having seen pornography" is the same as "I accuse myself of having seen impure images," "masturbation" can be referred to as "sins against the sixth commandment in reference to my own self," etc.

The confessor will try to foster trust and encourage the penitents to use their own words, and he will strive to answer any questions they may have. He must be understanding and welcoming, like the Good Shepherd who goes out in search of the lost sheep and carries them on his shoulders, or the father who welcomes the prodigal son without reproaches. A harsh or punitive approach—even when it is more an attitude than words—could result in distress or discouragement, possibly the same discouragement that the confessor himself may feel when he sees that the penitent does not progress as he thinks he should. It is therefore crucial that the confessor himself—or anyone involved in Christian formation—should be a prayerful person of faith.

The priest might make confession easier by asking a few questions if he thinks it is called for. The questions should be phrased in positive terms, in a refined manner that does not give the impression of curiosity but, on the contrary, shows trust in the penitent. It is better to remain silent than to give the impression that there is only one topic that matters. Specific questions about chastity make more sense if they are part of an encompassing view of the whole of Christian life. An example here would be helping the penitent to examine his conscience by looking at each of the commandments. It is even more useful to give the penitents a card or a booklet with age-appropriate questions that they can use to make a more meaningful examination of conscience before receiving the sacrament.[7]

If the priest feels that the penitent has omitted something because of a lack of formation it is best to invite him to return to confession at a later date, rather than wait until there are further falls, so that little by little he develops a more refined conscience.

I will end this section with a topic that is particularly delicate in today's environment: hearing the confession of minors or providing them with spiritual direction. The heinous abuses by certain clerics compel us to be particularly sensitive when dealing with children and teenagers.[8] Among the many precautions that should be taken, I would highlight two. First, one should never be alone with a minor, whether in the parish office—let alone in the home of the priest—or in excursions, camps, etc. The place to be with them is in church, making use of a grated confessional or a glass "reconciliation room," or in an open or busy area. The saying, "Caesar's wife must be above suspicion," remains true today.

---

7   As an example among many, refer to https://www.usccb.org/prayer-and-worship/sacraments-and-sacramentals/penance/examinations-of-conscience. (Accessed September 9, 2021)

8   Cf. F.J. Insa Gómez, "El escándalo de los abusos en la Iglesia: causas y líneas de prevención," *Toletana* 41 (2019) 311–347.

Secondly, it is better for a priest to explain these topics in large groups of boys or girls of the same age (and separately), and not one-on-one. It is better to give them age-appropriate material to read, and even better that they read it with their parents. This will spare the priest unnecessary conversations and will pre-empt questions that will no doubt surface at some stage. It will make the priest available to solve other questions: "Read this and we can talk about whatever you want."[9]

5. Professional Help

Moral problems should not be "psychologized." There have always been people who engage in inappropriate behavior, bad habits, deep-seated vices, etc., who managed to overcome them thanks to a resolute will and the grace of God that comes through the *traditional means*. St. Augustine offers a good example here:

> even these inferior things were placed above me, and pressed upon me, and nowhere was there alleviation or breathing space. They encountered my sight on every side in crowds and troops, and in thought the images of bodies obtruded themselves as I was returning to You.[10]

This passage and others like it remind us of the pathologies we looked at in the previous chapter. Yet, the future bishop of Hippo managed to get over his dissolute life, without any help from psychologists.

If we suspect someone has an addiction or a problem with compulsive behavior that does not mean we should immediate refer him to a psychologist. Tobacco is an addiction, and many people manage to quit on their own, although others are not able to. The problem is that out-of-control sexual behavior keeps on damaging the mind and the spirit, and possibly the body as well.

---

9   I suggest a short piece I wrote for 13– to 18–year-old boys on this very topic: F. Insa, D. Parker, *Why Purity? Navigating the Confusing Culture Messages*, Scepter, New York 2020.

10 St. Augustine, *Confessions*, VII, 11.

In the presentation of this book, we recalled the words of St. Thomas Aquinas, "grace does not destroy nature but perfects it."[11] However, what happens when the body is sick? Of course, God can always perform a miracle. But when someone is diagnosed with cancer no one thinks that prayer is the only remedy. They go to a doctor and look for the best treatment.

When is the best time to seek professional help? Even with the best of intentions and the use of *traditional means*, there are several tell-tale signs that can tip us off (Table 18). (From this point onward, we will assume that traditional means are lived and that they are not neglected in case professional help is sought.) The need for assistance could be summarized by the opposite of the words of St. Paul cited above (cf. 2 Cor 2:19): "Grace is not enough." It can be the sign that other factors—not ascetical ones—are at play and that they are pressing for a solution.

Time goes by and the person cannot get out of it.
Vulnerable people (psychiatric disorders and biographical wounds).
Behaviors are producing harm in some dimension of the life.
Presence of abstinence and tolerance.
Clearly abnormal behaviors.

Table 18. Warning signs to seek professional help.

The first sign is that *time goes by and the person does not get out of it.* A long time ago I heard the testimony of a man who had struggled with pornography for over thirty years without success. He had started as a teenager, and before getting married he alerted his future wife about the problem. Both felt that life as a married couple would help remove the vice. Once married they tried to lead a Christian life, although they became increasingly frustrated. He sought the assistance of many confessors, but the advice was always the same and was obviously not good enough. In the end, one of the confessors asked: "Don't you think that your problem is more complex than you thought? Have you seen a psychologist?" It took several years of treatment, of effort, of tears, of delving into his past life and his fears, but in the end he managed to get over the addiction. Now he uses

---

11 St. Thomas Aquinas, *Summa Theologica*, I, q. 1, art. 8, ad 2.

his experience to help others so that they don't have to go through the hardships he had to endure.

I would not venture to give a specific time frame in which to seek this kind of help, because I do not think that there is one. It depends on the effort the individual has made to try out all the remedies that have already been mentioned. Obviously, thirty years, like the case described above, is far too long. One's life of faith, relationships (especially within the family), and other values can be damaged—even unconsciously—and all this would suggest that the time for action should be rather early.

An important factor to consider is whether it involves *vulnerable persons*. We have already covered this in the previous chapter, and we can summarize these cases as psychiatric disorders and biographical wounds. People in this category need extra help, sometimes urgently so.

Thirdly, we need to consider the *harm that these behaviors cause*, whether it is in the area of family (marriage breakups, scandal for the children), work (loss of productivity, use of the work computer to access content that can lead to being fired, diminished academic performance), social life (falling away from one's social commitments or significant hobbies, isolation, the stigma that results from facts becoming public knowledge), vocation (temptations not to go forward along the path of following God more closely), health (sexually transmitted diseases, a possible gender identity crisis), financial, etc.

Let's now consider the *presence of the two key symptoms of addiction* already mentioned: *dependence* (sex is used not so much for pleasure but for the need to relieve the craving caused by abstinence) and *tolerance* (increased consumption, whether in frequency or intensity, to obtain the same result, or whether he engages in extreme behavior which he had promised he would not do).

It is urgent to act quickly when *behaviors are clearly abnormal*, either because they are very frequent, because of the length of time spent on them, because of their nature (paraphilias), or because they are illegal (violence, involving children, etc.).

In all these cases the individual more or less realizes that he is unable to change without assistance. However, agreeing to see a professional is another matter. It takes a lot of time, and often consists of significant expenses. More importantly it means acknowledging the serious nature of the problem. It is not only a vice to be excised, but pathological behavior. Thus, the individual often resists the idea of seeing a psychologist or a psychiatrist. He may even have to go through the five stages described by Kübler-Ross, which are applicable to accepting bad news in general. People trying to help him need to understand this, and give the person time to adjust. On the other hand, the individual might be relieved when the idea of a health professional is mentioned, because it helps him realize that he is ill, not depraved.

One way to introduce the idea of this kind of professional help is to talk about psychologists as specialists in behavior modification (or "mental skills coaches"). Anyone who has a neck spasm usually tries to fix it by himself, with rest, posture adjustment, or pain killers. If that's not enough, he may adopt various stretches, perhaps recommended by a friend or YouTube video. But if this is not enough or the pain gets worse—which happens often with unsupervised methods—he should go to a physiotherapist, the appropriate health professional who will give an appropriate exercise regime and treatment. The psychotherapist, then, is the specialist that helps people change their behavior. The change will be the result of a comprehensive process that includes delving into one's beliefs, character, past history, etc.

Once the decision to seek a health professional is made, the question is: who? There are two questions that follow from this.

First: *what kind* of health professional? A psychologist, a psychiatrist, or a general physician? The latter is usually easier to agree to because it is easier for most people to *medicalize* his problem rather than to *psychologize* it. However, it is not easy to find a general practitioner who is familiar with the complex psychological issues that are involved in problems related to sexuality.

I admit to my professional bias, but I think that a psychiatrist is best suited for an initial consultation. "I don't need a psychiatrist, I'm not crazy" is often the first line of resistance. But the truth is that most psychiatric patients are normal people, the same ones we see and spend time with on a regular basis, but who realize that they need assistance to overcome their anxiety, depression, or difficulties with particular behavioral habits. The medical training of psychiatrists allows them to assess physical or mental pathological processes that may have contributed to the problem. In addition, they are able to prescribe medication. If the psychiatrist feels that he is not proficient in psychotherapeutic techniques he will refer the patient to a trustworthy psychologist. The reverse might also work: initial assessment by a psychologist, followed by a referral to a psychiatrist (or another doctor with expertise in this area) to assess organic involvement and possible medication. But whatever clinician acts as the "case manager," it is usually a matter of teamwork.

The second question is: who is the best person to go to? Many Christian parents and spiritual directors say, "Look for a Christian doctor or a Christian psychologist." I partially disagree. We are not talking about just a moral problem. If it were only that, going to the psychologist would make no sense. Gary Wilson is one of the most vocal speakers on the harmful effects of pornography, and he is also an avowed atheist.[12] The approach should be to "look for a competent doctor or a competent psychologist." A health professional who shares the same anthropological underpinning, values, etc. as the patient can enhance the therapeutic relationship, but it is not essential. What matters is that he respects them. A competent professional will not pass judgment on the Christian lifestyle that a given patient has chosen for him or herself, or on that patient's understanding of sexuality (unless, of course, it is clearly mistaken or harmful), but will try to help the patient live according to his or her values.

Now, if the psychiatrist were to encourage the patient to give up Christian values, he would be a bad professional. He would not be showing respect for the patient and would display a poor understanding of the sexuality-related pathologies we looked at in the previous chapter. It would be time to move on to another health professional. The same would apply to other issues. For instance, if symptoms of anxiety or depression are having an impact on one's marriage or problems within a vocational calling, it would be inappropriate to advise the person to abandon the spouse or his vocational commitments without further reflection. The psychotherapist should be very careful about what advice he should give. Initially he should begin with strategies to face up to the problem, and so bring to focus the life project that the patient has in mind. The only reason to suggest,

12 Gary Wilson is the author of the book *Your Brain on Porn*, and runs the website www.yourbrainonporn.com. He is mentioned in the first footnote of this chapter.

however gently, the possibility of a change would be evidence that the lifestyle is harmful to the patient's health, and that there is no possible solution (i.e., recurrent failure of other alternatives, alienating or abusive relationships, etc.).

Confessors and spiritual directors must be cautious before they raise the possibility of referral to a health professional. It should not be done in a hurry, and only when it becomes obvious that the usual means are not working. By and large, this should not be recommended in the initial conversation unless the situation is dire (suicidal ideation or psychosis). It is better to wait until a trusting relationship is established. However, if it looks like there will not be another chance to meet with the penitent, a general statement can be made, such as: "It looks like you are going through a really tough time, and there may be a degree of anxiety worth tackling. Have you thought about talking to a good doctor?" The confessor should have a couple of names handy (better than just one) in case the penitent asks for a referral.

When dealing with minors any decision must be made together with the parents, not only because they will have to pay for the consultations, but mainly because they have the legal responsibility, and they are entitled to know that their child has a serious health problem. The best option is for the child to talk directly with the parents about the problems, and overcome any predictable embarrassment. It will help the parents realize the seriousness of the problem and take the initiative in the recovery process. The child will know who he should talk to first: father, mother, or both together. Often the parents will already be aware of the problem, or suspect it when they see that the boy switches off the phone when they are around, hides the screen, or spends hours on the computer locked in his room, and gives vague answers when questioned about it. Sometimes there are other clues, like his attitude, behavior, or facial expression, or clear proofs, like forgetting to shut the screen, or not clearing the browsing data. It is similar to teenagers who smoke (whatever it may be) and think that their moms are not aware of it, when in fact the smell of their clothes and hands, breath mints, and material found in their pockets or desk drawers gave the game away a long time ago. In fact, it is a relief when the parents find out. It means that they take note of his behavior, love him, and are taking care of him.

The spiritual director can support the boy in these conversations—in the initial one, or better yet as time goes on—and of course keep the content of their conversations confidential. The only information to be shared with the parents is what the kid has put on the table. Many times it will be necessary to explain to the parents how serious these behaviors are, as they might regard them as a minor issue or—even if they have a good Christian formation—because they may think that "boys will be boys."

How the treatment program is conducted depends a lot on the therapist, although there is a general pattern. Initially they will talk with the individual—sometimes also with the parents—to take stock of the situation and the extent of the problem. Discerning the history follows the initial step. It includes a "psycho-biographical history" to identify the most important events in the life of the patient and their impact on his affectivity. The next step would be psychotherapeutic techniques to improve anxiety management, promote healthier personality traits, teach behavioral strategies to cope with more difficult moments, etc. Sometimes it is necessary to delve into deeper issues: relationships, past psychological wounds, etc. A superficial understanding of psychology may give the false impression that the therapist is only giving common sense advice, much of which is already in place. It may seem like "a waste of time." Yet some common-sense suggestions could be useless or even counterproductive, and the good therapist will omit them. I will refer again to the example of the physiotherapist. Human psychology is a science, and treatment regimens are based on a combination of professional experience and knowledge of how the human mind operates.

Group therapy is known to be very effective, like in the case of other addictions. Many countries have set up associations of *sexaholics anonymous*. These treatment techniques help patients put their emotions into words, feel understood and encouraged, and see themselves accompanied and learning from others who have similar problems. The involvement of a trained moderator is paramount.

Sometimes medication to lower anxiety levels or raise low mood states is useful for a limited period of time. The usual drugs for these situations are selective serotonin reuptake inhibitors antidepressants—SSRIs—(which are also indicated for anxiety and obsessive compulsive disorders), or tranquilizers (benzodiazepines or a mild neuroleptic, like Sulpiride).

Medication is not given for moral problems, but to bring anxiety down to reasonable levels—daily stresses as well as *cravings*, that only end when the addictive behavior occurs. This allows the patient to become the master of his own actions once again because his out-of-control impulses are no longer compelling him to do things he does not want to do.

It takes a long time to overcome an addiction. According to some experts, the average length of time is around three years. Such a long time is required to dishabituate the brain (to "clean" oneself physiologically) and develop alternative strategies, heal past wounds, develop a mature personality, strengthen the will, improve relationships, etc. All these areas will benefit in the end. It is not about removing a symptom but about making the person better.

6. Moral Responsibility

The reader who agrees with everything that has been said may have a valid question: How responsible is a person who has fallen into an addiction or a compulsion of this sort? Whatever avoidable mistakes he has made to get to this point, it appears that the will is pathologically compromised, and resisting the impulses has become extremely difficult. Confessors and spiritual directors may ask themselves the following question: should this person go to confession after every fall? Could he go to holy Communion even if there has been a fall?

Several points of the *Catechism of the Catholic Church* deal with this situation. It is well known that mortal sin implies that the matter is serious, and that there is "full knowledge and complete consent. It also implies a consent sufficiently deliberate to be a personal choice."[13] If the latter is missing, we are talking about a venial sin because of the subjective circumstances of the sinner.[14]

The *Catechism* deals with insufficient consent in two other points that relate to this topic. The first is in the section that deals with morals: "The promptings of feelings and passions can also diminish the voluntary and free character of the offense, as can external pressures or pathological

13 *Catechism of the Catholic Church*, n. 1589.
14 Cf. *ibidem*, n. 1862.

disorders."[15] The second develops the idea further. It refers specifically to masturbation, but is also applicable to pornography:

> To form an equitable judgment about the subjects' moral responsibility and to guide pastoral action, one must take into account the affective immaturity, force of acquired habit, conditions of anxiety or other psychological or social factors that lessen, if not even reduce to a minimum, moral culpability.[16]

Therefore, the answer to the two questions raised above is Yes and Yes. There may be individuals who objectively have committed serious acts against the virtue of chastity (masturbation, pornography, etc.) but who have lost control of their will to the point that their consent is not "sufficiently deliberate." In these cases, we would not be looking at a free human act, and therefore it would be a venial sin.

The problem here is to work out whether the requirements are fulfilled in specific cases. General rules are not valid. A case-by-case assessment is necessary, which may even vary within the same person. There may be occasions where there was full consent because it was "avoidable," and others when the passion was so strong that it overcame their (pathologically reduced) capacity to resist. The following ideas can help to make a judgment call.[17]

To begin with, if there is a habit, a vice, or an addiction, liability is always reduced, as we saw in the *Catechism*, but *addiction is not incompatible with mortal sin*. There is also a grading of responsibility, and we can talk of greater or lesser malice. If someone assaults another person, we have a serious fault in principle, but it would be different whether it took place at the end of a conversation that had become heated, or the attack had been carried out after meticulously planning cold-blooded revenge.

15 Cf. *ibidem*, n. 1860.
16 *Ibidem*, n. 2352.
17 The basis of my opinion can be found in the conference by A. Rodríguez Luño at the Apostolic Penitentiary (Rome) titled "Valutazione della responsabilità morale in condizioni di dipendenza radicate," December 6, 2011, available at: http://www.eticaepolitica.net/eticafondamentale/Dipendenze.pdf. Accessed April 10, 2021.

This provides a practical way to assess the case: *check how elaborate the behavior is*. Having impure thoughts when a person is trying to get to sleep will be different from the person who is surfing the net, finds an inappropriate image, and is not able to get past it; or who lets curiosity take over, switches on the computer, removes the safe mode from the settings and looks for images on purpose; or who drives for half an hour to visit a house of ill repute. In this last case he had to jump over several obstacles and probably had time to backtrack, which makes it more difficult for him not to have had a moment of mental clarity to rectify.

Predisposing factors have already been mentioned and should be considered. Two examples taken from real life can help us understand it. A boy on his way to class notices two young women sitting on the bus, his sensuality is awakened, and he has impure thoughts. He tries to resist, but the images remain with him all day. The distress continues as he gets home in the evening and in the end he gives up, goes to pornographic websites, and masturbates.

The second case is a young man who could not fall asleep unless he looked at pornography and masturbated. He was aware that this was not a normal habit, and tried to resist, leaving his cell phone outside his bedroom, trying to fall asleep without going through the nightly ritual, but to no avail. In the early hours of the morning he finally got up, did it and then managed to fall asleep, ashamed and remorseful.

Both cases have a point in common. The promptings lasted an unusually long time, certainly longer than normal temptations, and there was a degree of obsession, along with other facts of personal history that would take too long for us to consider here. They tried long and hard to overcome the problem by themselves, but in the end they sought specialists' help and managed to overcome the problem, with patience and personal effort. They both wanted to lead a truly Christian life, and ultimately found that persevering in prayer, sacraments and spiritual direction was beneficial.

One final criterion would be a diagnosis from a reliable psychologist or psychiatrist. That would be a compelling argument in favor of the idea that the individual's freedom is seriously compromised. But it would not be a *definitive* argument, because it should be looked at together with other dimensions having to do with the person. In my opinion, a clinical diagnosis is necessary but insufficient to form the opinion that a person does not need to go to confession in a specific case. It should be noted as well that the very fact of seeking treatment indicates a willingness to change.

With all these factors in mind and after due consideration, if a confessor thinks that a person does not need to go to confession after falling, he should not hesitate to say so, and should not think that he is running contrary to the teachings of the Church. On the contrary, not saying so would run the risk of overloading the conscience of someone who could be suffering from a pathological condition.

Even then, spiritual directors and confessors may find it difficult to reach moral certitude on how to proceed. This is not surprising because we are facing complex mental disorders and scientist are still learning about them. In a case such as this they would benefit from asking someone with more experience and good formation, while always respecting confidentiality. They should also see whether the specific individual has a well-formed conscience. The penitent should examine himself in the presence of God and consider how much he has struggled and what means he has applied—both human and supernatural—in each specific circumstance. It is important not to fall into scruples or casuistry at the time of this examination.

Throughout the healing process, the spiritual director should provide support: by offering spiritual accompaniment, helping the individual to keep up a life of piety, guiding his struggle, and providing hope in God's goodness and mercy. The Lord will not forsake anyone who rectifies, who keeps on trying—although the person could always try harder—and especially anyone who is committed to growing in love for him regardless of personal frailties. "The saying is sure: If we have died with him, we will also live with him; [...] if we are faithless, he remains faithful—for he cannot deny himself" (2 Tim 2:11–13). His very struggles and every defeat are the crosses he has to sanctify, precisely where the Lord awaits him.

The sacrament of penance has features of its own. There is no need to receive the sacrament if the conditions outlined above are fulfilled. But it is a good thing to receive it frequently, even more often than before they became addicted. Going to confession after every fall can also help. In addition to receiving the grace to help them in their struggle it will be a reminder of how evil these actions are. But they also should be encouraged not to focus on them too much, lest they overload their consciences or develop scruples. The combination of acts of sinful behavior and scruples is highly explosive. They should also be reminded that confession is not a remedy for staying calm or only for mortal sin—rather, it is an encounter with God's mercy to beg forgiveness for the evil that has been committed willingly. How the will was committed is a different question that sometimes cannot be answered. God, who knows us better than we know ourselves—he is "more inward to me than my most inward part"—knows it too, and this should be enough for a person who has faith.[18]

Those who have a deep-seated habit usually only need to confess external acts (completed actions or images looked at with evil intent). On the other hand, internal acts (imagination, slow reaction to withdraw from something found by chance) will only rarely constitute a serious matter for them, but rather the opposite: if they didn't go any further it could even mean that these internal acts that were not completed could in fact be occasional, partial successes.

It is also helpful to confess the occasions where they had not been prudent in preventing situations that often lead to falls. That may include watching TV or going on the internet late at night, spending more time on the internet than scheduled, neglecting one's schedule, etc. This will help them to remember that even in these situations they could be in control, and if they are more careful in these moments they will be in a better position to break the habit.

Above all they need help to look beyond this limited horizon. Their examination of conscience should not be limited to the virtue of chastity, but should be centered on the virtue of charity. Love of God and concern for others will be the guide that leads them out of themselves.

The best help a spiritual director can give these individuals is to remind them that God loves them in spite of their problems. He loves them always and at all times, even when they act badly. God does not like it, but he continues to accept them as persons and as children, and yearns for them to come home just like the prodigal son, as often as necessary, provided he continues to try.

I offer one final thought that has helped many restless souls to find rest. Anyone who sees himself in the situations that have been described over the past two chapters should not blame himself excessively or unduly. True

---

18 St. Augustine, *Confessions* III, 6, 11.

enough, things would be different if he had been quicker to withdraw, been more prudent, and asked for help earlier. But this is a much broader issue. We are facing a social problem in which unscrupulous individuals are damaging a whole generation of young people, often by exploiting impoverished and unfortunate young women. God will call those who perpetuate this industry from above to account for the harm they are causing and for the souls that are lost because of them. It is worthwhile that those who have fallen into these scenarios pray for them, the men and the women. It will be a way of atoning for the sins of others, and for one's own. Prayer is a way of seeing someone else as a person, not as a body. Therefore, prayer is a way to come out of oneself, one of the steps required for healing. It can be done, and it is worthwhile.

CHRISTIAN CELIBACY

1. Gift and Mystery

The content of the previous three chapters on the virtue of chastity applies to everyone, Christians and non-Christians alike, in keeping with each person's state in life: men and women, young and old, single or married, lay or priests. However, the latter—and many others who receive a specific vocation—have a distinctive feature. They are called to a particular lifestyle, and one of its features is to renounce marriage. Why should the Church demand it from some people?

A close friend of mine asked me this very question. He is rather skeptical and likes to be provocative. He understood that someone who remains single has more time available to work on pastoral matters, but he thought that that was not a good enough reason to be celibate. The same could be said of teachers, researchers, the military, politicians, etc., but it would be an abuse. "Watch out," he would tell me, "the Vatican is exploiting you." His argument gave me the chance to point out to him the three traditional reasons for celibacy: availability to look after the faithful, configuration with Christ, and the eschatological sign (celibacy as a foretaste of heaven).[1] When I mentioned the third point, he could not resist a jab: "If total abstinence is a foretaste of heaven, I'd rather go to hell." One thing was clear. My answer was not good enough. My friend is not sex-obsessed, he's a good father and husband, and a man with a high level of professional prestige. I decided that the key to the misconception was that I had not highlighted the second reason enough: configuration with Christ.

All Christians are called to identify themselves with Christ. Celibacy is a specific way to do it. The Lord chose a celibate lifestyle for himself, in

1   Cf. Vatican Council II, Decree *Presbyterorum Ordinis,* December 7, 1965, n. 16; St. Paul VI, Encyclical Letter *Sacerdotalis caelibatus,* June 24, 1967, nn. 22–23; *Catechism of the Catholic Church,* n. 1579.

stark contrast to his peers. Jewish priests were able to marry (e.g., Zachariah, the husband of Elizabeth, Our Lady's cousin) and many prophets of the Old Testament (Hosea, Isaiah) were also married. Yet, some others remained celibate (Jeremiah, Elijah, Elisha), and in the New Testament John the Baptist stands out for remaining celibate, which appears to be the norm in some Jewish communities (like the Essenes). We are faced with a transcendent reality because the humanity of Jesus Christ is a mystery. We can delve deeply into it, but we cannot encompass it totally.

Jesus chose not to found a family of the flesh, although among his followers some women were helping to support them out of their own means (cf. Lk 8:3). He wanted to establish a relationship with his disciples that went beyond the bonds of blood: "My mother and my brothers are those who hear the word of God and do it" (Lk. 8:21). Above all, he made his exclusive union with the Father very clear. Marriage is about a man who "leaves his father and his mother and clings to his wife, and they become one flesh" (Gen. 2:24), however Christ states that "the Father and I are one" (Jn. 10:30).

Jesus not only took up a celibate life, but he also asked his closest associates to do likewise. He also told them of the rich reward they would get, both in this life and in the next: "Truly I tell you, there is no one who has left house or wife or brothers or parents or children, for the sake of the kingdom of God, who will not get back very much more in this age, and in the age to come eternal life" (Lk 18:29–30). The answer of the Twelve was to renounce marriage, both those who were single (like St. John, barely out of his teens) and those who had been married, like St. Peter (whose mother-in-law is mentioned in the gospel in Lk 4:38–39). If he had not already become a widower, he renounced life with his wife to give himself totally to the life of the newborn Church. Of course, whether he was a widower yet or wasn't makes a huge difference. It's not quite the same to leave wife and children behind for the sake of the Kingdom of God and just leaving one's mother-in-law behind.

In imitation of Jesus Christ, the apostles were not called to give extra time to the evangelizing mission, but to have an exclusive relationship with the Father, and give him all their affection, all their mind, and all their soul. This exclusivity would not hurt their relationships with others. On the contrary, it is this very exclusivity that underpins their love for other people.

Jesus Christ can give of himself totally to serve them because he has given himself completely to God. In my opinion this is key to understanding the call to Christian celibacy. It allows us to love the Father with the heart of Christ and expands that heart so that it can give itself to each of our brothers and sisters.

In fact, celibacy predisposes us toward service, and they reinforce each other. When it becomes difficult to serve others, celibacy reminds us that self-giving to others is the sign of one's self-giving and love for God. And when celibacy becomes hard, looking at those we are called to serve helps to keep going when facing difficulties: "For their sakes I sanctify myself, so that they also may be sanctified in truth" (Jn 17:19).

I insist: this is a mysterious reality where we are out of our depth. It can only be reached by a gift of God. Jesus said so himself: "Not everyone can accept this teaching, but only those to whom it is given" (Mt 19:11). Above all, a gift from God is necessary to transform one's heart such that it can live out a complete self-giving to him and to the others cheerfully and in a wholesome way. Love of God and the mission to evangelize support each other.

Therefore, celibacy does not undercut marriage. That would only happen by spurning the vocation to celibacy. Renouncing something bad or poor has little merit. On the contrary, we have already said that marriage is so great that St. Paul calls it a mystery or great sacrament, and he relates it to the love Christ has for the Church (cf. Eph 5:32). The deeper we delve into the dignity of marriage the better we can understand how great the vocation to celibacy is. If it is worthwhile to renounce something so precious, it means that the path undertaken is even more excellent. Comparing it to marriage will help to understand some of the traits of celibacy.

Pope Francis has reminded us that marriage is a vocation and a path to holiness.[2] Each spouse is a path to holiness for the other. One aim of marriage is for both spouses to go to heaven holding hands (guiding the other in difficult times, if necessary), along with the children and the extended family. Holiness in marriage is an individual matter, but it is somehow mediated by the other spouse:

---

2   Cf. Francis, Post-Synodal Apostolic Exhortation *Amoris Laetitia*, March 19, 2016, nn. 69, 72, 317; Apostolic Exhortation *Gaudete et exsultate*, March 19, 2018, nn. 14, 141.

For the married person, marriage implies that the path of self-giving to God goes through the love for the spouse, the dedication to the family, by bringing the love of God into it.[3]

In celibacy there is no such mediation. The celibate meet God face to face and establish a more direct relationship with him, with no third party. Along with Jesus Christ they can say, "the Father and I are one" (Jn 10:30). This is the reason why Christian tradition speaks of the "objective superiority" of celibacy, based on St. Paul's own teaching (cf. 1 Cor 7:8, 25–40).

There is one more feature of marriage that can help us to understand better the vocation to celibacy. When we looked at the stage of adulthood, between the ages of forty and sixty in Erikson's life cycle, the evolutionary competence was *generativity*. The obvious answer to that need is given by children. Is a celibate person doomed to *stagnation* because of the lack of children? Do celibate people have to skip an evolutionary competency?

Nothing could be further from the truth. Celibacy brings someone to self-transcendence through service to others, and helping them find Christ and advance in their Christian life, not to mention help them reach heaven. This is the reason that it is called *apostolic* celibacy. It is a *spiritual fatherhood* or *motherhood*, which is just as real and psychological fulfilling as biological parenthood, even if it is not so in the material sense.

Something similar happens in marriage. What really satisfies generativity is not the fact of bringing children to the world, but raising them in both a human and supernatural way. The greatest joy children give their parents is setting up their own homes, finding their place in society, and living their own Christian lives based on what they have learned from their parents. Spiritual paternity is as fulfilling for the spouses as it is for the celibate person. In this sense, Pope Francis says that:

> Fathers are not born, but made. A man does not become a father simply by bringing a child into the world, but by taking up the responsibility to care for that child. Whenever a man

3 F. Ocáriz, *Cristianos en la sociedad del siglo XXI*, Ediciones Cristiandad, Madrid 2020, p. 102.

accepts responsibility for the life of another, in some way he becomes a father to that person.[4]

Celibacy *empowers* people to practice paternity in a wider sense because it opens their heart to everyone, without them having to focus on a wife and kids. St. Paul puts it in these words, "My little children, for whom I am again in the pain of childbirth until Christ is formed in you" (Gal 4:19).

Ultimately, celibacy is not a burden or a toll from God, but a gift of self that the celibate person makes to God. Above all it is a gift that he receives from God to configure himself to Christ more fully in his undivided love for the Father, and in him, in his love for all men.

> Jesus wanted everyone to see in him the preferential and total love for the Father. He asked the apostles to live out virginity so that everyone would see in them the preferential and total love for Christ.[5]

I will refer to apostolic celibacy in general, that is, one lived out in a specific vocation within the Church, whether it refers to men or women, to priests, religious, or lay people, who feel a particular call to serve God. I will refer to the priesthood specifically on several occasions for two obvious reasons: it has been studied more extensively, and to a certain extent it is the paradigm for other kinds of celibacy.[6]

---

4   Francis, Apostolic Letter *Patris corde*, December 8, 2020, 7.

5   M. Camisasca, "Christian Paternity, Mature Fruit of a Chaste Life," in F. Insa, D. Parker (eds.), *Loving and Teaching Others to Love. The Formation of Affectivity in Priestly Life*, Independently Published, 2021, pp. 169–170.

6   A lot has been published on priestly celibacy in recent times, dwelling on its rich content from various perspectives. I highlight some of them: T. McGovern, *Priestly celibacy today*, Scepter–Four Courts Press–Midwest Theological Forum, Princeton (NJ)–Dublin–Chicago (IL) 1998; S. Guarinelli, *Il celibato dei preti. Perché sceglierlo ancora?* Paoline Editoriale, Milano 2015; M. Ouellet, *Friends of the Bridegroom: For a Renewed Vision of Priestly Celibacy*, EWTN Publishing, Irondale (AL) 2019; W. Vial, *El sacerdote, psicología de una vocación*, Palabra, Madrid 2020; C. Griffin, *Why Celibacy? Reclaiming the Fatherhood of the Priest*, Emmaus Road, Steubenville (OH) 2019; Benedict XVI, R. Sarah, *From the Depths of Our Hearts: Priesthood, Celibacy and the Crisis of the Catholic Church*, Ignatius Press, San Francisco (CA) 2020.

2. Affectivity and Celibacy

A vocation to apostolic celibacy entails a particular way of living out one's affectivity, and it results in specific ways to grow in maturity. The usual path to grow in maturity is marriage. The practical implications that come with marriage help people to mature. One factor here, already mentioned, is generativity, to which we should add the affective support given to and received from one's spouse. There is also the gift of self and acceptance of the other in the sexual union, living together and with other family members, the responsibility of raising a family, the difficulties that must be overcome (financial, balancing family and work obligations), etc. This all raises the question: can a person mature by a different route?

Before we proceed, we should point out that the way celibate people live out their sexuality is unique only to a certain extent. Single people practice abstinence for lots of reasons, not all of them religiously motivated. They do so waiting to find a spouse, or in the decision not to marry, or after undergoing a separation or being widowed, etc. Married people are also expected to abstain from sex when they cannot have marital relations with their spouse for whatever reason. The difference is that for the celibate person abstinence is forever. He has renounced it permanently in order to give himself to God, body and soul. It requires a somewhat greater self-mastery, but only somewhat. A father of a family once told me that he was convinced that chastity is easier for priests than for married people like him, because priests choose never to have sex and are used to it, but for him not having sex depended on circumstances outside of his control: a trip, an illness or the spouse not feeling well, and many other reasons could frustrate his legitimate desire and force him to abstain from sex unexpectedly.

Whether abstinence is easy or not, the celibate person must (to use the words of the Catechism) properly integrate and live out his sexuality within his life project, his vocation. For those called to serve God as a celibate person, living celibacy becomes part and parcel of their identity. If the intrinsic value of such a lifestyle were not fully understood, they could view it as an external yoke or penalty, which gives back nothing as it takes away something actually desired. Such an approach would be the source of potential conflict. Such a framework should be avoided when one discerns a vocation. The reasons behind a celibate lifestyle should be part of one's formation during the period of discernment. Formators should offer a positive outlook regarding what celibacy gives the individual and the apostolic work it enables people to carry out.

In my opinion, the main affective trait of celibacy is not so much abstaining from sex as renouncing a life project shared with a person of the opposite sex, with all their unique traits, and the physical and emotional company that person provides. The second chapter of Genesis narrates God's words after he created Adam: "It is not good that the man should be alone; I will make him a helper as his partner" (Gen 2:18). The help that Adam needed would not come from domestic or wild animals, nor from the birds of heaven, but from God's intervention, in the creation of Eve (cf. Gen 2:20–22). That's where Adam would find the company he needed. As the Second Vatican Council recently explained, the spouses "render mutual help and service to each other through an intimate union of their persons and of their actions."[7]

Celibacy for the sake of the kingdom of heaven (cf. Mt 19:12) does not mean that the person cancels their biological sex, be it male or female, because our sexual dimension cannot be renounced. Curiosity and attraction for the opposite sex remain. Choosing this lifestyle does not mean that passions and emotions will disappear, nor will temptations in this area. It is important to realize that the need to love and feel loved remains.

Apostolic celibacy is open to a wide range of relationships. In some of these relationships there may be a good dose of personal intimacy, in which they will share aspirations, worries, joys, and sorrows. That's friendship. These relationships are not exclusive and bodily, as in the case of marriage, and it is fair to say that they will not be as intense. But they are—or should be—greater in number and of a more spiritual nature. That's how they can fulfill the need for affection. After all, spiritual does not mean unreal, abstract or unsatisfactory. Of course, it requires the spiritual *inner environment* that was referred to in chapter five.

Isolation would be contrary to man's natural tendency. There are indeed certain types of vocations that eliminate contact with others or reduce it to a minimum, as in the case of hermits or strict monastic orders. I will refer

---

7   Vatican Council II, Pastoral Constitution *Gaudium et spes*, December 7, 1965, n. 48.

to this calling later, but I will mention here that in these cases God must supplement these absences with the so called "grace of state" to enable these souls to develop their own personality and live out their self-giving in a happy and healthy way (even humanly speaking).

Spouses are often referred to as "our better half," but the expression has serious limitations.[8] It implies the idea that each spouse—and in general everyone—is incomplete, and that everyone is under duress until each person finds unity, or the encounter with a person of the opposite sex. This is not the case. We are all—single, married, widowed, priests— a "whole" and need to relate to many other "wholes." We can find a good counterpart in the other sex, but there are other ways to meet the real aspirations of human nature, which consist in flourishing by relating to the others.

If this weren't true, our Lord would have been a frustrated person or not a true man. I do not think it is cogent to say that he used his divine condition to hide such an important human dimension. The early Fathers of the Church asserted that "that which he has not assumed he has not healed; but that which is united to his Godhead is also saved."[9] Thus the Second Vatican Council stated that

> For by his incarnation the Son of God has united himself in
> some fashion with every man. He worked with human hands,
> he thought with a human mind, acted by human choice and

8   The expression "better half" hearkens back to Plato's *Symposium*, in which Aristophanes claims that the original human beings had four arms, four legs, two faces, a single head and two reproductive organs. They were androgynous. People were so strong that they dared to climb the sky, so Zeus punished them by separating them in two to reduce their strength, so as not to compete with him. That's how sexual diversity came about and also the fact that man and woman are, according to Plato's Aristophanes, incomplete and in continuous tension until they unite with each other: "Now when our first form had been cut in two, each half in longing for its fellow would come to it again; and then would they fling their arms about each other and in mutual embraces yearn to be grafted together, till they began to perish of hunger and general indolence, through refusing to do anything apart" (Plato, *Symposium,* 191a–b).

9   St. Gregory of Nazianzus, *Letter 101*, I, 32. This Christological expression is usually connected with St. Irenaeus of Lyons, who lived in the second century, two hundred years before St. Gregory.

loved with a human heart. Born of the Virgin Mary, he has truly been made one of us, like us in all things except sin.[10]

Well then, Jesus took on human affectivity as well—and specifically the affectivity that is lived in apostolic celibacy— he lived it, healed it, and showed us how man come closer to God and his neighbor by achieving his potential, humanly and supernaturally.

The reason behind one's choice of celibacy is the key for a healthy development of one's personality. It must be love, love of God and our neighbor. That is what develops a person's full potential, to help him mature and find fulfillment. Man finds himself in the sincere gift of himself to others.[11] Celibacy does not undermine a person's normal development, but on the contrary "it develops the maturity of the person, making him able to live the reality of his own body and affectivity within the logic of gift."[12]

We can think of Jedi, who are also celibate. Although *Star Wars* is obviously fiction, we can admire the Jedi for their high moral rectitude and dedication to the service of others. But their motives for celibacy are quite different than a Christian's. They give up human love because love entails the danger of losing the beloved, which can lead to the dark side. As master Yoda explains it: "Fear is the path to the dark side; fear leads to anger, anger leads to hate, hate leads to suffering." The Jedi are not an example of priestly celibacy, but rather of the stoic outlook we saw several chapters back. For a Jedi it is better not to love so as to avoid suffering. This has nothing to do with the life of Jesus Christ.

3. The Affectivity of Jesus Christ

The gospel shows that the Lord had a great many feelings. We are told that he loved the apostle John (cf. Jn 13:23), the rich young man (cf. Mk 10:21) and the family of Bethany (cf. Jn 11:5). He was a true friend of Martha,

---

10 Vatican Council II, *Gaudium et Spes,* n. 22.

11 Cf. *ibidem,* n. 24.

12 Congregation for the Clergy, *The Gift of the Priestly Vocation.* Ratio Fundamentalis Institutionis Sacerdotalis, December 8, 2016, Libreria Editrice Vaticana, Città del Vaticano 2016, n. 110.

Mary, and Lazarus—he went to the house at Bethany as if it were his own, the sisters spoke to him in a spirit great friendship, and even dared to reproach him for having let Lazarus die (cf. Jn 11:21, 32). Jesus calls the twelve his friends (cf. Jn 11:15). There are moments when he shows his desire to be loved (I would not dare say need because he is God). He regrets the lack of manners shown by the Pharisee who invites him to eat (cf. Lk 7:44–46), he is thankful for the anointing at Bethany (cf. Jn 12:1–8) and he asks his three closest apostles to be near him in Gethsemane (cf. Mt 26:36-45). In this last episode we also see our Lord's fear, sadness and anguish to the point that an angel comes to comfort him to replace the sleeping apostles (cf. Lk 22:43). Jesus sometimes withdrew to be alone and pray (cf. Lk 5:16), but on other occasions he preferred to be accompanied.

Jesus Christ allows himself to be touched by the needs of men, such that he feels *compassion* (co-suffering) for them. This happens in the case of the widow who goes to bury her son (cf. Lk 7:13), the crowds of people who are like sheep without a shepherd (cf. Mt 9:36; Mk 6:34), the multitude of sick people (cf. Mt 14:14; Mk 10:46–52; Jn 5:6) or the daughters of Jerusalem (cf. Lk 23:28). He even weeps before the tomb of his friend Lazarus (cf. Jn 11:33–36) and before the city of Jerusalem, which he knows will be destroyed (cf. Lk 19:41). And he is moved by the alms of the poor widow (cf. Lk 21:2–3) and by the repentance of the Good Thief (cf. Lk 23:43). All these characters received the saving glance of Jesus.

He also became angry when the occasion required it and gave forceful corrections, as we see when he drove the merchants out of the Temple (cf. Mt 21:12–13), or when he considered the unbelief of those who witnessed his miracles (cf. Mk 3:5), or when Peter tried to dissuade him from the passion (cf. Mt 16:23). But he only got angry when the situation called for it, and he calmed down quickly after the correction was given. After driving merchants from the Temple, he goes to heal the sick (cf. Mt 21:14).

Some of Jesus' friends were women. "Jesus loved Martha and her sister and Lazarus" (Jn 11:5). It seems to me that the order is significant, and the gospel seems to confirm this. Lazarus is never shown addressing our Lord directly, but on three occasions we see the two sisters having deeper conversations with him. Yet we get the impression that he did not spend much time alone with women. There is a subtle take-away in the episode of the Samaritan woman. His disciples "were astonished that he was speaking with a woman" (Jn 4:27). In short, he had female friends and treated women with affection and refinement, without fear or aloofness, but he avoided an intimacy that would have been inappropriate to his time and place. This is what has traditionally been called *guarding the heart.*

Jesus loves the men and women he meets and enjoys a deeper friendship with some of them; John defines himself as "the one whom Jesus loved" (Jn 13:23). Christ rejoices, gets angry and weeps with them. He seeks affection, is grateful for it when he finds it, and is disappointed when it is not shown to him. It must have been fun to be at his side and this is probably why he attracted so many people, such that when he delivered the transcendental invitation—"follow me"—many did leave everything to follow him.

Let us dwell on an episode that shows the richness of Jesus' emotions: the story of the rich young man (cf. Mk 10:17–31). Jesus looks at him with loving eyes and invites him to follow him. The young man, however, turns his back on him. Our Lord respects his freedom and lets him go. But this young man goes away sad, and it seems that he also made Jesus a little sad, because he takes a look around and says: "How hard it will be for those who have wealth to enter the kingdom of God!" It is a situation that would have tested an ordinary man's frustration tolerance, as psychologists put it. Peter jumps in to console the master: "Look, we have left everything and followed you." Jesus moves on from his sadness at the "no" of the rich young man by his joy at the faithfulness of his friends. He promises them happiness in this life and heaven as a reward for their self-giving.

4. A Psychologically Healthy Celibacy

The crisis caused by clerical sexual abuse, which we learned about in the early 2000s and of which the effects are still being felt, has raised an old question: is celibacy psychologically healthy? Is it beautiful but utopian, accessible to few, and stressful for many others?

As for the first question: yes, celibacy is psychologically healthy. A single person can achieve emotional balance, a mature personality and a successful, serene and happy life. Hundreds of thousands of people throughout history confirm it by the testimony of their lives. To assert that marriage is the *only* healthy lifestyle—or that in order to have a healthy life it is necessary to exercise one's sexual ability at least occasionally—would mean declaring many people of many different religions unhealthy when they renounce the exercise of this capacity for all the variety of reasons that they may have. It is tantamount to saying that the person is incomplete.

Nevertheless, the crisis has made it ever more evident that we need to select those who present themselves for a celibate vocation very carefully, no matter which institution of the Church they aspire to be part of. Some of the required features (Table 19)[13] are discussed below.

A mature, harmonious and balanced personality.

A settled moral life.

Fulfilment in the lifestyle implied by the vocation.

Good people skills.

A frustration tolerance.

An intense interior life such that God fills their heart.

Table 19. Psychological requirements for Christian celibacy.

The first feature would be having a *mature, harmonious, and balanced personality*. A celibate lifestyle implies the ability to make stable commitments (i.e., to understand the reason behind and consequences of one's choices and be able to carry them through), adequate mastery of one's passions (especially with regards to the sexual dimension), the ability to welcome everyone despite the normal ups and downs in mood, being able to serve very different types of people of either sex, etc. In short, it requires a degree of maturity at least equal to what we might call average. At the same time, we can rarely say that a person is *completely mature*. It is a dynamic concept, subject to progress, stagnation and setbacks. This is why the Code

---

13 I will take make use of certain classes offered by Prof. Julio Diéguez (Pontificia Università della Santa Croce, Rome) on the formation of candidates to the priesthood. These can be applied to other types of vocation. I am grateful to him for allowing me to use his ideas, which have not been published yet, and adapt them within the content of this book.

of Canon Law speaks of a "sufficient maturity" to assume these commitments as a requirement for ordination when it refers to the priesthood.[14]

Next, we might mention a *settled moral life*, that is, steadfastness in the human and Christian (cardinal and theological) virtues. In the field of the moral virtues, we see the relationship between grace and nature, and how human growth helps supernatural growth. This is what led St. John Paul II to establish the motto, "human formation, the foundation of all priestly work," which can also be applied to other types of vocation.[15] The document that regulates the formation of candidates to the priesthood[16] contains a long list of virtues that formators should be able to detect in their candidates: "simplicity, sobriety, serene dialogue, authenticity" (n. 42), prudence (cf. n. 43), the theological and cardinal virtues (cf. n. 69), "humility, courage, practicality, magnanimity of heart, upright judgment and discretion, tolerance and transparency, love for the truth and honesty" (n. 93), obedience (cf. n. 109), chastity (cf. n. 110), poverty (cf. n. 111), "faithfulness, integrity, consistency, wisdom, a welcoming spirit, friendliness, goodness of heart, decisive firmness in essentials, freedom from overly subjective viewpoints, personal disinterestedness, patience, an enthusiasm for daily tasks, confidence in the value of the hidden workings of grace as manifested in the simple and the poor [...], humility and compassion towards the People of God at large, especially those who feel themselves strenuous to the Church" (n. 115).

The third criterion is that *the lifestyle of this vocation should fulfill the individual*. One day, when I mentioned this principle, I was presented with an interesting objection: "What about the cross, self-denial, fulfilling the will of God, even when it is hard?" An example will make the point easier to understand. If during courtship someone realized that it would be very difficult to live with the other because of the person's character, habits, tastes, etc., it would be a great risk to go ahead with the marriage. Even if there were other pleasing aspects, and sincere love, a lifetime commitment in these conditions could condemn someone to a lifetime of misery. Yes,

---

14 *Code of Canon Law*, c. 1031, can. 1.
15 Cf. St. John Paul II, Post-Synodal Apostolic Exhortation *Pastores do vobis*, March 25, 1992, n. 43.
16 Congregation for the Clergy, *The Gift of the Priestly Vocation*.

the cross will come and it should be accepted. But if there is not a minimum of pleasure or affinity with the vocation, it will be hard to persevere. What this criterion means is that the person is able to say, "I could be happy living this way."

Jesus Christ did not promise his followers that only in heaven would things be tolerable, and that life is one long arduous sacrifice. Rather he said that there would be joy and rewards even on earth:

> Truly I tell you, there is no one who has left house or brothers or sisters or mother or father or children or fields, for my sake and for the sake of the good news, who will not receive a hundredfold now in this age—houses, brothers and sisters, mothers and children, and fields, with persecutions—and in the age to come eternal life (Mk 10:29–30).

St. Josemaría summed up this idea by affirming that "the happiness of heaven is for those who know how to be happy on earth."[17]

In his Apostolic Exhortation on young people and vocational discernment, Pope Francis stated the same thing:

> I want you to know that, when the Lord thinks of each of you and what he wants to give you, he sees you as his close friend. And if he plans to grant you a grace, a charism that will help you live to the full and become someone who benefits others, someone who leaves a mark in life, it will surely be a gift that will bring you more joy and excitement than anything else in this world. Not because that gift will be rare or extraordinary, but because it will perfectly fit you. It will be a perfect fit for your entire life.[18]

Next is *good people skills*. Apostolic celibacy is geared toward self-giving to others, to serve people of multiple backgrounds equally, without preferential

17 St. Josemaría Escrivá, *The Forge*, Scepter, London—New York 1988, n. 1005.
18 Francis, Post-Synodal Apostolic Exhortation *Christus vivit*, March 25, 2019, n. 288.

treatment or exclusivity. That doesn't mean becoming a professional entertainer, but it does require basic interpersonal skills like kindness, courtesy, a sense of humor, a ready smile, feeling good when surrounded by people, working as a team, etc. It implies having the flexibility to devote substantial amounts of time to people (a priest can be called at any time to attend to a dying person) or losing a bit of intimacy. In short, it is a matter of manifesting to others the kind and affable face of Jesus, to be a living and transparent image of Christ, so as to be (and sense that one is) an instrument to bring all kinds of people closer to the Father.[19]

Vocation indeed helps timid people come out of themselves and become more people oriented. But whoever cannot relate to what we just wrote or who finds most of their comfort being by themselves could experience self-giving as a burden or would tend to shy away from certain apostolic tasks, which would so damage one of the main reasons for their self-giving.

Fifth, anyone who wants to lead a life of self-giving must have a *frustration tolerance.* In the first years of self-giving, there is often the excitement of bringing people closer to God, inventiveness in carrying out new activities, etc. But the honeymoon doesn't last forever, in any vocation. Sooner or later there comes a time when the fruits—conversions, increased reception of the sacraments, new people participating in formation activities, vocations, etc.—are not so quick in coming. This can open the door to disenchantment or even second thoughts about whether lack of results speaks against the sacrifice being worthwhile. This is not new. Jesus described a similar situation in the parable of the wedding guests (cf. Lk 14:15–24).

We have already looked at some of the human factors that help us develop a frustration tolerance. Although it arises in childhood, people must develop it throughout their life and adapt it to different circumstances. Two supernatural considerations can also help. First, in the eyes of the world, Jesus' death may have appeared to have been fruitless, or a failure. Christ died on the cross almost alone, abandoned by all except his mother and a handful of disciples. But death was not the last word. There was resurrection, and he went looking for the lost sheep one by one. A Christian's life ends in victory, even if we do not see it on this earth. Secondly, understanding the

---

19 Cf. St. John Paul II, *Pastores dabo vobis,* n. 72.

apostolic aspect of celibacy means taking a step back. Jesus "called to him those whom he wanted, and they came to him. And he appointed twelve, whom he also named apostles, to be with him, and to be sent out to proclaim the message" (Mk 3:13–15). The first thing for those who have given themselves is not the mission, but the fact of being close to Jesus. We highlighted this when we spoke of the three motives for celibacy. Arguments for celibacy based on availability to carry out apostolic work and those based on happiness in the world to come are not enough. This opens the way to the sixth and final consideration.

The vocation must be sustained by an *intense interior life, such that God fills the heart* of the one who has given himself, and gives meaning to the individual's life regardless of the challenges that may come. A life of prayer, the experience of God's love and of his providence directing one's life, knowing oneself to be a son before the Father who protects him, the desire to give glory to God and to show him love in all one's actions—these will be reminders that self-giving is worthwhile. And it will be a refuge in times of difficulty. The celibate person must have great interiority, able to fill the silent times in his life with a contemplative prayer that will be the best way to fill his soul with God.

We mentioned earlier the distinct vocation of hermits or cloistered religious, who withdraw to a life of prayer and have minimal contact with other people. It is astonishing that one can renounce so much without impairing one's personality. I think that their secret is their experience of God, which is difficult to conceptualize for those of us who have not experienced it first hand. It is an experience that leads them to say with St. Teresa: "God alone is enough."[20] Those who are illuminated by the sun don't need lights. Of course, those who enter strict religious life must *already* have developed a deep interior life.

5. Some Situations that Require Special Discernment

If we admit that celibacy is not of itself a risk of mental illness, there is an even more insidious question that demands an answer. *Could celibacy be damaging in specific cases?* I think that the answer to this question is also

20   St. Teresa of Ávila, Poem "Nada te turbe" (*Let nothing disturb you*).

Yes. A person who enters this state but does not have the necessary capabilities may experience undue stress and endanger his mental health. Let us look at some particular situations (Table 20).

Special affective needs

Difficulty establishing healthy interpersonal relationships

Difficulty with authority figures

Difficulty being alone

Difficulty living chastity

History of abuse

Certain sexual identities

Table 20. Situations that require special discernment
regarding a vocation to celibacy.

There are people who have what we could call *special affective needs*. To feel loved they require explicit, palpable, perceptible and frequent manifestations of affection. They may have suffered deficiencies in childhood (unloving parents), they may be very insecure (external locus of control, need to be reaffirmed), they may have poor self-esteem, or various other conditioning factors. The celibate person, as we have already seen, will find many occasions to feel loved throughout his life, but in general they will be more immaterial in nature. These immaterial forms of affection will leave some people feeling unloved and may lead them towards an unsatisfactory existence. They may need the affection that comes from the constant support of a spouse who shares the same roof and with whom physical affection can be shared.

Another obstacle would come from *difficulty establishing healthy interpersonal relationships*. There are excessively dependent, invasive, and unstable individuals, who are more at ease with people much older or younger than themselves than they are with people their own age. In short, these people seek to satisfy their own affective deficiencies in relationships, perhaps unconsciously. This is an obstacle to the selflessness that is a necessary feature of vocational self-giving.

Special attention would also be required for those who show *difficulty with authority figures.* This often comes from a poor relationship with one's father figure. Dealing with superiors becomes a continuous source of conflict, either through rebelliousness (difficulty in living docility) or subservience (falling into a blind and alienating obedience). It is even more dangerous when a person with this limitation is in a position of authority. He may fall into certain vices of excess (authoritarianism) or defect (permissiveness), and this will hinder his apostolic work. In the first case he runs the serious risk of falling into an abuse of power or of conscience, and in the second case it will be difficult for him to exercise the gentle exigency that characterizes spiritual direction.

Difficulties being alone would be another obstacle. We could also call it poor emotional autonomy. Even when one enjoys a wide range of relationships and friendships, or lives with others who share the same vocation, there is an element of loneliness in a celibate person's life, because some affections cannot be shared with anyone but a spouse. The fact that married people share a bed seems quite significant to me. It does not only imply sexual relations, but always being at the side of another person. Let us recall some words of St. Paul VI directed to priests, but applicable to other kinds of self-giving to God: a priest's

> "solitude is not meaningless emptiness because it is filled with God and the brimming riches of his kingdom. [...] [That solitude] should be an internal and external plenitude of charity [...]. He will not be lacking the protection of the Virgin Mother of Jesus nor the motherly solicitude of the Church, to whom he has given himself in service.[21]

The celibate's identification with Jesus Christ should lead him to say with him: "I am not alone because the Father is with me" (Jn 16:32).

Difficulties living chastity would be a problem on a different level. The complete abstinence involved in such a vocation includes the absence of sexual experiences with oneself or with other people, the absence of pornography and of conscious recreation in inappropriate images, etc. In the case of sins committed with other persons, one must take into account the risk of scandal for that person and for any third parties.

---

21   St. Paul VI, *Sacerdotalis caelibatus*, nn. 58–59.

This does not mean being impeccable nor automatically excluding any person who had a slip-up of any kind. In addition, it is not possible to set a standard of "maximum frequency of sin permitted" because that would be a superficial, legalistic, and minimalistic vision. The point that the candidate should reach—with the help of a spiritual director—is knowing *why* he is not capable of leading a chaste life. That means asking whether there are ingrained habits, a lack of self-control, dependence on sensitive pleasure, dissatisfaction with his lifestyle, the need for easy rewards, affective immaturity, lack of integration of body-mind-spirit, etc. We have already seen that many troublesome sexual behaviors are the tip of the iceberg, which can hide (and at the same time point out) more basic hidden conflicts.

Formators and candidates may wrongly assume that "trusting in God's grace" means that the candidate can prudently commit himself to a celibate lifestyle even if he has not managed to lead a chaste life, in the belief that this step will prevent him from falling in the future. This present book has never questioned the efficacy of grace, but we have repeatedly pointed out that grace *ordinarily* relies on a healthy nature. St. Paul VI appears to be of the same opinion in his affirmation that the

> life of the celibate priest, which engages the whole man so totally and so delicately, excludes in fact those of insufficient physical, psychic and moral qualifications. Nor should anyone pretend that grace supplies for the defects of nature in such a man.[22]

Of course, God's grace comes to the aid of human endeavor. But grace is just as much at work during the discernment phase as it is after making the commitment. I would venture to say that an authentic grace of discernment will usually lead candidates with these difficulties to wait. In the meantime, he will grow in chastity and many other virtues, in prayer and in love of God, and eventually he may reach the balance necessary for a celibate vocation. To do otherwise would endanger the incipient vocation, not to mention the conscience of the person in question. After trying but failing to live chastity for some time, he could fall into a self-defeating sort

22 *Ibidem*, n. 64.

of attitude, in which the beautiful ideal of chastity would be attainable only for a privileged few. The formator should be the first to be convinced that chastity and continence are eminently possible.

Yet we should not conclude that such individuals should simply get married, an opinion that is often inspired by St. Paul's advice to the young men of Corinth: "But if they are not practicing self-control, they should marry. For it is better to marry than to be aflame with passion" (1 Cor 7:9). St. Paul's words must be interpreted correctly. It would be false to derive the conclusion that marriage is the vocation for people with no self-control. The incontinent will have difficulties living conjugal chastity as well. They would struggle to respect each other's times, live continence when they cannot have relations for whatever reason, or even remain faithful. The vision of marriage as *only* a *remedium concupiscentiae* (remedy for concupiscence) is narrow and even offensive, as we read in Unamuno's novel *Aunt Tula*. The main character lives with the obsession of not being a remedy for the concupiscence of any incontinent pervert, so she decides to remain single forever and encourage those who depend on her to follow her example; but she does so at the cost of sacrificing her noblest affections and the possibility of starting a life project with the person she loves.

Regarding this virtue, those who have had *previous sexual experiences* deserve special attention, because those experiences leave a mark that can play a role in their self-giving. Let us remember that sexual relationships are meant to signify a total gift (spiritual and bodily). Therefore, they are in direct conflict with the complete gift of self to God of a celibate person. People in this category may have difficulties living continence, but there is a subtler and, in my opinion, more important consideration: a person who has been in a sexual relationship—or who has been widowed—may have become accustomed to giving and receiving affection in a very "physical" way. In the initial phases of self-giving, enthusiasm may emotionally satisfy him. But with the passing of time, the difficulties of self-giving and of dealing with other people can make him long for more physical forms of affection. Their absence may make it difficult for him to express affection for others in a more spiritual or "understated" way. He may be left, so to speak, with "repressed affection." Conversely, he may not feel loved by only receiving more "spiritual" forms of affection, which are more difficult to appreciate because they tend to make more of a difference in the long term.

Obviously, I am not talking about an absolute exclusion of people who have had sexual relationships. That would mean excluding no one less than St. Augustine from the priesthood, or so many others who gave themselves to God after their conversions or simply after being widowed. It is a matter of letting time pass, being reasonably sure that they have no particular problem with guarding their hearts, or with continence.

People who have been *victims of abuse* deserve special care. This horrible situation leaves a wound in their self-understanding, especially in the understanding of their own bodies. A young man who had gone through this ordeal in his early adolescence told me that in the first three years after the fact, any physical contact put him under stress. He could not stand a handshake, a slap on the back, collision sports, etc. It took years—many years—of patient psychotherapy together with an intense prayer life, a strong desire to forgive, and competent spiritual guidance for the wounds to heal. In his early adulthood he decided to give his life to God. When he concluded his story, he stretched out his hand and I found no sign of tension as I shook it.

Finally, we should consider the case of certain sexual identities. In 2005 the Congregation for Catholic Education issued an instruction that confirmed previous doctrine. It clearly states,

> The Church, while profoundly respecting the persons in question, cannot admit to the seminary or to holy orders those who practise homosexuality, present deep-seated homosexual tendencies or support the so-called 'gay culture' [...]. Different, however, would be the case in which one were dealing with homosexual tendencies that were only the expression of a transitory problem—for example, that of an adolescence not yet superseded. Nevertheless, such tendencies must be clearly overcome at least three years before ordination to the diaconate.[23]

---

23 Congregation for Catholic Education, *Instruction Concerning the Criteria for the Discernment of Vocations with Regard to Persons with Homosexual Tendencies in View of Their Admission to the Seminary and to Holy Orders*, November 4, 2005, n. 2. The Instruction quoted a previous letter from the Congregation for Divine Worship and the Discipline of the Sacraments, "Letter, May 16, 2002," *Notitiae* 38 (2002) 586.

Eleven years later the same words were repeated in a document issued by the Congregation for the Clergy on the formation of candidates to the priesthood.[24]

The reason for this exclusion was not based on possible difficulties living chastity. Instead, the document says that the

> candidate to the ordained ministry, therefore, must reach affective maturity. Such maturity will allow him to relate correctly to both men and women, developing in him a true sense of spiritual fatherhood towards the Church community that will be entrusted to him.[25]

Pope Francis has also spoken along these lines. In a recent book-interview, he mentions an objection made to him by a religious:

> "In short"—he said—"it is not very serious; it is only an expression of affection." This is a mistake. It is not only the expression of affection. In the consecrated life and in priestly life, there is no room for this type of affection. For this reason, the Church recommends that those who have this ingrained tendency must not be accepted into the ministry or the consecrated life. The ministry or the consecrated life is not their place.[26]

It is a decision that clashes with the prevailing mentality, and it is not understood even within some Catholic circles. But many authors (who have sometimes been misunderstood or subject to attacks) have shown that from the psychological, pastoral and moral point of view,[27] those with same-sex attractions

---

24 Congregation for the Clergy, *The Gift of the Priestly Vocation*, n. 199.
25 Congregation for Catholic Education. *Instruction Concerning the Criteria for the Discernment of Vocations with regard to Persons with Homosexual Tendencies in view of their Admission to the Seminary and to Holy Orders*, n. 1.
26 Francis, *La fuerza de la vocación. La vida consagrada hoy. Una conversación con Fernando Prado*, Publicaciones Claretianas, Madrid 2018, p. 82.
27 The following articles are only a sample: A. Cencini, "Omosessualità strutturale e non strutturale. Contributo per un'analisi differenziale (I)," *Tredimensioni* 6 (2009) 31–42; idem, "Omosessualità strutturale e non strutturale.

usually have a conflicted relationship with one or both parents, which has led to a lack of identification with the parent of the same sex and difficult relationships with some types of people. Surely these problems are not specific to people with same-sex attractions. Many heterosexuals report even worse relationships with their parents. There may also be people with same-sex attraction who claim to have had a good relationship with their parents, but my experience and that of many others supports what I have said. It is a complex issue and there are certainly other factors involved, although they appear to be much less decisive.[28]

All the circumstances we have studied in this section do not necessarily mean a permanent exclusion from a vocation to apostolic celibacy. But a careful discernment is always required. First by the person concerned, and secondly by those who have the authority to admit him to a particular path of self-giving to God. On some occasions the most prudent thing to do will be to let some time pass—even years—rather than having the person concerned make a commitment that he may not be able to fulfill. It is important to highlight the welfare of the candidate as the most important thing. A hasty decision would lead him to taking on commitments that he might not be able to fulfill in his current psychological and affective state. This would make his self-giving onerous and jeopardize his fidelity to the charism he had received. Hence the best thing is for the candidate himself to be sincere about his situation with those who can help him. Then, if he realizes that the difficulties outlined above are unresolved, he should reconsider his noble decision to give himself to God in celibacy.

Contributo per un'analisi differenziale (II)," *Tredimensioni* 6 (2009) 131–142; J. de Irala Estévez, *Comprendiendo la homosexualidad*, EUNSA, Pamplona 2006; J. Nicolosi, *A Parent's Guide to Preventing Homosexuality*, Liberal Mind Publishers, 2017; J. Harvey, *Same Sex Attraction: Catholic Teaching and Pastoral Practice*, Knights of Columbus Supreme Council, New Haven (CT) 2007 (available at: http://www.kofc.org/un/en/resources/cis/cis385.pdf. Accessed 14 November 2020).

28 Cf. A. Ganna, K.J.H. Verweij, M.G. Nivard, et al., "Large-scale GWAS reveals insights into the genetic architecture of same-sex sexual behavior," *Science* 365 (30 August 2019), DOI: 10.1126/science.aat7693. This article is well documented and has been well accepted by the scientific community. It explains that there is not a single gene that determines homosexuality (the influence is polygenetic) and that homosexuality is genetically determined between 8% and 25% (the remaining percentage is due to environmental factors).

We should not forget that the Christian faithful have a right to find mature and well-formed pastors.[29] A person who has given himself to God enjoys a certain status in the eyes of the Christian community that he is called to serve, who will see in him an instrument of God for their own good. The faithful often try to thank priests through gifts of a spiritual or material kind. A mature person will appreciate these details but will always keep in mind that, like Jesus, he "came not to be served but to serve, and to give his life a ransom for many" (Mt 20:28). An imbalanced person may find in this lifestyle a refuge for his affective shortcomings, for his difficulties relating to people of one or the other sex, for his desire to dominate, for his fear of facing life, etc.

I conclude with a text from the *Ratio* on priestly formation, which again is applicable to other types of vocation to celibacy:

> It would be gravely imprudent to admit to the sacrament of Orders a seminarian who does not enjoy free and serene affective maturity. He must be faithful to celibate chastity, through the exercise of the human and priestly virtues, understood as openness to the action of grace rather than the mere achievement of continence by will power alone.[30]

29   Cf. Congregation for the Clergy, *The Gift of the Priestly Vocation*, n. 82.
30   *Ibidem*, n. 110.

IV. WHEN AFFECTIVITY IS DISTURBED

AFFECTIVE DISORDERS

1. Mental Illness

The last section of the book will deal with mental illness, and how spiritual accompaniment and formation can help people suffering from it. It may be helpful to begin by describing the three classic types of mental illness.

The first group are *psychoses*, the more obvious mental disorders. Their main trait is having an altered sense of reality, and its basic symptoms are delusions and hallucination. *Delusion* means that a patient holds a false belief despite all evidence to the contrary. For instance, that someone wants to harm the individual (persecution mania), that one's spouse is having an affair (jealousy), that a famous public figure is in love with him or her (erotomania), that one is called to save the world (messianism) or has particularly gifted (megalomania), etc. *Hallucinations* are "percepts arising in the absence of any external reality—seeing things or hearing things that are not there."[1] Typical examples of psychotic illnesses are schizophrenia and the manic phase of bipolar disorders (previously called manic-depressive psychosis).

The second type are the *neuroses*. Patients with neuroses, unlike those with psychoses, perceive reality as it is. They exhibit what are known as *affective symptoms*. These include anxiety and depression. Both symptoms are normal from a qualitative point of view, as everyone experiences them at some point. They are usually in response to something, although the trigger is not always clear. But the anxiety and depression become pathological when they are out of proportion with the trigger, whether by the *intensity* or *duration* of the symptom. For instance, it is normal to mourn after the loss of a loved one. But occasionally it can lead people to lock themselves up for months and refuse to meet other people, which is a pathological

---

1   O. Sachs, *Hallucinations*, Random House, New York (NY) 2012, p. ix.

reaction. Similarly, many people have a fear of dogs or storms, but for some the reaction is so intense and limiting that it becomes pathological. At that point it becomes *cynophobia* and *lilapsophobia*, respectively.

The term neurosis has fallen into disuse for many reasons, but mostly because of its negative overtones. It survives in common parlance, as people who are emotionally unstable, worriers, etc. are often called "neurotic." In the field of mental health, we now talk about affective disorders, mood disorders, depressive disorders, or anxiety disorders.

The third group consists in *psychopathic disorders*. Nowadays they belong to the so-called *personality disorders*. They are different from the other two in that they do not have specific symptoms. They involve the whole of a patient's personality, the stable pattern of their relationships with themselves, with others, and with the world. The main feature of psychopathic disorders is an altered pattern of relationships and reactions.

The three categories are interrelated. For instance, when some of the personality traits we saw in the first chapter are very prominent they predispose someone to neurotic disorders. There is ample evidence of their association with high levels of neuroticism. On the other hand, low levels of neuroticism and high levels of extroversion, agreeableness, and conscientiousness are protecting factors against neurotic disorders.

This chapter and the next will deal with the second and third groups only. Psychotic disorders take us too far afield, although these patients undeniably need all the help they can get to endure their illness with a Christian outlook.

As in previous chapters, we will initially address the medical aspects, and then consider what assistance a formator can give to these individuals.

2. Anxiety

Anxiety is the most frequent psychiatric disorder, with a prevalence of almost 25%.[2] This means that throughout the world one in four people will

2   The figure 25% includes all anxiety disorders: generalized anxiety disorder, panic, social anxiety disorder, specific phobias, panic disorder, etc. Here we will cover anxiety in general terms, with no reference to any specific syndrome. Further information can be obtained in American Psychiatric Association,

suffer one or other of the clinical illnesses described below to the point of requiring the intervention of a doctor or a psychologist.

Anxiety is a normal reaction, its purpose being to signal a threat and the need to be prepared to face it. When faced with danger, we usually say that the brain "produces adrenaline" (which is in fact a standard neurotransmitter), and the individual gets ready both psychologically (heightened awareness, unrest, distress) and physically (rapid heartbeat, sweating, insomnia).

This is an adaptive reaction to address the cause that triggered it. A modicum of stress helps to prepare people for exams by helping them make better use of their time, or to speak in public or to get ready for a sports competition or a fight. It helps us not faint on the dentist's chair or during a blood test, or to make a difficult maneuver while driving. Adrenaline moves us to avoid a car that comes through a pedestrian crossing, move away from an animal that seem like it is about to attack us, etc.

There is a basic level of activation, which varies from person to person. It is like the idling of a car. Each model has its own level of revs. Some people are active (they are usually said to be the *nervous type*) and others are more sedated. The basis of the difference is mainly inherited, but there is also a learned component. Making or avoiding reasonable demands on oneself, being proactive or passive in solving one's problem, keeping an internal or external locus of control, balancing work and leisure, etc., all play a role.

Stress is another related concept. It is a borderline state between normality and pathology. It means a high level of anxiety maintained over time due to a lifestyle that requires sustained high levels of activity. Some professions are particularly prone, for example those involving responsibility and quick decisions (executives, businessmen, investors, politicians) or those involving serious danger to oneself or one's dependents (military personnel, airline pilots, merchant captains, surgeons, high-risk or high-competition athletes, air traffic controllers, firemen, etc.).

Both anxiety and depression become pathological if their levels remain high for an extended period of time, a time that depends on the individual's resistance. When it becomes pathological the clinical symptoms become

Diagnostic and Statistical Manual of Mental Disorders (DSM-5), American Psychiatry Association, Arlington (VA) 2013, pp. 155–188.

independent from its source—the reaction is no longer proportional. Levels of stress remain high during leisure, vacations, when trying to sleep, etc., which makes rest impossible. Such anxiety does not help people resolve the situation and reduce stress. Rather it renders useless any attempt to "problem solve."

There are further symptoms: physical (tiredness, insomnia, sweating, tremor, muscle cramps, headaches, digestive problems, loss of appetite) and psychological (irritability, scattered attention, low mood, etc.). Each person has a typical symptomatology because anxiety is like a leak in the roof—water enters by the way of least resistance, and comes down far from the point of entry. Therefore, if we know our weak points (or those of the people who depend on us), we can anticipate the problem and take appropriate measures to reduce the stress and prevent the problem from developing further.

3. Sadness and Depression

We saw earlier (Table 5) that *sadness* is a normal passion in man. We experience sadness when we become aware of *physical or psychological ailments that cannot be avoided*. It becomes pathological when the reason for sadness does not exist, or the symptoms it causes are disproportionately intense or long lasting with respect to the cause. It must last at least two weeks and prevent normal functioning before it can be classified as pathological.[3]

Depression affects 14% of the population, more than 264 million people throughout the world, and it is the leading cause of disability worldwide. Women are more affected by depression than men.[4]

The main symptom is sadness, usually associated with other psychic manifestations. People lose the desire to do anything (apathy), don't enjoy anything (anhedonia), have high emotional reactivity (affective lability), frequently cry, are anxious, restless, irritable, and experience a general change in their character. It can lead to despair and suicidal thoughts. The clearest sign that we are in the realm of pathology is anhedonia: there is no

---

3   I refer the reader to *DSM-5* once more to check the different syndromes associated with depressive disorders. Cf. *ibidem*, pp. 189–233.

4   Data from WHO: https://www.who.int/news-room/fact-sheets/detail/depression. Accessed June 9, 2021.

desire to do anything, but even when the patient tries to get going, he does not even enjoy the things he used to.

In addition, one's vital tone becomes generally impaired. There is a lack of energy that can present itself as chronic tiredness, lethargy, or a physical or mental block. Physical symptoms similar to those of anxiety are often present. From a cognitive point of view, there is a diminished ability to concentrate and a reduced attention span, difficulty making decisions, pessimistic outlook (everything looks grey), feelings of worthlessness and guilt, and death-related thoughts.

Finally, there is a significant social impact. Work or academic performance suffers, one becomes unable to fulfill basic obligations, suffers a loss of interest and enthusiasm, and forms a tendency towards isolation.

The main types are *major depressive disorders* and *persistent depressive disorder* (also called dysthymia). The former is related to what was classically called endogenous depression. It has a greater biological component and symptoms typically improve in the afternoon. On the other hand, dysthymia, previously known as neurotic depression, is associated with one's underlying personality (emotional instability, need for affection, low self-esteem, insecurity, difficulty to adapt to changing circumstances). The onset is more insidious. It has a longer clinical course, with ups and downs. Symptoms are not so intense or disabling, and it worsens in the evening. There is a closer relationship to triggers (family, social, or work-related problems) and the clinical course is more dependent on external events (a piece of good news can result in a "good week," and vice versa).

There are clinical reasons for the differences between endogenous and neurotic depression. However, these diagnoses are no longer in regular use because both share similar personality factors and similar brain changes as shown by their biochemistry and neuroimaging. In addition, the response to drugs and psychotherapy is similar in both conditions. This has led to a change in the interpretation of the depression model, and of mental illness generally. The current *bio-psycho-social model* takes into account structural and functional changes, personality and biographical features, external stressors and the support network available to the patient.[5]

5   Cf. G.L. Engel, "The Need for a New Medical Model: A Challenge for Biomedicine," *Science* 196 (1977) 129–136.

4. Burnout Syndrome

This condition is not included in the main disease classification and it does not have a clear definition nor a unanimously accepted name (it is also called professional exhaustion and professional stress). More than a disease it is a syndrome, a pathological state with a mixed clinical picture of anxiety and depression which can be triggered by multiple causes.

The clinical picture of burnout syndrome is typically psychological exhaustion due to excessive amounts of work. It can present itself as listlessness, lack of interest, a worsening mood, and many of the symptoms associated with anxiety and depression.[6]

Burnout is more common among women and in the service professions: teachers, nurses, social workers, and in priests.[7] In the last case it has been called the *illness of the gift of self*.[8] It usually occurs in people who commit themselves to a job and invest an excessive amount of time into it, in the hope of better results, and eventually become frustrated. They complain that those who benefit from their hard work do not respond or appreciate their effort, their work colleagues are not as committed, their boss does not recognize their achievements, work becomes repetitive and unrewarding. In short, the project that they enthusiastically embarked upon becomes unsatisfactory after a few years, and this leads to physical and mental exhaustion.

This would be the case of a teacher who has to teach the same subject every year to students who are (in his estimation) increasingly uninterested in the subject, or a doctor whose patients mention the same complaints

6   Cf. C. Maslach, *Burnout: The Cost of Caring*, Malor Book-ISHK, Los Altos (CA) 2003; P.R. Gil-Monte, *El síndrome de quemarse por el trabajo (burnout). Una enfermedad laboral en la sociedad del bienestar*, Ediciones Pirámide, Madrid 2005; M. Bosqued, *Quemados. El síndrome del Burnout. ¿Qué es y cómo superarlo?* Paidós, Barcelona 2008.

7   Cf. G. Ronzoni, *Ardere, non bruciarsi. Studio sul «burnout» tra il clero diocesano*, Edizioni Messaggero, Padova 2008; S.J. Rossetti, *Why Priests Are Happy: A Study of the Psychological and Spiritual Health of Priests*, Ave Maria Press, Notre Dame (IN) 2011.

8   Cf. P. Ide, "Le burn-out, une urgence pastorale," *Nouvelle Revue Théologique* 137 (2015) 628–657.

day in and day out, or a priest who gives himself to his parishioners, but sees little improvement in their Christian life, and all of them expect that they will be doing the same thing indefinitely. In one way or another they picture their life to be like the myth of Sisyphus. They must carry a huge stone to the top of a mountain to find it back down the next morning, restarting their futile work without hope or reward.

People who suffer from this condition have several traits in common. They are usually responsible, sincerely concerned about working well and about helping others. Careless workers rarely burn out. They often have strong obsessive or perfectionist personality traits, which lead them to make exaggerated demands on themselves and on others. In the following chapter, there is a long section on this personality style, and the reader is referred to it to complete the description. Other typical personality traits are excessive dependence on results and external gratifications, and a mainly external locus of control. The clinical picture usually presents itself after one works on the same job for a long time, which leads to the sensation of increasing monotony. This is often influenced by lower levels of resistance to fatigue (both physical and mental), which occur with age and during a midlife crisis.

Sometimes burnout can be misunderstood as a lack of dedication to one's vocation, a lack of patience or faith that the fruits are supernatural. Undoubtedly these can be elements of the problem, but it is important to go deeper into the factors that psychological condition the patient. Otherwise, burnout patients may try to overcome their affective deficiency and personality shortcomings merely by increasing the demand on themselves, in the form of more prayer and ascetical struggle. In some cases it may work, but in other cases it can lead to a breakdown.

5. Preventing Affective Pathology

We said in the introduction that a spiritual director or formator is not and should not pretend to act as a psychologist. However, part of his job is to help the person concerned to develop a harmonious personality that will help to relate to himself, to others, and to God in a healthy manner, carrying out his tasks in a serene, ambitious, and realistic way. Several suggestions follow to help form people on the more natural level, and prevent the development of affective pathologies. (Table 21)

a) A healthy lifestyle:

    Lifestyle habits

    Mental hygiene

b) Taking care of rest:

    Getting enough sleep

    Having a rest period every day

    Resting within the daily routine of family life

    Longer periods of weekly and monthly rest

    Resting with other people

    Non-productive rest

    Passive rest should be avoided

    Relaxation techniques

    Protecting our inner peace and joy

    Being calm and transmitting serenity

c) Amending cognitive distortions

d) Optimizing working time:

    Getting organized before starting work

    Living in the present

    Concentrating on the process rather than on the results

    Doing well, even if we are not appreciated

    Learning to go to bed with a long to-do list

    Delegating

    Saying *no*

    Breaking out of the tyranny of other people's expectations

    Beginning the day with something pleasant

    Taking advantage of the golden hours

    Removing sources of distraction

    Making work more motivating

    Watching out for prolonged periods of overwork and accumulated stress

    Changing job

e) Stress-proofing one's life of piety:

A vision of God as a Father who loves us

Looking forward to the reward awaits us in heaven

Revising and amending the concept of holiness

Valuing unproductive prayer

Meditating on the Passion of our Lord

Sanctifying illness

Giving suffering an apostolic meaning

Table 21. Prevention of affective pathologies.

a) A Healthy Lifestyle

We can begin with the basic stuff, which is to adopt healthy lifestyle habits. That means avoiding a sedentary lifestyle, having a healthy and balanced diet, eating at regular times and spending enough time at each meal, maintaining the right weight, doing regular physical exercise, avoiding tobacco and stimulants, etc. All these measures not only lengthen our lives but also allow us to be in better shape for the time we have left.[9]

It is also necessary to take care of *mental hygiene*. Every day we put time aside to take care of our physical hygiene, and we do not even think of allocating this time to other things. We do not think it is a waste of time but as an investment for our body, which helps us to feel better and present ourselves in a more dignified fashion to others.

Similarly, there are habits that help us feel psychologically better. They require us to slow down, stop producing, and dedicate some time to ourselves. At times, we may wonder whether we are stealing this time from our work, from our family, from the apostolic work to which we are committed.

9   Regarding the habits that have greater influence on the length and quality of our life I recommend this book: M.A. Martínez-González, *Salud a ciencia cierta. Consejos para una vida sana (sin caer en las trampas de la industria)*, Planeta, Madrid 2018.

We shouldn't worry. Mental hygiene is an investment that will be of benefit to all these areas because if we are doing well, we will be better able to carry out all these activities. The last of Stephen Covey's *The 7 Habits of Highly Effective People* is to *sharpen the saw*, i.e., stop cutting down trees for a while and getting around to repairing a tool that is becoming increasingly blunt.[10]

But I do not want to fall into the trap of pragmatic activism. We must take care of ourselves so as to be healthy because we deserve it, because we need our nature to be in good working order to receive grace properly, and because charity begins with ourselves. Additionally, we will be in a position to love and care for others.

b) Taking Care of Rest

It is important to *get enough sleep*. One of the main temptations of our fast-paced society is to cut down on sleep. Sometimes it cannot be avoided, but then it is necessary to work out how to make up the lost sleep. It may mean a nap after lunch, getting up later on weekends, a day of *sleep therapy*, figuring out which spouse will get up to take care of small children, etc. Accumulated sleep deprivation leads to major psychological problems. Conversely, sleep is one of the main *water leaks* mentioned earlier. Chronic difficulty falling asleep, frequent waking, waking up earlier than planned or waking up regularly with the feeling of not having rested can be a sign that one's lifestyle cannot be sustained. Sometimes a small adjustment will be enough, but other times a more substantial change will be in order. It may mean taking medication for a period of time, though always with a doctor's prescription and with this caveat: if you start medication without making life adjustments, the bad habits will become chronic, and sleeping pills will become lifelong companions.

We should *have a rest period every day* to regain strength before returning to work. It is said that some people "do not know how to rest." They string one activity to the next without stopping, and over the years they fall victim to physical and mental exhaustion. The nature of this rest will depend on the circumstances of each person, but everyone can take a few minutes to "switch off" by reading a book or the news, or listening to music,

---

10 Cf. S.R. Covey, *The 7 Habits of the Highly Effective People*, Simon & Schuster, New York (NY) 1989, pp. 285–307.

preferably in the peace and quiet of one's own bedroom or another place that allows someone to disconnect from the hustle and bustle of everyday life.

It is not possible to switch off for long periods of time. Therefore, it is necessary to know how to *rest within the daily routine of family life*. Family life involves a lot of rushing around: getting the children dressed, making breakfast, taking them to school, and then picking them up, helping them with their homework, bathing them, preparing dinner, and putting them to bed. In between, making sure they leave their room tidy, intervening when they fight, reminding them to do their chores, etc. Every family also needs to have leisure time together, without rushing. Meals are a good chance to do this, and with a little patience and a sense of humor (without feeling the need to correct everything) they can be an occasion to enjoy time together and discuss the day's incidents. For this to happen, the television should be turned off, the children should help set and clear the table from an early age, and everyone (parents and children) should be on time and not be in a hurry to go on to do other things.

Similarly, *longer periods of weekly and monthly rest* should be arranged. Weekends are an opportunity to make special plans, which do not need to be elaborate. It may mean going out for donuts after Sunday Mass, taking a walk in the park, going to a museum, etc. It should not be done in a hurry. A good resolution might be "at least once a week, spend a morning or afternoon taking it easy."

These periods of time are occasions to catch up with extended family, friends, social clubs, etc. This idea of *resting with other people* fulfils a need that is even greater than that of rest itself: the need *to love and to feel loved*, which we have talked about at length elsewhere in this book. I agree with what I have often heard, that one should know how to "put oneself out there for others." But I also think that first it is necessary to learn to "enjoy oneself with others," and having a wide range of tastes and friends so that it is easy to find someone to rest with.

In the area of leisure I usually recommend—especially to people with perfectionist traits—*non-productive rest*: taking a walk, reading a book, visiting an art exhibition, listening to music, playing an instrument, painting, doing puzzles, having a conversation about unimportant subjects (when we often discover the true interests of those around us). In short, enjoying the many good things in life and "wasting time" with others, which is sometimes the best way to make the most of it.

On the other hand, *passive rest should be avoided* as far as possible. Who has not had the almost reflex reaction of switching on the TV or computer in a free moment "to see what's on," to end up with the feeling of having wasted time. And what a feeling of emptiness after a weekend spent watching sports, movies or series one after another. It is not just a matter of avoiding moral hazards, but of using these times for activities that rest the body, mind and spirit, which leave behind a certain intellectual or cultural "aftertaste" (which can also be found in movies or TV, when used in moderation).

Sometimes it is not easy to find enough time to wind down. When this happens, *relaxation techniques* can be useful. Some—diaphragmatic breathing and deep muscle relaxation for example—are very easy to learn and can be practiced while doing other activities, like walking or driving, talking with someone else, etc.

By now many readers must be thinking: "I wish I had the time to get to all these forms of rest." All we can do is to try to practice some of them, as many as realistically possible. But remember that this is not a whim or an escape from one's obligations, but a physical and psychological necessity.

Chronic tiredness has very negative effects on several fronts. One of them is losing the freshness of joy and having to force oneself to smile when we are confronted by life's challenges, be they large or small. It is important to *protect our inner peace and joy*, even if it requires slowing down a little. A bad temper, a bad mood, our own tension or the tension we create around us are all some of the *water leaks* that indicate that something is seeping in from somewhere. It is important to *be calm and transmit serenity* and to remember that charity is more important than efficiency.

Formators can greatly help those that depend on them by reminding them of the obligation to rest (which is part of the third commandment applied to oneself), suggesting healthy ways of resting and encouraging them to develop various strategies to rest, whether alone or in the company of others.

c) Amending Cognitive Distortions

In the field of cognitive psychology, Aaron Beck and Albert Ellis developed the concept of *cognitive distortions*. They were originally defined by Beck in 1967 as "the result of processing information in ways that predictably resulted in identifiable errors in thinking."[11] They are very deeply internalized maladaptive beliefs that determine the interpretation of reality (including internal reality) and the reaction to problems. The list has grown as other authors have studied the topic further. We will now comment on the 17 proposed by Yurica and Di Tomasso.

Arbitrary inference/jumping to conclusions. Negative interpretation of an event or situation without evidence supporting such a conclusion: "This exam is important; I will fail for sure."

Catastrophizing. Taking for granted the worst possible conclusion: "She did not like my surprise present, I am sure she will leave me."

Comparison. The tendency to compare oneself whereby the outcome typically results in the conclusion that one is inferior or worse off than others: "I wish I were as comfortable with women as my brother is."

Dichotomous/black-and-white thinking. Thinking about everything in terms of "all or nothing," like black/white; good/bad; possible/impossible: "If I do not get 100% in this assessment, I will be a failure."

Disqualifying the positive. Dismissing positives as something of no value: "I did well only by chance."

Emotional reasoning. Basing the way I feel as a reflection of reality: "I get nervous when I board a plane, therefore planes must be dangerous."

Externalization of self-worth. To base one's self concept exclusively by the opinion of others: "If they have laughed at me it is because I am worth nothing."

Fortunetelling. Predicting a negative result and taking for granted that it will happen: "I will never get better."

Labelling. Giving oneself a derogatory label: "I am a loser."

Magnification. Exaggerating negative events or traits: "My presentation was so bad that the teacher has labelled me as a bad student."

Mind reading. Taking for granted that another person reacts negatively or thinks poorly of oneself without any evidence: "I know he does not like me."

11   C.L. Yurica, R.A. DiTomasso, "Cognitive Distortions," in A. Freeman, S.H. Felgoise, A.M. Nezu, C.M. Nezu, M.A. Reinecke (eds.), *Encyclopedia of Cognitive Behavior Therapy*, Springer, New York (NY) 2004, pp. 117–121.

Minimization. Downplaying positive events or traits: "He said he was happy to see me but that doesn't mean anything."

Overgeneralization. Drawing conclusions based on limited experience, or applying them to situations that have nothing to do with them: "He did not give me the ball at all during the game, therefore he does not want me in his team."

Perfectionism. Constant striving for a high standard of quality without considering whether that standard is reasonable, usually to avoid a subjective experience of failure: "If I can't get all the details, I might as well not try."

Personalization. Believing that we are responsible for events or other people's reactions that are out of our control: "Someone was laughing, I am sure it was about me."

Selective abstraction. Focusing on only one aspect of a negative situation, so that the whole event takes on a negative consideration: "The exam went badly, I got one of the dates wrong."

"Should" statements. A pattern of internal expectations or demands on oneself, without examination of the reasonableness of these expectations in the context of one's life, abilities, and other resources: "I should be more talkative."

Of course, we all have these *automatic thoughts*, as cognitivists call them, to a greater or lesser extent. Their origins can vary widely. They are definitely not innate, although there may be a certain genetic predisposition related to temperament. They are ways of thinking that we have learned from parents or other educators, from friends and significant others, from life experiences and inevitable setbacks, and so on. If they have been learned, they can be "unlearned," i.e., replaced by more conscious, reasonable, and realistic ways of reasoning. Formators play an important role here, by pointing out the incongruities of this style of thinking and helping people formulate judgments and approaches that are more in keeping with reality and with the individual's possibilities.

d) Optimizing Working Time

I once attended a course for priests given by a married couple—a role reversal—who were involved in family enrichment. One of the classes was called, "What does a married person expect from a spiritual director?"

Among other things, they said that it was a great help to them when their spiritual director, in addition to giving them advice about their life of piety and about practicing charity toward others, prompted them to organize their time better, reminding them of their priorities and proposing alternative strategies for times of difficulty.

In this section I will look at several ways that a family can manage their various commitments (work, social, family activities, etc.). But before we start, it needs to be said that *we can't do everything*. However, a little creative thinking helps us get more things done, at least the most important things, and helps us avoid mad rushing.

The first thing is *getting organized before starting to work*. Using a pen and paper or a task app, we can work out pending matters and an order of priorities, and set up a schedule for each task. The *Eisenhower matrix*, named after the president, is a classic tool for implementing this plan (Figure 3).[12] We will take a look at it in reverse order, from least to most important.

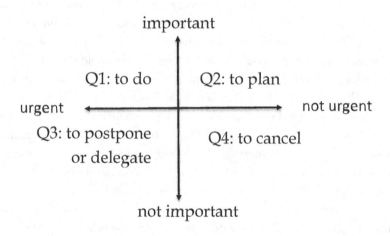

Figure 3: Eisenhower matrix of time management.

We could call activities in sector Q4 (not urgent and not important) *a waste of time*. If they are not urgent and not important, why are we doing them? Especially when we have many other things to do. Many Google

12   A more detailed description can be found in Covey, *The 7 habits of the Highly Effective People*, pp. 144–182.

THE FORMATION OF AFFECTIVITY

searches, empty conversations, endless text messaging, constant refreshing on social media or news websites, trivial activities and seminars we do not really care about would fall into this category. These activities are *time predators* in which we engage because we let ourselves be carried away by our first impulse or they are relaxing or because. In the first case, they should be moved to the category of rest and leisure; we have already covered the topic, now we want to concentrate on how to better organize our work. It is easy to realize that we have wasted time after the fact; a good goal would be to be able to realize in advance whether a given activity will do so.

Sector Q3 (urgent and not important) are *avoidable distractions*. They are things that crop up and require our attention, but prevent us from doing what we consider important. Examples include responding to emails that cannot be postponed, taking phone call, unexpected requests for help, the details of planning for events. How do we manage these tasks? Two possible strategies are delaying and delegating.

Delaying a task allows us to fit it into a *plan*, and not just *react*. It also gives us the pleasure of being in control of our time. I once heard a team manager say, "the fact that someone sends me a message does not give him the right to a response, let alone an immediate one." Otherwise, we would spend the whole day looking after other people's problems, at the expense of our own! Responses need to be reconciled with good manners and dialogue. We can ask, "When do you need this job done? Can you come back before lunch?" or "I am tied up right now, can you call me later?" Delaying has the added bonus of teaching us new skills: we will be more comfortable saying *no* in an assertive way, accepting that sometimes we have to look bad (by rejecting a favor or not doing it immediately) or not meet expectations, being seen as limited, etc.

Delegating is quite a challenge, particularly for perfectionists and micromanagers ("I would rather do it myself because others will not do it right"), or those who only have a short-term view of things ("It's quicker for me to do this than explain to someone else how to do it," which often means "I will always do it myself, even if it is someone else's job").

Unavoidable distractions belong in sector Q1. They are like those in the previous sector, except that we have to drop everything else and do them ourselves, because they fall under our responsibility, and any delay would be detrimental. Here we find things like handing in documents before a deadline, medical emergencies, repairing tools or gadgets that are necessary for work, etc. They are the extras, though part of our daily life. They remind us that planning needs to be flexible—we should make allowances for these things to happen. For example, it's common knowledge in the medical field that the ideal occupancy of a hospital is 85%. I was surprised when first I heard that. What's the point of leaving so many beds empty? Well, a full hospital is unable to cope with accidents, the seasonal flu, staff sickness, or an equipment malfunction that would require closing a ward. In other words, planning cannot be so tight as to exclude unexpected changes. Of course, it is key to do Q3 activities as quickly as possible so as to return to the really important things.

These *really important things* are in sector Q2. These are the activities that require time and planning. They allow medium and long-term goals to be achieved by calm and steady work. The idea is to schedule most of our time for these important but not urgent tasks, and protect them from interruptions.

How can this planning be implemented in practice? We can start with Eisenhower's phrase: "Important matters are seldom urgent, and urgent matters are seldom important." The problem is that urgent matters produce an itch that is hard to resist, whereas we usually have no qualms about delaying what is important but not pressing. Time management experts recommend the following sequence: 1) make a list of tasks; 2) rank them by importance; 3) only now judge each item according to urgency; 4) act on the assumption that we will never achieve perfect planning and execution, but that we can always improve on it.

Eisenhower and his matrix aside, there are other strategies to help us work more calmly and efficiently.

As a general rule, we should begin by *living in the present*. That does not exclude anticipating what comes next, but we must enjoy the task at hand. This means *concentrating on the process rather than on the results*. The world of work is marked by productivity—manufacturing, sales, reducing waiting lists, winning a trial—but success is not always up to us, and having our peace of mind depend on it is a dangerous slide towards an external locus of control. On the contrary, if we can compliment ourselves on a job well done (which is not the same as "doing *everything* possible," which is impossible), regardless of the results, our peace of mind will depend on ourselves to a larger extent, among other things because we can examine the process and improve upon it.

This will help us to *do well, even if we are not thanked or appreciated,* but with the satisfaction (both human and supernatural) of fulfilling our duty. We have already mentioned that we should value ourselves first of all. In this way we prevent a source of stress in the form of *competitiveness* and *comparisons.* They are useful if we know how to handle them because they help us to improve through emulation and a healthy desire to shine. But those who only feel at ease when they have done better or have more than everyone else run the risk of being under stress all the time, as he has placed his locus of control outside himself (it is always possible to improve, but it is not always possible to be the best). We can't always keep up with the Joneses, and that's OK.

To-do lists can be an enemy of interior peace. Indeed, we must *learn how to go to bed with a long to-do list* and sleep soundly. If there were thirty hours in a day, we would do many more things and some of them would do a great deal of good to many people. The problem is that the day has only twenty-four hours, and seven to eight should be set aside for sleep.

The to-do list can be shortened by means other than work. We have already talked about how important it is to *delegate.* Another way to prevent work from overwhelming us is to *say no* to requests that can put our own well-being at risk. This means thinking twice before accepting a new responsibility when we already feel overburdened, while accepting that we will look bad. Dissatisfaction can arise when after devoting ourselves to other people's tasks we are prevented from taking care of our own needs and duties. In other words, the idea is to *break out of the tyranny of other people's expectations.*

When the workload becomes heavy, or we are particularly tired, it often helps to *begin the day with something pleasant.* That may include a chat with a friendly colleague, catching up on sports, listening to music—in other words, some of the content in Eisenhower's Q4 block. As we can see, the suggestions given here can be flexible, adapted to one's personal situation. It is better to perform at some level than not at all. This can help us look at work with a different attitude: yes, it can be heavy, but it brings rewarding moments.

Once we get down to work, we must *take advantage of the golden hours,* the times when we are at our productive best. These are usually the first hours of the day. This is when we can think at our best and are more productive in

Q2 tasks. Easier and more routine activities can be left for the end of the morning or afternoon, or used as a break after an hour or two of work.

In order to prevent distractions during these more productive times, it is a good idea to *remove sources of distraction*, like notifications, email, texts, phone calls, social media, etc. Only after a time set in advance can we check the inbox, answer only what is important, or take a break with the idea of returning to the important and non-urgent stuff as soon as possible.

It is always possible to *make work more motivating*. One strategy is Mihály Csíkszentmihályi's (a Hungarian-American psychologist with an unpronounceable surname) *theory of flow*.[13] According to Csíkszentmihályi, in order to enter a state of *flow* one must strike a balance between the challenge of the task and one's own skill. The flow state is an optimal state of intrinsic motivation, where people are pleasantly absorbed by what they are doing. Contrarily, a minimally challenging task is boring and excessive amounts of challenge becomes a stressor (Figure 4).

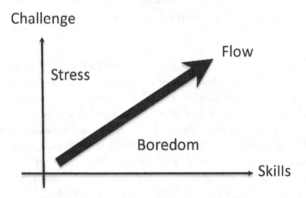

Figure 4: Flow, according to Mihály Csíkszentmihályi.

We should *watch out for prolonged periods of overwork and accumulated stress*, which sooner or later degenerate into affective disorders of one kind or another, as we have already seen. It is especially important for people who have unusual schedules (night shifts) or demanding levels of activity (competitors, tight deadlines, etc.). These people and those they live with will have to provide for periods

13 M. Csíkszentmihályi, *Flow: The Psychology of Optimal Experience*, Harper and Row, New York (NY) 1990.

of rest and pay attention to any *water leaks* so that they can go back to work in better shape and avoid what in orthopedics are known as *stress fractures*.

Finally, when health begins to suffer, a *change of job* is a good idea, at least for some time. It may not be easy or even possible to pull off, with changes in employment depending as they do on one's personal qualifications and the state of the market. Before considering a change, one must be realistic and avoid *unreasonable expectations*. One's occupation will change but not one's character, which is often the real problem. One cannot leave excessive self-demand, poor social skills, difficulty in relating to authority figures, or whatever it may be, at the old workplace. An external change must be accompanied by a willingness to make internal changes.

e) A Stress-Proof Life of Piety

There is ample evidence in the relevant literature that participating in religious activity and holding certain religious beliefs are at least moderately protective against depression and suicide,[14] and improve coping

14 Cf., among many other publications, M.E. McCullough, D.B. Larson, "Religion and Depression: A Review of the Literature," *Twin Research* 2 (1999) 126–136; P. Murphy, J.W. Ciarrochi, R.L. Piedmont, S. Cheston, M. Peyrot, G. Fitchett, "The Relation of Religious Belief and Practices, Depression, and Hopelessness in Persons With Clinical Depression," *Clinical Psychology* 68 (2000) 1102–1106; C.H. Hackney, G.S. Sanders, "Religiosity and Major Depression in Adults at High Risk: A Ten-Year Prospective Study," *Journal for the Scientific Study of Religion* 42 (2003) 43–55; T.B. Smith, M.E. McCullough, J. Poll, "Religiousness and Depression: Evidence for a Main Effect and the Moderating Influence of Stressful Life Events," *Psychological Bulletin* 129 (2003) 614–636; H.G. Koenig, "Research on Religion, Spirituality, and Mental Health: A Review," *The Canadian Journal of Psychiatry* (2009) 283–291; L. Miller, P. Wickramaratne, M.J. Gameroff, M. Sage, C.E. Tenke, M.M. Weissman, "Religiosity and major depression in adults at high risk: a ten-year prospective study," *The American Journal of Psychiatry* 169 (2012) 89–94; R.D. Hayward, A.D. Owen, H.G. Koenig, D.C. Steffens, M.E. Payne, "Religion and the Presence and Severity of Depression in Older Adults," *The American Journal of Geriatric Psychiatry* 20 (2012) 188–192; M. Jongkind, B. van den Brink, H. Schaap-Jonker, N. van der Velde, A.W. Braam, "Dimensions of Religion Associated With Suicide Attempt and Suicide Ideation in Depressed,

skills.[15] However, these same studies point out that, despite the overall positive effect, there are aspects of piety that can make affective symptoms worse. One may be more prone to feelings of guilt, rigidity, or scrupulosity, or experience stress in the attempt to conform to lofty ideals. In this section we will look at some ways in which Christian faith, when it is lived to the full, can prevent the onset of affective disorders and, should they arise, help us to cope better. Ideas which we saw in the chapters on illness and death are applicable here, but I will not repeat them.

A vision of God as a Father who loves us. "God is my Father! If you meditate on it, you will never let go of this consoling thought. —Jesus is my dear Friend (another thrilling discovery) who loves me with all the divine madness of his Heart. —The Holy Spirit is my Consoler, who guides my every step along the road. —Consider this often: you are God's and God is yours."[16] I would venture that the most repeated idea in this book is the need to love and to feel loved. Well, God fulfills this need superabundantly. God loves us as a good father, even when he allows us to go through hard times. This awareness of God's fatherhood, which can always be deepened, is a solid point of support that made St. Paul exclaim, "If God is for us, who is against us?" (Rom 8:31).

When faith has been internalized it is able to withstand the onslaughts that challenge it. We know that *a reward awaits us in heaven.* It is not simply a matter of passing through the "valley of tears" with dignified resignation, but of enjoying life and looking on difficulties as opportunities to show love and trust in Our Father, God, and to prepare ourselves for the eternal reward. "I consider that the sufferings of this present time are not worth comparing with the glory about to be revealed to us" (Rom 8:18).

In some cases, it is necessary *to revise and amend the concept of holiness,* which does not consist in the absence of faults or just "doing things" (acts

Religiously Affiliated Patients," *Suicide and Life-Threatening Behavior* 49 (2019) 505–519.

15 Cf. B. Cyrulnik, *Psychothérapie de Dieu*, Odile Jacob, Paris 2017; S.M. Southwick, M. Vythilingam, D.S, Charney, "The Psychobiology of Depression and Resilience to Stress: Implications for Prevention and Treatment," *Annual Review of Clinical Psychology* 1 (2005) 255–291.

16 St. Josemaría Escrivá, *The Forge*, Scepter, London—New York (NY) 1988, n. 2.

of piety, works of service, apostolic tasks), but in loving God. Some people are sincerely committed to a Christian path and burden themselves with "obligations to God or to others" and fall into an activism that Pope Francis described as "today's Pelagianism."[17] It can be summed up as focusing on the means and forgetting the end, of "missing the forest for the trees." St. Augustine's advice "love, and do what you will" can help here, being a source of freedom of spirit.[18] It also reminds us that sometimes our wills are wrong, that we want things that we later regret. We have seen that virtue is a key to loving the good even affectively—that is, that we desire it and enjoy it, even when it is arduous and involves renouncing other goods.

In connection with what we have mentioned above, it is appropriate to *value unproductive prayer*. A few pages ago we used a similar expression when speaking of rest. Now I want to apply it to how we pray. We should not make excessive use of vocal prayers because they may not be spontaneous, having rather the feel of fulfilling a duty. We should also avoid the pragmatism of speaking to God exclusively about apostolic tasks, catechesis, talks or homilies we have to give, or even exclusively about the people who depend on us, the resolutions that we want to draw, etc.

Two ways of praying fit in with what I am trying to say. One is a meditative reading of the gospel, trying to discover the figure of Jesus. The other is silent prayer before the blessed sacrament, even if no words come out. It is enough to remain at his side, keeping him company. In the words of St. John Paul II,

> It is pleasant to spend time with him, to lie close to his breast like the Beloved Disciple (cf. Jn 13:25) and to feel the infinite love present in his heart. If in our time Christians must be distinguished above all by the "art of prayer," how can we not feel a renewed need to spend time in spiritual converse, in silent adoration, in heartfelt love before Christ present in the Most Holy Sacrament? How often, dear brother and sisters, have I

17   Cf. Francis, Apostolic Exhortation *Gaudete et exsultate*, March 19, 2018, nn. 42–62.

18   St. Augustine, *Homilies on the Letter of Saint John*, VII, 8.

experienced this, and drawn from it strength, consolation and support![19]

When illness and suffering come to us it is useful to *meditate on the Passion of our Lord*, to look at the crucifix—without feeling like a victim—and consider the love that led him to suffer and thus makes our pain more relative:

> Jesus, compared to your Cross, of what value is mine? Alongside your wounds, what are my little scratches? Compared with your Love, so immense and pure and infinite, of what value is this tiny little sorrow which you have placed upon my shoulders?[20]

It will be a time to seek union with God in life as it is, which means *sanctifying illness,* even mental illness. Like everything in life, it should lead the Christina to ask himself: "How am I to show my love for God and for others here and now, how am I to use these circumstances to grow in 'love, joy, peace, patience, kindness, generosity, faithfulness, gentleness, and self-control' (Gal 5:22–23)?" It isn't a list of acquired human virtues, but the classical catalogue of "gifts of the Holy Spirit," which the Paraclete gives freely to those who ask for them.

Finally, even these painful occasions—as we studied in the stages of mourning—can have an *apostolic meaning* if they are united to the redemptive zeal of Christ on the Cross.

6. When Illness Comes

The reality of mental illness can involve all kinds of people. There are predisposing risk factors and protective lifestyles, but the former are not the determining factors, and the latter are not 100% effective in preventing them. An individual with a mature personality and a solid life of piety may

19 St. John Paul II, Encyclical letter *Ecclesia de Eucharistia*, April 17, 2003, n. 25.
20 St. Josemaría Escrivá, *Friends of God*, Scepter, London—New York (NY) 1981, n. 310.

come to suffer from an anxious condition or a depressive illness that requires the assistance of a psychologist or psychiatrist. Symptoms should not be confused with "thinking too much about oneself," nor should one be too hasty in dismissing such people with the advice "pray and think more about other people." People who have tasks of formation can use the following criteria to help people suffering from depressive illness.

First of all, a sensitive formator will be able to bring about an *early diagnosis*, because in his conversations with the person concerned he will be able to perceive the person's affective state, difficulties in carrying out ordinary activities, initial warning signs and symptoms of a depressive condition: anxiety, sadness, crying, change of character, irritability, insomnia, apathy, and—the most defining ones—anhedonia and suicidal ideation. The presence of the latter two should set off alarm bells. It is also necessary to be alert when these manifestations are less intense but long-lasting, for example fatigue or somatizations that do not subside after a weekend's rest or a vacation.

It is important to *see a doctor* when these symptoms begin to appear because the prognosis depends to a large extent on how early therapy is started. It is not the same to repair an instrument slightly deformed by tension as it is to fix a broken one. Something similar happens with the human mind. If the subject has "broken down," i.e., fallen fully into a pathological situation, it will take longer to improve the condition, and it may not be entirely resolved. As it is not possible to know the exact moment someone will break, it is better to see a doctor too early rather than too late.

Usually, the first person to consult is one's general physician, who can confirm the diagnosis and rule out other conditions that sometimes mimic mental illness: anemia, hormonal or metabolic imbalances, tumors, etc. After the diagnosis is confirmed he can begin specific medication. The usual ones are SSRIs (Selective Serotonin Reuptake Inhibitors) and/or anxiolytic drugs. The family doctor can also point out suggestions regarding one's lifestyle, character, cognitive style, etc., that may assist both in management and recovery. If the clinical picture is more severe, or the physician does not feel confident treating it, he may refer the patient to a psychiatrist. The patient is often reluctant to see a doctor (especially a specialist) and take medication. Being involved in an adverse event, the mentally ill will have to go through the five stages of mourning that we saw in earlier chapters. We already know that the first stage is denial.

Psychotherapy is another important treatment tool, either on its own or together with medication, as is often the case. It is not just the advice that a non-specialist can give regarding unhealthy lifestyle habits, but a thorough look at maladaptive personality traits. It is about changing them, improving coping strategies with regard to stress, and looking at past life events that may have left undiscovered wounds.

Family support is extremely helpful throughout the treatment period. A patient with depression is a challenge for all those who live with him. As they try to serve him, they should remember that "to treat the sick, to welcome them, to serve them, is to serve Christ: the sick are the flesh of Christ."[21] It is indeed one of the seven corporal works of mercy that our Lord will reward as if he himself had been the recipient (cf. Mt 25:34–36).

Caring for someone with depression is often not easy, as they can give the impression of "not doing their best," "complaining about everything," "being unhappy about everything," or being reluctant to go out, fill their time, socialize, etc. Their loved ones need to combine words of encouragement with silence, patience and understanding. These patients are very grateful to be shown affection and empathy, not to be judged, and not to have their feelings dismissed ("you shouldn't feel this way"). I refer to what we said when we talked about the depressive phase of mourning, especially words like "whatever happens, I will be here for you," which carry great affective meaning.

Patients in this situation may have problems controlling their thoughts and with their decision-making processes. It will help them to receive suggestions on how to organize their work and rest periods, with simple and easy short-term goals that will help them to be useful, to be recommended pleasant activities (although they may not enjoy them as they used to), etc. Rather than telling them what to do, it is even better to do it with them. It is important to balance their desire to be alone with their need (even if they do not perceive it) to feel accompanied, listened to, and loved. This requires spending time with them (which is not wasted time). Often it will be enough to stay nearby, quietly doing something else, or asking them to accompany someone on a trip to the store or on an outing.

Patients may suffer from pathological pessimism. They must be given *hope*. They should know that mental illness usually improves, and those

21 Francis, *Angelus* February 8, 2015.

who suffer it often achieve a full recovery. They *can* go back to their normal lives, if only gradually. Now, hyper-responsible individuals may show a counterproductive haste to return to their previous activity, so it is important to ensure that they have sufficiently improved and have made the required changes to their lifestyle, so that there are no relapses in the future.

We end the chapter by recalling that those who suffer from affective pathologies still need *spiritual accompaniment*. Indeed, they will need it more than ever, just like in any other extraordinary circumstance of life. The spiritual director, and if possible in contact with the family—obviously if the patient wishes and with due discretion—can help the directee to use the illness to draw closer to God. We have already seen that a mature faith facilitates the process of healing.

Anyone who has overcome a mental illness tends to be much more sympathetic to the subjective state of other individuals. They gain a great capacity for empathy that equips them to be excellent support for others who suffer similar issues. In this sense their experiences, however painful, are enriching.

PERSONALITY DISORDERS

1. Personality and Its Disorders

In the first chapter we described personality as *a stable way to relate to oneself, to others, and to the world*, and developed the "criteria of maturity" as proposed by the American psychologist Gordon Allport. In this chapter we will approach personality from a different perspective. Instead of focusing on "maturity" and "immaturity," we will talk about health and illness. Both approaches are closely related, but they are not the same. An immature person is not necessarily sick, although some degrees of immaturity are thought to be pathological.

Personality disorders can be defined as a global alteration of one's way of being, thinking, and relating to others. They therefore affect the individual at different levels.

From a *structural* perspective, personality disorders typically show very marked traits. If we apply the *big five* personality traits, people suffering personality disorders would be in the extreme range in one or more of the five categories. They are cautious to a fault or extremely sensitive or introverted or callous, etc.

Consequently, their *behavior* is hopelessly rigid. They always act in the same way at all times regardless of the circumstances, even though those strategies have failed in the past, because they have no resources to act otherwise. We can think of Abraham Maslow's dictum: "I suppose it is tempting, if the only tool you have is a hammer, to treat everything as if it were a nail."[1] They lack flexibility, and therefore it is difficult for them to adapt to changing circumstances.

Such people have *affective disturbances*. It may be the result of deficient

---

1   A.H. Maslow, *The Psychology of Science: A Reconnaissance*, Harper & Row, New York (NY) 1966, pp. 15–16.

relationships early in life, poor education, or other past wounds. They have little affective autonomy, and exhibit sadness, insecurity, fear, anxiety, and feelings of inferiority (manifest or hidden behind compensation strategies). They handle frustration poorly, lack control of their passions and emotions, are impulsive and have difficulty understanding medium and short-term goals (such as delaying rewards or understanding the consequences of their actions). They are ambivalent, meaning that they show love and hatred towards the same person, or idealize and disregard them, which leads to intense but unstable relationships.

They try to overcome their affective deficiencies by setting up *unhealthy relationships*, as ineffective as they are harmful. They tend to exclude third parties, invade the other's personal space, not respect otherness, and use other people. This last part is known as "manipulation," that is, forcing a relationship for one's own benefit.

Strategies to achieve this are their attempts—not entirely conscious—to make other people do or feel what they do not want to do or feel, such as neglect themselves so that others take care of them, exploit their virtues or defects for their own benefit, put them in extreme situations, apply pressure on them to create certain feelings (emotional blackmail, inducing pity or guilt or inculcating a sense of inferiority), etc.

Consequently, they find it difficult to establish "equal footing" in their relationships, i.e., to make friends with their equals on equal terms. The usual pattern is either dominance or submission. It is therefore rare for their relationships to be long-lasting or varied. The other person eventually withdraws, exhausted, and only those who also have unbalanced personalities stick around. The relationship between a psychopath and a dependent is a classic example. One needs to step on the other to assert himself and the other needs someone for support, even if he or she is mistreated in the process.

If we look at them from a different perspective, some of these disorders can be described as *persistent infantile self-centeredness* at the expense of self-transcendence and the extension of the sense of self (the latter was the first of Allport's maturity criteria). The subject focuses his attention on himself—it is important to stress that he is not entirely conscious of it—and he seeks to feel good or not to feel bad at all costs. Indeed, he is not capable of appreciating the needs of others and perhaps does not even realize that others also have their own needs. Consequently, he claims attention for himself, gives priority to his own satisfaction, does not pay attention to the implications that his actions or demands have on others, etc.

From a *cognitive* point of view, they have what we called in the previous chapter *cognitive distortions* or *automatic thoughts* that lead them to interpret reality wrongly. "They want to harm me" (paranoid), "The other person is to blame" (antisocial), "If things won't work out 100% it is better not to try" (obsessive-compulsive), etc.

Typically, they are not aware that they have a problem, which makes it very difficult for them to seek treatment. The best they can achieve (in many cases) is to receive treatment from a doctor for the management of other secondary symptoms (e.g. insomnia, anxiety or depression).

Personality disorders appear as early as childhood or adolescence, and become evident at the beginning of adulthood or maturity. Given that we are not talking about specific behavior but about one's overall personality, the alterations must be stable, long-lasting and of long evolution, and interfere significantly in different areas of the individual's life (family, social, work, etc.) before a definite diagnosis can be made.

In addition to the personal interview and the data provided by the family, psychological tests are part of the diagnosis. These may include the Rorschach test, which consists of sheets of undefined drawings or multiple-choice questions (MMPI, 16-PF), etc. In less severe cases, it can be difficult to establish a diagnosis, which creates a grey area between normal and pathological personalities.

Treatment is often challenging and can take a long time (years). Not surprisingly, medication is only helpful to alleviate some manifestations (e.g., to reduce impulsiveness) or to mitigate secondary symptoms (anxiety and low mood). Prescription drugs will not fix the condition. Psychotherapy is necessary to identify the root causes, correct cognitive distortions, and help to develop healthy relationships and strategies to cope with problems.

2. How to Help from a Formation Perspective

Individuals who suffer from these conditions can be helped in various ways by those involved in tasks of formation and spiritual accompaniment.

Healthy people may find it very difficult to understand these patients because they appear to do things on purpose that lead to failure over and over again. Indeed, they lack a sense of reality—not in the sense of the psychotic who has altered beliefs or perceptions, but they are not aware of their own needs or the needs of others.

Though they may instinctively provoke rejection, their difficulties are real pathologies rather than manias or character defects, and so we should approach them with the awareness that these abnormalities make them (and society) suffer.[2]

We should also note that formators are not immune to the pattern of abnormal relationships that these individuals tend to establish. They will also try to use and manipulate them. Consequently, not everyone is in a position to help these individuals. Special preparation, experience and a sincere capacity for self-observation and self-control are required to prevent a relationship that would be harmful for both parties.

The formator should start by pointing out inappropriate behaviors and reinforcing adaptive ones. This is often not easy, as these individuals—as part of their disorder—usually do not perceive any disturbance in their behavior, beliefs or relationships, and therefore do not feel the need to establish healthier patterns of behavior. They often place all the responsibility on others. Making them face reality will help them, and it will be a step toward overcoming self-centeredness. They need to look beyond themselves and transcend themselves. This can be done by pointing out the bad consequences that their behavior has on themselves and on others, and by showing how people with integrated and happy lives behave, so that they can try to imitate a healthy alternative.

A possible approach is to provide a book in which they can recognize themselves. It can be a psychology book or a novel (or even a movie) where one of the characters has similar traits. The latter is often less aggressive to the person concerned and leads to conversations where similarities and strategies for change arise.

Formational conversations will also be opportunities to point out more adaptive traits and defense mechanisms they can use to deal with various

2   Cf. K. Schneider, *Psychopathic personalities*, C.C. Thomas, Springfield (IL) 1958.

situations in life. The study of the traits associated with each of the *big five* personality factors will help them to set realistic and concrete goals.

When setting these goals, great care should be taken not to demand what the individual is not in a position to give, or to force him to do what he is not in a position to do. These individuals are fragile and may end up breaking down. For example, one could advise a young person with few social skills and difficulties relating to others to participate in an activity— a camp, community project, etc.—with people his age. That may help him, but if the person concerned does not feel he can manage it or comes to believe that his attempts were not successful, it would be harmful to keep encouraging him. It would end up reinforcing his fears and undermining his self-esteem even further. It is better to move forward gradually, keeping an eye on his reactions and letting him set the pace of his own progress.

Formators can also help by keeping an eye out for hidden pathologies behind maladaptive behaviors, and encouraging the individual to seek professional assistance (medical or psychological). It is common for people who are around these patients to minimize the problem or think that there is no solution: "That's how he is and he has always been the same, and nothing can be done about it." At other times they just hope that with time and effort the problem will go away. But all this only makes the problem chronic and harder to overcome. The natural course of these conditions is often to deteriorate.

We can think of individuals with chronic tiredness. A moderate walk or a flight of stairs makes them short of breath, they look worn out and exhausted by the end of the day. If there is no obvious cause, like old age, making an appointment with a doctor would make sense. The doctor will take a history, carry out a clinical examination, and possibly order some blood tests. Let's imagine that the doctor discovers that the patient has anemia. He will prescribe iron supplements, and more importantly he will try to find the cause of the problem. However, if those close to the patient— relatives, formators, a spiritual director, etc.—had simply encouraged him to be tougher and forget about himself, give himself more to the others, have a break and abandon himself in the hands of God, they would have done him a disservice, both physically and spiritually. Good will, either in the sick person or in the loved ones, is not enough when someone is ill.

When faced with a "peculiar" or chronically maladapted person, who cannot work things out despite personal effort and the help of formators, it is worthwhile to recommend an assessment by a professional and not wait for things to get worse. Early diagnosis and treatment make for a better prognosis. Since the person concerned is often unable to acknowledge his or her maladaptive personality traits, it may be appropriate to rely on the so-called secondary symptoms or on their need to improve their relationships. Even if he or she does not take responsibility and blames others, a professional will help him to develop strategies to improve social harmony.

We have seen that people in similar situations—mourning, addictions, depression—ought to use their real-life situation to grow in their love for God and for others. In these patients it is especially important to separate psychological factors from their interior life. We have also seen that this is a difficult thing to do because the distinction is somewhat artificial. The person is one and all the dimensions of a person are interrelated. Having said that, it is often wrong to look at the manifestations of his altered personality in moral terms. Self-focus is easily confused with selfishness, the tendency to isolate oneself with lack of concern for others, impulsiveness with a lack of temperance, etc.

Such people suffer from a major obstacle for self-giving, both in marriage and in other vocations. Personality disorders are a frequent cause of annulments, but we would note that maladaptive behavior can become apparent even during courtship: excessive control, jealousy, angry outbursts, etc.[3] One cannot naively trust that the other will improve with time, or that one can change the other. When in doubt, it is a good idea that both parties be assessed by a professional, who would be able to gauge the personality of each one and show how they complement each other.

For similar reasons, it would be inappropriate for those who suffer from these conditions to commit themselves to a vocation of total dedication to God. These illnesses have a profound effect on the individual, and would make their relationship with God and with other people very difficult.

3   Cf. F. Poterzio, *Il dialogo tra il giudice e il perito nella prospettiva del perito*, in H. Franceschi, M.A. Ortiz (eds.), *La ricerca della verità sul matrimonio e il diritto a un processo giusto e celere. Temi di diritto matrimoniale e processuale canonico*, Edusc, Roma 2012, pp. 254–304.

Difficulty forging healthy bonds would become obvious in their relationships with other people, whether their brothers or sisters in vocation or the beneficiaries of their apostolate. Using others, manipulation, dominance, dependence, etc.—even if they are not completely aware of it—are the precise opposites of this sort of lifestyle.

Yet it is not uncommon for people with these disorders to seek religious life in order to hide there or compensate for their affective shortcomings and relationship difficulties. It would be a wrong way to start their self-giving because it would be a way of fleeing or hiding and not of serving. During the period of discernment, it is necessary to be aware of people who have problems integrating with their peers or who are known to have had problems of this sort. The past history of the candidates should be addressed in conversations with them, particularly the relationship they had with their parents. When conflicts or serious deficiencies are identified, the process of discernment should be particularly thorough. But since it is difficult to know about someone's past life just from interviews, it is a good idea for formators to get to know the families of candidates as well, if possible within their own family environments and in their homes, and not just inviting them to the institution where the formation or process of discernment takes place.

Ultimately, the presence of a personality disorder reduces one's freedom to give oneself and puts the ability to live out a vocation's charism in danger, not to mention the fulfilment of that charism's apostolic mission. Again, in case of doubt, a psychological assessment should be carried out.

Whenever there are doubts it is wise to proceed slowly, even if the candidate shows a sincere desire to give himself and a valid eagerness to follow down this path. As he grows in his life of piety and gets to know the charism he wishes to follow, it is better for him to work on resolving his pathological traits, to ensure that his motives are sound, to help him achieve a normal relationship with God and other people, and to reach a reasonable conviction that the lifestyle he chooses will allow him to serve God and religious brothers and sisters happily and in a healthy way. To do otherwise would run the risk of the person concerned becoming unhappy and dissatisfied with his life. He could be tempted to abandon his vocation and even the whole of his Christian life if he blames it for his unhappiness.

3. Classification of Personality Disorders

The *Diagnostic and Statistical Manual of Mental Disorders* identifies ten personality disorders, grouped into three clusters (see Table 22). Some specific suggestions are offered after each cluster.[4] DSM-5 also includes changes of personality due to medical conditions that impact the central nervous system (tumors, trauma, epilepsy, infections, vascular and endocrine diseases, etc.) and two other more general disorders that do not meet all the specific criteria, or mixed clinical processes.

Cluster A:

    Paranoid

    Schizoid

    Schizotypal

Cluster B:

    Antisocial

    Borderline

    Histrionic

    Narcissistic

Cluster C:

    Avoidant

    Dependent

    Obsessive-compulsive

Personality change due to a separate medical condition

Other specified personality disorder

Other non-specified personality disorder

Table 22. DSM-5 Classification of Personality Disorders.

One final word of caution before moving on. Occasionally, when speaking about these disorders (they are not personality types but pathological personalities), some people have told me, "I think I have all of them." My usual reply to these people is that they should not be particularly worried because

---

4   Cf. American Psychiatric Association, *Diagnostic and Statistical Manual of Mental Disorders (DSM-5)*, American Psychiatric Association, Arlington (VA) 2013[5], pp. 645–684.

if they have traits of each of the personality types, they are unlikely to have a personality disorder. Typically, personality disorders have only a few traits that are put to use in all kinds of scenarios. There would be more cause for worry if someone identified himself with only one personality type.

Cluster A: The Eccentrics

These patients are very similar to those we studied at the beginning of the previous chapter, those with psychotic conditions. These personalities probably involve the greatest genetic component. Three categories have been identified.

The first is *paranoid personality disorder*, the key to which is *mistrust*. The term "paranoid" refers to delusions or paranoia, which was discussed at the beginning of the last chapter. Paranoid people do not have false and incurable beliefs, but have suspicions (without much basis in reality) and see crooked intentions in others. Harmless comments are looked upon as attacks, they imagine that people want to harm or take advantage of them, they suspect disloyalty in friends and adultery in their spouse, etc. They are generally very spiteful.

Schizoid personality disorder could be conceptualized as *low emotional reactivity*. The name is borrowed from schizophrenia, another psychotic disorder. The schizoid person does not have the more severe and obvious symptoms (delusions, hallucinations), but shares the flattening of affect and social isolation. Unlike in Cluster C disorders, the schizoid person does not withdraw out of fear of failure or rejection (he is not merely shy), but he sees no point in socializing, he feels better when he is on his own.

The *schizotypal personality disorder* is closer to a psychotic condition because in addition to the traits of the two previous conditions he has *eccentric interests and behaviors*. He may engage in magical thinking, superstitions, esotericism, bizarre language, etc. Within the religious sphere he may have excessive interest in extraordinary apparitions, diabolical possessions, stigmata, revelations, etc.

Accompaniment of these persons is extremely complex in the setting of formation because they do not realize how strange their behavior and beliefs are, and they do not feel the need to socialize. Therefore, one's goals for them must often be limited. The basic guideline is to help them to face reality with regards to events and people. In so far as other people are concerned, the idea is to point out that although they may not see the need to relate to other people, others do need to establish relationships and therefore it is worthwhile to overcome their own character in order to give themselves to others, just like other sorts of people.

Their tendency to isolation and their lack of social skills makes them unsuitable for a life of dedication to God in the priesthood or in apostolic celibacy. However, the question may arise as to whether they may be suitable for a life of self-giving to God in the solitude of the cloister. At first glance it would appear to be a style very much in keeping with their capabilities, but a more careful consideration raises serious doubts. First of all, their relationship with God needs to be assessed because it can suffer from the same limitations they have in their relationships with others. Remember that a life of dedication to God and a solitary life are not the same thing. Dedication to God implies a life of intimate union with him, and this can be difficult for someone who cannot easily establish close bonds with others.

The schizotypal person's peculiar view of some aspects of the Christian life deserves special scrutiny. Initially, his strange interests may be confused with a healthy interest in spiritual development, a high degree of union with God, and even with truly extraordinary mystical phenomena.[5] Therefore they need accurate discernment from wise and experienced people. On this point, it is worth remembering that the great mystics—St. Francis of Assisi, St. Teresa of Avila, St. John of the Cross, St. Padre Pio—handled their extraordinary mystical experiences with great discretion, their day-to-day manner was very normal, and above all they always submitted to their superiors and allowed their spiritual directors to guide them. They also knew how to combine their mystical experiences with a simple life of ordinary work (St. Teresa of Avila was fond of saying, "God is also found among pots and pans"), of service to others, and long periods of the dark night of the soul.

Cluster B: The Extrovert or Self-Centered

If we draw a parallel with the classification of mental disorders (neurotic and psychotic), the disorders in cluster A would be qualitatively abnormal,

---

5   Discernment of extraordinary phenomena is a difficult area, cf. J.B. Torelló, *Psicología y vida espiritual,* Rialp, Madrid 2008, pp. 229-250; M. Belda, *Ars artium. Storia, teologia e pratica della direzione spirituale,* Edusc, Roma 2020, pp. 193–205.

while in groups B and C there is a quantitative disruption, an exaggeration of traits that we all have to a greater or lesser extent. At first glance, these individuals appear normal and even very pleasant to deal with; however, as time goes by, it becomes clear that there are significant shortcomings in their way of being.

Antisocial personality disorder consists in *exploiting others*. It is a complete disregard for people and rules that leads to using others (by manipulating them, deceiving them, making promises that are systematically broken) and breaking rules without having any feeling of guilt or remorse. In some cases, they harm people or animals for no other reason than the simple enjoyment of doing it. When confronted with such acts, they tend to rationalize their abusive behavior, and project responsibility onto others. If they are contradicted, they may become irritable and aggressive. They are unable to establish genuine intimate relationships and have a gross lack of empathy for the needs and suffering of others, except when they fake it in order to gain their trust, to control them or to manipulate them. This pattern is common in criminals, but it can also happen in "unscrupulous leaders" who seek their own benefit or that of their company or institution without caring about whether they use others or cause them harm.

Borderline personality disorder is probably the most severe, and a patient's prognosis is worse.[6] The main feature is extreme *instability*, both internally (intense and ever-changing emotions, affective ambivalence, feeling of emptiness, depressed mood, impulsiveness) and in their relationships, which are usually intense and fragile. Deep down these patients have a very unstructured self-image, they fear being abandoned and find it difficult to give themselves to others trustingly. Suicidal ideation and self-harming behaviors to release their stress are common. In the most severe cases, there may be psychotic episodes.

Histrionic personality disorder can be summarized as *seductive behavior* (a Freudian concept that means excessive attention-seeking, but not exclusively from a sexual point of view). It is a tendency to be the center of

---

6   Cf. P.T. Mason, R. Kreger, *Stop Walking on Eggshells: Taking Your Life Back When Someone You Care About Has Borderline Personality Disorder*, New Harbinger Publications, Oakland (CA) 2020. This book may be useful to understand and help these people.

attention. When they are not being noticed they feel uncomfortable and try to come to the fore. They are very dependent on the esteem and affection of others, and they rely on childish or theatrical comments and behavior, provocative dress styles, and provocative behavior to gain it. Their moods are shallow and volatile, and their character is very impressionable, so that external events have an excessive effect on them.

Finally, the *narcissistic personality disorder* is characterized by delusions of grandeur. These persons have an exaggerated sense of their own importance and abilities. They seek a coterie of fans who follow and admire them as a matter of course, but they treat them with little empathy, as they feel entitled to look down on them and act in an arrogant, haughty and overbearing manner. They tend to exploit and humiliate others, but unlike the antisocial person, they do not do so for the pleasure of seeing them suffer or to gain material advantages, but because contrasting with their humiliation makes them shine more brightly. They take it for granted that they are owed everything, that only special or high-status people deserve to spend time with them, and that they are destined to succeed. They are envious of other people's successes. Deep down they lack affective autonomy. They are dependent on the acceptance and recognition of others because their apparent grandeur hides a very weak core. That explains why when they see themselves alone, rejected, or having failed, they suffer what psychoanalysts call a *narcissistic wound* that leads to anger or a depressive collapse.

An experienced formator will soon realize that these four categories of people tend to use and manipulate others in a pathological way to compensate for their psychological needs. However, it is worth remembering that they do so unconsciously, or at least they are not fully aware of it. The problem is not one of selfishness but of self-centeredness, it is not about virtues but about personality. Obviously the two concepts are intertwined and reinforce each other both positive and negatively, but they need to be discerned correctly.

A first way to help these people is to make them see the effect their actions have on other people, the harm they are causing others or the pressure they are putting on them to comply with their own demands. It means pointing out, for example, that their attitude is forcing a great deal of work onto others that they are not obliged to do (and therefore the person with the personality disorder should not feel offended if is not done) and above all that there is a lack of correspondence in the relationships they are trying to establish. They are giving themselves much less than what they receive. This needs to be done gradually and gently because if external support is abruptly withdrawn, the weak structure of their personality could collapse.

It is often useful to connect their behavior with their upbringing: lack of affection, an overprotective mother (common among narcissists), rigid or loose rules (typical of antisocials), a dysfunctional family, traumatic events, etc. The formator should not psychoanalyze, which would only be confusing and disastrous. It is about getting to know the person as a whole, in the context of his or her past history, so that—this is the key—the individuals learn to understand their own selves and to interpret what they are really looking for in their dealings with others: support, recognition, affection, etc., and adjust their behavior to find it out in a mature way, without harming others or harming themselves.

All that has been said throughout this book about the maturity of one's character and affections, as well as about two-way relationships (especially friendship between equals), is particularly relevant for these people. In so far as they learn how to form healthy bonds, respect otherness, and endure frustrations, they will develop a more solid and stable personality and grow in self-confidence.

Narcissistic and antisocial personalities deserve special mention. They tend to show great leadership qualities and initiative, so they would appear to be ideally suited for tasks of direction and governance in apostolic undertakings and institutions. Big mistake. They may perceive their appointment as the acknowledgement of their personal worth, and it would reinforce their more maladaptive traits. It is true that at first, they seem to be very charismatic and attractive, but over time their lack of empathy and respect for the needs of others becomes obvious. They confuse adherence to their person with loyalty to the charisma or the institution —"I am the State," as Louis XIV used to say—so that questioning their decisions is taken as a personal offence or a lack of obedience or commitment to God. Given their small capacity for self-criticism and introspection, it will be difficult for them to recognize their responsibility and to change what they need to change in their own selves.

Normal people end up either distancing themselves from them or even from the institution, or they will confront them, and the result will be resistance, disputes, tensions, triangulation, involvement of other leaders, etc. They often find it difficult to obey, so that they end up being a source of conflict with both their superiors and their subordinates. Only weak people with deficiencies on the opposite end follow them uncritically, especially those who have a dependent personality, which we will look at next. Finally, their lack of scruples makes them candidates for abuse of power and of conscience, which Pope Francis has rightly put at the origin of the sexual abuses we have had to lament in recent decades.[7]

A solid interior life will help them to deepen their understanding of the value of selfless service, without seeking anything in return or making cost-benefit balances.

Cluster C: The Introvert or Anxious

Individuals in this cluster are similar to the previous group insofar as their personality defect is quantitative, but their defining traits are at the opposite extreme. Instead of trying to act to compensate for their shortcomings, their inclination is to remain passive.

The main feature of the *avoidant personality disorder* is *withdrawal* from interpersonal contact. We saw this trait in the schizoid personality, but it is not difficult to draw a distinction between the two. The dependent does not display autonomy, excessive coldness or insensitivity toward relationships. He realizes that he needs them. However, he has an insurmountable fear of rejection because he feels inadequate, inferior to others and has poor social skills. He is very sensitive to criticism, embarrassment, hurtful jokes, ridicule, and neglect. Consequently, he is inhibited in social situations unless he is sure that he will be accepted. On the other hand, he is reluctant to take up challenges and risks because of his fear of failure.

The main feature of the *dependent personality disorder* is *subservience.* Dependent individuals are very insecure, which leads them to avoid making decisions, leaving responsibility (even for important personal matters) to others, or persistently to seek reassurance when they have made a decision.

7   Cf. Francis, *Letter to the People of God on pilgrimage in Chile,* May 31, 2018; idem, *Address of his holiness pope Francis at the end of the eucharistic concelebration at the Meeting "The Protection of Minors in the Church"* February 24, 2019.

Their great fear is being abandoned and they experience an exaggerated need to be cared for, protected and supported. To achieve this, they are willing to give up their own dignity. They are submissive, do things they dislike, allow themselves to be exploited, do not express disagreement, and give up all kinds of rights. When left alone, they feel uncomfortable or helpless because they feel incapable of taking care of themselves.

Obsessive-compulsive personality disorder (formerly called anankastic, and not to be confused with obsessive-compulsive disorder) can be summarized as a desire for *control* over the material world and others. They try to control the outside world in order not to be overwhelmed by their own insecurity. They are orderly and perfectionist, concerned with details, rules, lists, order, organization and schedules. They are rigid, stubborn, and obstinate to the point of losing sight of the main object of the activity at hand and putting its success at risk. They have trouble delegating and try to get others to do things their own way. They tend to work too much, and they focus on productivity at the expense of leisure activities and relationships with friends and family. In the area of morals, they are scrupulous and inflexible, and very demanding of themselves and of others. Their eagerness to secure future needs leads them to be greedy and not to get rid of damaged or useless objects even when they have no sentimental value.

People suffering from these three disorders usually have a greater awareness of their own illness than the two previous groups, i.e., they are aware of their maladaptive personality. I will cover them in greater detail in the following sections because people with these problems often are encountered in the work of Christian formation and vocational discernment.

Rather than strictly follow the psychopathological classifications, I will look at them from a broader perspective, which can be applied to people with similar traits but who do not strictly speaking suffer from a personality disorder. Therefore, I will refer more generally to the avoidant-dependent personality and the obsessive-perfectionist personality rather than those in the first two clusters.[8]

---

8   I will use many of the ideas included in F. Insa, "Affective Dependency and Perfectionism: A Proposal Based on Attachment Theory," in F. Insa, D. Parker (eds.), *Loving and Teaching Others to Love. The Formation of Affectivity in Priestly Life*, Independently Published 2021, pp. 83–101.

3. The Avoidant-Dependent Personality

The attachment theory discussed earlier in the book (at the beginning of the life cycle) can help us identify the origin of these personality types: an overly close relationship with a mother figure, which makes it difficult for the child to achieve the self-esteem, autonomy, and security necessary to explore and interact with the world on his own.[9] As the years go by, the youngster leaves the family environment, goes to school, and begins to relate to his peers, but finds it very difficult to establish contact with them. He would like to get closer to them, but he suffers from two fears that fight against each other: the fear of rejection and the fear of being left alone.

If the avoidant overcome their fear of being excluded, they will avoid relationships and live in loneliness. If, on the other hand, they overcome their fear of neglect, they will seek to establish a bond with someone who makes them feel safe, a *substitute attachment figure* to replace the maternal figure. Dependent relationships are thus established. In extreme cases, this relationship can involve a two-way exploitation. On the one hand, the dependent is willing to do anything in order to be accepted, which is a breeding ground for being used or abused, not daring to say no or to break off the relationship for fear of being left alone. On the other hand, he tries to control the other person by absorbing their time and affection, which they want to monopolize for themselves (they are very jealous), and he demands total availability. The autonomy of the other is taken as a personal offense. Sometimes there is an attempt to control others through service, which in Italian is graphically called *sindrome della crocerossina* (Red Cross volunteer syndrome), which could be defined as the tendency to help, even in an invasive way, in order to receive affection.

Such an individual may accumulate anger and resentment toward the reference figure, but is not capable of bringing them out to the open because of his difficulties channeling his emotions and fears of being left alone. Thus they respond with a passive-aggressive attitude: he shows his resentment through resistance, obstructionism, reproach, forgetfulness, or

---

9   To delve further in these types of personality, cf. L. Balugani, "La personalità dipendente," *Tredimensioni* 10 (2013) 133–146; F. Sarráis, *El miedo*, EUNSA, Pamplona 2014.

a dour expression, together with an unconvincing "there is nothing wrong with me."

The avoidant or dependent youngster may find it more comfortable to deal with adults than with people his own age, as they give him security, accept him (in the peer group he has to earn it), and respect him (which unfortunately is not always the case among children). As a result, adults may be under the false impression that they are dealing with a very mature child.

He can also find the security he lacks in a religious group: the parish, a movement, a youth club. There he feels loved, welcomed, and respected. The search for this type of bond is even greater when he not only has difficulties in his relationship with his peers but also when he is not at ease in his own home because of cold, absent or unaffectionate parents, or because he comes from a broken home. The contrast with the atmosphere of joy, service, and concern for others that he finds in the various groups we have referred to may lead him to think that this is the way to find happiness, and therefore that is where God is calling him. It would mean confusing vocation with the fulfillment of affective needs.

Undoubtedly one of the signs that God can use to make someone see that he is calling the individual down a certain path is that the person feels humanly at ease in that particular environment. But this motive needs to be purified and matured. God calls us to serve him, to have a personal relationship with him. The bond, the secure attachment that has to be established, must be with God in the first place, not with formators or with the group. On the other hand, in following that vocation, the person may try to remain in the secure comfort of the institution instead of launching into an apostolic task. This creates a dichotomy between the vocation itself and the mission that the vocational call entails.

From a human point of view, the first task of formators is to help these people improve the relationship with themselves and with others. It is important to keep this order: it starts with themselves, which is why we started the section by going back to attachment theory. The main objective is to overcome insecurity and low self-esteem in order to achieve the freedom that will allow them to decide what to do with their lives.

Maintaining a positive tone during conversations with them is always helpful in assessing everything and encouraging him to take risks without delegating them to others. An individual with an avoidant or dependent personality finds the compliments from people in authority when goals are achieved very encouraging, but it is also necessary for them to acknowledge apparently unsuccessful, "wasted" efforts. At least they have tried. Yet it is important not to exaggerate compliments because they may encourage dependence or insecurity in the youngster when they are not acknowledged. The aim is for the young person to become more autonomous and for him to be the one to value and congratulate himself when he achieves success, be it great or small.

A delicate balance is required in order not to fall into a dependency trap, because he is likely to seek it out with authority figures. A formator should not lose sight of the fact that it may be pleasant to know that someone is dependent on him—that he has become a *secure base* for one of the pupils—and may therefore unintentionally foster a relationship that would be unhealthy for both.

This does not mean abandoning the subject before he is ready to be autonomous. It is rather a matter of going forward one step at the time, for example by spacing out meetings further than what he would want, by not always answering phone calls, etc. It should be explained that one's reluctance to be a secure base does not mean rejection, but on the contrary, is due to confidence in the individual's abilities, even if he is not able to appreciate them at the time.

On the other hand, inappropriate manifestations of affection, either by excess or by defect, must be corrected gently but firmly. Exclusive and engrossing relationships, a lack of sympathy or empathy with other people, episodes of emotional overflow, not taking into account different tastes, interests, or ways of being, excluding certain individuals from their relationships, lack of interest in others, and a tendency to isolation, complaints, criticism, envy, sarcasm, bitter jealousy, etc., should be corrected.

Periodic discussions will be a great help for them to get to know themselves, realizing and appraising their talents while also recognizing their affective shortcomings, the causes of their fears and anxieties, etc. This knowledge will allow them to overcome their difficulties showing their own emotions, verbalizing their needs, fears and moods, including the negative emotions of anger and resentment. They will thus be able to resist possible attempts at manipulation by third parties and to do so in an assertive way, i.e., asserting their rights without being uncharitable or disrespectful.

Regarding relationships with peers, social skills should be promoted. He should be encouraged to break down his insecurity by dealing with everyone (especially his peers) without confining himself to the restricted circle where he feels safe or limiting himself to dealing with people much older or younger than himself. The relationships and friendships he needs to establish, maintain and promote are, let us repeat, with his peers. For example, in a parish setting it will not help him to be entrusted with young children—first communion catechesis—but with people his own age. That may mean preparing candidates for confirmation, teaching pre-Cana courses, etc.

People with an avoidant or dependent personality can be encouraged to work out what they expect from their relationships. They should seek the good of the other, not their own in the guise of affection or recognition. In this regard, it is interesting to know that the so-called *depressive personalities*, in whom we often find many of the traits described above, tend to engage in helping others—such as volunteering, teaching or the health professions—as a way of compensating for their low self-esteem and fulfilling their need for affection.[10] It would not therefore be unusual to find a subject with these characteristics in one of the various forms of dedication to God.

Finally, attention should be paid to abnormal relationships, i.e., relationships that are too close, exclusive, or inappropriately intimate. In short, where we can foresee an emotional dependence that can end up destroying the person because they do not respect otherness. A couple made up of a person with markedly dependent personality traits and another with narcissistic or antisocial traits—they are psychologically complementary—is particularly dangerous because it leads to the double exploitation referred to above. This would be a clear example of a *toxic relationship*.

4. The Obsessive-Perfectionist Personality

We come to the second personality type: the obsessive-perfectionist.[11] This individual does not seek security and attachment in people but in their own actions in a way that removes all uncertainty.

10   Cf. M. Fierro, J. J. Ortegón, "Trastorno de personalidad depresivo: el sinsentido de la vida," *Revista Colombiana de Psiquiatría* 34 (2005) 581–594.
11   Regarding etiological aspects and a proposal for strategies to change, cf. C.

Usually there is an obvious positive substratum: such a person shows a high sense of duty, is orderly, dutiful, and reliable. He is therefore ideal for tasks involving high responsible because he inspires confidence that whatever task he does will be done properly.

However, a closer look reveals a very marked obsessive component that conditions his working style and how he relates to others. It would take too long to talk about the causes of these obsessive traits, and we will simply point out that educational (usually a rigid and very demanding father) and biological factors can be found in their origin.

A background of insecurity lies behind the obsessive personality, just like in the avoidant and dependent personalities. The individual cannot tolerate uncertainty, is afraid of failure, and therefore tries to secure everything and prevent any mistake. This makes him extremely rigid. He must follow rules and protocols rigorously, trying to anticipate every possible outcome.

On the other hand, he does not tolerate unforeseen events or changes of plans, he is distressed by to-do lists (he has an excessive sense of pleasure every time they manage to tick off a task from the list), he demands more from himself than the circumstances require, and he is incapable of leaving things undone. He has a typical cognitive distortion, "If I am not sure that I can finish this task to perfection, I won't even try."

When confronted with problems, he tends toward activism. He tries to solve everything by working harder. But as he is not very flexible, he usually insists on doing things the same way even if they have not worked out in the past, and he is not very open to alternative solutions (both thinking about them and accepting them from others). Some attribute the phrase "insanity is doing the same thing over and over again and expecting different results" to Einstein, and it applies to the obsessive. They are not very

Ciotti, "La personalità ossessivo-compulsiva," *Tredimensioni* 5 (2008) 75–87; M.M. Antony, R.P. Swinson, *When perfect isn't good enough. Strategies for coping with perfectionism*, New Harbinger Publications, Oakland (CA) 2009; A.E. Mallinger, J. De Wyze, *Too Perfect: When Being in Control Gets Out of Control*, The Random House Publishing Group, New York (NY) 2011[3]; J. Schlatter Navarro, *Ser felices sin ser perfectos*, EUNSA, Pamplona 2016[3]; M. Álvarez Romero, D. García-Villamisar, *El síndrome del perfeccionista: el anancástico*, Almuzara, Córdoba 2017[4].

creative and have little *lateral thinking*.[12] On the other hand, their difficulty in acquiring a wide, global vision is very distinctive. They are often very attentive to details but they get lost in them and neglects the overall result. They cannot see the wood for the trees.

This often leads to a paradox. Although the obsessive individual is usually very effective in his tasks, he can be difficult to work with precisely because of his lack of flexibility. He demands that everything always be done his way, that everything be finished down to the last detail without exception. He concentrates on the smallest details and has little understanding of other people's ways and feelings. In the end he gets cranky and does everything himself. He thinks that others work less or worse than he does, and with less sense of responsibility. He is prone to burnout. Women in this category are also more vulnerable to anorexia nervosa.

From an affective point of view, he tends to have little ability to discover and talk about emotions, which makes him very demanding and unsympathetic to his own and other people's subjective needs. For example, he may find it difficult to understand that he or others may be tired and need a break, and he is unable to enjoy these same breaks without becoming anxious about the pressure to get back to work.

A permanent state of anxiety is also typical. Because he does not "get there," does not meet his objectives, does not reach the expectations others have placed in him. These reasons may be more or less justified in the present moment or in past experiences, but the main idea is the lack of proportion between the state of inner stress and the causes that drive it.

From an ascetical point of view, he may lack abandonment and trust in God. He prefers to have everything under control, to fulfill a schedule, a program, practices of piety, and he may lack reflection (and therefore internal adherence) in living out obedience. He will not ask himself for the reason behind what he is doing. He lacks authentic freedom of spirit. As a consequence, perfectionist people are prone to collapse when they see their limitations, their weaknesses, and above all their downfalls. "I can no longer

---

12 Cf. E. de Bono, *Lateral Thinking. Creativity Step by Step*, Harper Perennial, New York (NY) 2015; idem, *Six thinking hats. The power of focused thinking. Six proven ways to effectively focus your creative thinking*, International Centre for Creative Thinking, Mamaroneck (NY) 1985.

be perfect." Finally, a personality with these traits is a breeding ground for scruples.

In a word, the perfectionist may forget that the driving force of his actions must be love of God and the love of others, not the achievements that results from his own deeds. It may be helpful to remember the Lord's words: "you tithe mint and rue and herbs of all kinds, and neglect justice and the love of God; it is these you ought to have practiced, without neglecting the others" (Lk 11:42).

Given that the core of the obsessive-perfectionist personality is insecurity, the assistance that a formator can give is firstly to facilitate the development of self-confidence by encouraging them to live with the uncertainty of not having everything figured out down to the last detail. The outline of a talk to be read verbatim, the exam revised down to the last comma, a briefing that covers every possible detail to prevent anyone from misunderstanding it, and so on. In short, it is a matter of helping them to detach themselves from their confidence in their own security in order to establish a *secure attachment* to more mature and higher realities.

It must be clearly stated that a rigid or a perfectionist formator (or spiritual director) is the worst thing that can happen to a person who has obsessive-perfectionist personality traits. Such a formator might be satisfied with demanding (and getting) things done externally—respect for rules and objectives or the fulfillment of certain practices of piety—without looking at how they impact the interiority of the individual.

It is also essential that a formator be always very understanding. Any ironic comment about such people's way of doing things will only reinforce their fear of failure, undermine their low self-esteem, and therefore increase their anxiety. On the contrary, it is much better "to walk with them" so that they can gradually take new risks without feeling overly lonely. Sometimes it will be better to encourage them to "jump with a safety net" so that they do not hurt themselves when they fall, while on other occasions it will be better to remove the net so that they can learn by trial and error. In any case, any attempt should always be appreciated, even if the results are not good.

It is wise not to give them too much work. They are certainly efficient and reliable, but it is difficult for them to say no and they can easily take on too much without realizing it and without voicing it.

It is important to insist in the area of flexibility. Perfectionists must learn that there are many ways of doing things, many ways of reaching the same goal, and they need to know how to discern what is important from what is secondary. Life is not only *black and white*, but there are also many shades of grey. And in the context of flexibility, it is useful to develop a healthy sense of humor. To laugh at oneself, at one's limitations and short-comings without feeling humiliated by them.

Therefore, they need to reassess their concept of duty. This does not mean they should do away with it, but rather find the right balance. Indeed, it is not uncommon for these people to feel confused when they are made to realize that the way they have approached their endeavors up to that point (often successfully in various areas: family, social, academic and even vocational) is no longer valid. But this conclusion would not be correct. It is rather a matter of broadening the range of their responses, depending on the challenges that life presents, so that different problems can be tackled differently.

This reframing can help them to slow down, to give them necessary breaks for rest and leisure activities without feeling that they are wasting their time. It will help them to be more understanding of others when they also take a break. Moreover, it will allow them to enjoy these moments not only as intervals between one job and another, but as a chance to enjoy the pleasant moments that life has to offer and to *waste time* with others, i.e. to dedicate time to rest and having fun with other people.

In their relationships with others, therefore, charity is more important than efficiency. This is why perfectionists needs to attain and transmit serenity and peace—to accept that they are imperfect persons, in an imperfect world and surrounded by imperfect people.

We have left to the end the most important point, the relationship that the candidate with an obsessive-perfectionist personality establishes with God must become for them a solid point for a *secure attachment*.

Their conversations with formators are a chance to see how they relate to God. They may have internalized a very partial vision of the gospel, related to rules, duties and fulfillment, rather than love and mercy, and this partial vision would shape their relationship with God. It is therefore useful for them not to look at demands in terms of duties, actions and results, but as a way to live out one's love for God, who is above specific works and their results:

Love, and do what you will: whether you hold your peace, through love hold your peace; whether you cry out, through love cry out; whether you correct, through love correct; whether you spare, through love do you spare: let the root of love be within, of this root can nothing spring but what is good.[13]

Emphasis should be placed on an upright intention, on the supernatural value of actions (as distinct from their human efficacy), on the priority of prayer, especially prayer that does not lead to resolutions but facilitates a personal relationship with Jesus Christ, e.g., meditation on the gospel and silent, contemplative adoration before the tabernacle.

When they face their own mistakes (and also the failures of others), it will help them to rediscover the wonder of a God who does not ask us to be flawless. Love for God is compatible with things not going perfectly right, and when we fall, he forgives us. Sometimes the problem is that perfectionists do not forgive themselves.

Finally, both the formator and the person concerned have to be realistic about their goals. It is not a matter of having a completely balanced personality, but rather that the trusting relationship with God leads to self-acceptance and to trying to be ever more patient with oneself and with others.

13 St. Augustine, *Commentary on the Letter of St John*, VII, 8.

EPILOGUE

A HEALTHY FORMATIVE STYLE

1. Two Ways of Forming People

As we come to the end of the book, I would like to make some observations about what it means to be a formator. Thus far, we have talked about how to help people looking for guidance in their lives. Now is the time to look at ourselves and ask: can this important task be carried out by anyone, or only by a few special people? What specific skills should be acquired or improved in order to carry out this task? What aspects of one's own personality should be tempered so that they are not a negative influence? How does one combine affection and high demands, or high goals with the directee's potential?

First of all, we should point out that there are two ways of forming, which depend on where one's emphasis is placed. Both can lead to the same external results—people acting righteously—but the learner's interiority will be very different depending on the case.

A *healthy formation style* produces free people. They understand what is good for them, make it their own, and try to put it into practice in the various circumstances of their lives. This model is based on explaining the "whys" and "how comes" from the point of view of the person concerned, i.e., not by listing externally imposed rules or criteria, but by showing that the content of these rules has deep roots and that it is in their best interest to internalize them, that they will help them become better people. As a direct consequence, the person concerned will know how to apply general criteria to specific situations with initiative, creativity, flexibility and *epikeia*.[1] Let us go deeper into the concept of *epikeia*.

Epikeia is a virtue that perfects moral judgment by enabling it to reach

---

1   "Epikeia: A liberal interpretation of law in instances not provided by the letter of the law. It presupposes sincerity in wanting to observe the law, and interprets the mind of the lawgiver in supplying his presumed intent to include a

the right decision even in exceptional circumstances, or circumstances not foreseen by the rule.[2] It is not a simple exception to a rule, or of applying a rule in a flexible or progressive manner, but of doing so by this criterion: whoever understands the meaning of a rule knows that in a specific case it should not be followed because the same person who established it would not have considered it appropriate in the particular circumstance. For example, a teacher may say, "You have to be on time for class." But if on my way to class I come across someone in serious need, my obligation would be to attend to that person, even if makes me late and it breaks the rule. It is not really an exception (otherwise we would have to add a long list of exceptions to every rule) but rather an understanding that the complete sense of the rule would be: "We must be on time for class unless a serious need requires our attention." What exactly is serious enough to warrant tardiness, the measure of charity toward the needy and charity toward one's classmates, etc., is something that a virtuous person is capable of discerning more fluidly. There are different ways to err in this virtue. One type of person abuses *epikeia*—sometimes under the mask of freedom of spirit—as a way to lower his standards when he finds something difficult or unpleasant. On the other end of the spectrum, rigid types cling to the letter of the law and so pass over the need of their neighbor, like the priest and the Levite did in the parable of the Good Samaritan (cf. Lk 10:30–37).[3] This example can be applied to many situations in life where conflicting interests and obligations are impossible to reconcile.

situation that is not covered by the law. It favors the liberty of the interpreter without contradicting the express will of the lawgiver," J. Hardon, *Modern Catholic Dictionary*, Eternal Life, Bardstown 2000 (https://www.catholicculture.org/culture/library/dictionary/index.cfm?id=33347. Accessed: September 19, 2021.

2   Cf. St. Thomas Aquinas, *Summa Theologica*, II-II, q. 120, art. 1; A. Rodríguez Luño, A. Rodríguez Luño, *Scelti in Cristo per essere santi. Elementi di teologia morale fondamentale*, Edusc, Roma 2003, pp. 296–301 (English edition: *Chosen in Christ to Be Saints: Fundamental Moral Theology*, Createspace Independent Pub, 2014).

3   There is a famous social experiment that illustrates the above. It was conducted in 1973 at the American University of Princeton. In brief, some students at Princeton Theological Seminary were asked to give a lecture on the Good Samaritan. On the day of the conference, an urgency factor was put in place: some were told that people were waiting for them for a few minutes; others

There is also an *unhealthy formative style* that constricts people because it does not encourage or respect personal freedom. It insists on the subject improving in certain areas but forgets about the person as a whole. It is satisfied if they fulfill their obligations regardless of whether they understand the reasons, and sometimes it overloads them with rules, fosters mistrust, and can lead to excessive control or even coercion.

We will now look at some features of both styles by drawing from educational sciences.

2. Parenting Styles

When we talk about formation, the "main analogue" is the work that parents do with their children. This has been studied from several points of view and can shed light on our reflections. Many authors have tried to categorize the various styles of parenting. Here I will use a model with two intersecting parameters: demands and affection (Figure 5).[4] The dashed lines emphasize that the quadrants are not watertight compartments. Usually there are no pure styles, but rather a mixture of all of them with a greater or lesser proportion of each of the ingredients.

were told that the participants were ready; and finally, a third group was told that the conference would begin a few minutes earlier than scheduled. In other words, high, intermediate, and low 'rush' conditions were created. Everyone had to cross the campus to get to the lecture hall, and on the way they "accidentally" found a man with clear signs of suffering a severe respiratory crisis. Well, only 10% of those in a high state of urgency hurry, 45% of those in an intermediate state, and 63% of those in a low state stopped to attend to this man. The researchers reported that "on several occasions, a seminary student going to give his talk on the parable of the Good Samaritan literally stepped over the victim as he hurried on his way!" (cf. J.M., Darley, C.D. Batson, "From Jerusalem to Jericho: A Study of Situational and Dispositional Variables in Helping Behavior," *Journal of Personality and Social Psychology* 27 (1973) 100–108.)

4   Cf. E.E. Martin, J.A. Maccoby, "Socialization in the Context of the Family: Parent-Child Interaction," in E.M. Hetherington, P.H. Mussen, (eds.). *Handbook of Child Psychology*, Vol. 4. Socialization, personality and social development, Wiley, New York (NY) 1983[4], pp. 1–101. I also use S. Torío López, J.V. Peña Calvo, M.C. Rodríguez Menéndez, "Estilos educativos parentales. Revisión bibliográfica y reformulación teórica," *Teoría de la Educación* 20 (2008) 151–178; C. Chiclana Actis, "Formación y evaluación psicológica del candidato al sacerdocio," *Scripta Theologica* 51 (2019) 467–504.

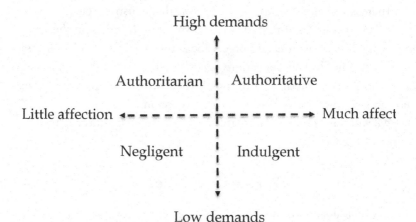

High demands

Authoritarian | Authoritative

Little affection ◄ ─ ─ ─ ─ ─ ─ ─┼─ ─ ─ ─ ─ ─ ► Much affect

Negligent | Indulgent

Low demands

Figure 5: The parenting styles

The combination of the two parameters determines four styles: authoritative, authoritarian, negligent and indulgent. Table 23 shows the main features of each of them, both from the point of view of the educator's behavior and the consequences they have on the child.

	Parental behavioral traits	Educational impact on children
Authoritative	Overt affection.	Social competence.
	Sensitivity to the child's needs: responsibility.	Self-control.
	Explanations.	Motivation.
	Promoting desirable behavior.	Initiative.
	Inductive discipline or reasoned punitive technique (deprivation, reprimands).	Autonomous morality.
		High self-esteem.
	Promoting exchange and open communication.	Cheerfulness and spontaneity.
		Realistic self-conception.
	Home with affectionate warmth and a democratic environment.	Responsibility and faithfulness to personal commitments.
		Prosociability inside and outside the home (altruism, solidarity).
		High motivation for achievement.
		Parent-child conflicts decrease in frequency and intensity.

Authoritarian	Detailed and rigid rules.	Low autonomy and self-confidence.
	Frequent punishments and infrequent praise.	
	No parental responsibility	Low personal autonomy and creativity.
	Closed or one-way communication (no dialogue).	Low social competence.
	Assertion of power.	Aggressiveness and impulsiveness.
	Home marked by an autocratic climate.	Heteronomous morality (avoidance of punishment).
		Less cheerfulness and spontaneity.
Negligent	Indifference to the children's attitudes and behaviors, both positive and negative.	Low social competence.
		Poor self-control and heterocontrol.
	Responsiveness and attention to children's needs.	Low motivation.
	Permissiveness.	Little respect for rules and people.
	Passivity.	Low self-esteem, insecurity.
	Low assertion of authority and imposition of restrictions.	Emotional instability.
		Weak self-identity.
	Infrequent use of punishment, toleration of all children's impulses.	Negative self-conception.
	Particular flexibility in setting rules.	Severe lack of self-confidence and self-responsibility.
	Easy accommodation of children's wishes.	Poor school performance.
Indulgent	No emotional involvement in the children's affairs.	Poor social competence.
		Poor control of impulses and aggressiveness.
	Disengagement in the educational task, they invest as little time as possible in their children.	Low motivation and capacity for effort.
	Low motivation and capacity for effort.	Immaturity.
	Immaturity.	Cheerfulness and vitality.
	Cheerfulness and vitality.	

Table 23. Family education styles and child behavior.[5]

Obviously, the authoritative style is the best option. Demands are properly balanced with affection and dialogue.

The personality of children will be strongly conditioned by these patterns. For example, the authoritarian style fosters a rigid, perfectionistic

5   Cf. Torío López, Peña Calvo, Rodríguez Menéndez, "Estilos educativos parentales," pp. 164–165.

and anxious mindset. Alternatively, it may result in rebellion against authority and rules. The negligent style, on the other hand, generates affective shortcomings that the subject will attempt to fill with relationships that are not always healthy, like what we saw in the previous chapter.

The relationship established with one's parents in childhood tends to be replicated in adult life with other educators or authority figures: teachers, formators, bosses, superiors, etc. The subject will usually be equally submissive, compliant, tense, rebellious, dependent, etc. And when they take on a formation role, they may act in either of two ways. The usual approach is to repeat the pattern of behavior with which they were raised, which reproduces the mistakes they made and perpetuates them. On the other hand, their desire to avoid these mistakes leads them to fall into the opposite extreme, i.e., the person who was brought up in an authoritarian or negligent manner becomes excessively overprotective.

Finally, we point out that parenting styles influence the image of God that the student will internalize.[6] In the authoritative model, God will be seen as someone close, who takes care of the person's needs; in the authoritarian model, as someone who demands and punishes; in the negligent model, as a distant being who ignores us; finally, in the indulgent model, God is seen as someone who is permissive and inconsistent.

It is therefore wise for the formator to know the family of his charge in order to correct any shortcomings he may have had and not perpetuate them by his own attitudes. But we have already talked about this in previous chapters. The aim of this chapter is rather to point out that the formator must be aware of the way he himself was brought up and how it impacts his own formative style. The formator should ask himself what parenting style he experienced, and try to correct its limitations as far as possible. This brings us to the last section of the book.

3. The Personality of the Formator

What are the skills required of a good formator? The present chapter began with several questions pertaining to this topic. The first question was a bit

---

6   Cf. Chiclana Actis, "Formación y evaluación psicológica del candidato al sacerdocio," pp. 467–504.

extreme: can anyone perform this task, or is it only for a few people? In my opinion, anyone who has a healthy mind can do it. In fact, being a father or a mother is the most natural thing in the world and no special qualifications are required to perform this task reasonably well. However, I doubt that anyone is satisfied with being a "reasonably good" parent, teacher or spiritual director. Fortunately, we all aspire to do better than that.

In this section I will discuss some skills that will help us carry out our educational tasks in a healthier and more effective way, by which everyone, educator and educated, will emerge humanly and spiritually more solid, more serene, confident, joyful, and self-assured, people who can face life's ups and downs successfully.

a) Mature Personality and Life of Virtue

"Apostolic soul: first of all, yourself," St. Josemaría recommends.[7] What we have set out in this book has to be lived first of all by the formator, who needs to have a solid piety if he is to transmit a living faith and not merely abstract concepts. He must also have self-confidence, self-esteem, self-critical capacity, a consistent life, emotional stability, mastery over his moods and impulses, empathy, sensitivity to the psychological needs of others, social skills, listening skills, joy, stable human and supernatural virtues, etc.

It is important that his emotional needs are covered, otherwise he will easily seek inadvertently to compensate for them in the formative relationship, when what is expected of him is to give selflessly without seeking anything in return (although obviously a formator finds many affective gratifications in his task).

It is definitely not a matter of being perfect, and later we will look at ways to compensate for one's limitations. It is simply a matter of reflecting on one's own person with regard to what is being taught, not because it is lived perfectly well in the formator, but because one tries to live it. In the words of St. Paul VI, "modern man listens more willingly to witnesses than to teachers, and if he does listen to teachers, it is because they are witnesses."[8] The one who tries to acquire the skills we have mentioned makes himself attractive to the learner and will then be able to refer him humbly to his own model: Jesus Christ. It is from dealing with him in prayer and

---

7   St. Josemaría Escrivá, *The Way*, Scepter, New York–London, 1979[9], n. 930.
8   St. Paul VI, Apostolic Exhortation *Evangelii nuntiandi*, n. 41.

in the sacraments that a Christian formator will ultimately draw the strength to be available and smiling always, in spite of the difficulties. This is why Pope Francis said, "Teach prayer by praying, announce the faith by believing; offer witness by living!"[9]

A particularly important attribute for those involved in formation is frustration tolerance. We have already mentioned that burnout is particularly prevalent among educators. People do not always move at the pace we would like, nor do they keep up with our efforts. That is why those who are engaged in these tasks must have a clear objective from the outset: to do good regardless of the results. This requires an inner balance which has been discussed repeatedly in previous chapters.

Together with psychological competence, a Christian formator must have the optimism that comes from trusting in the power of grace and in the ability of the person who resolves to respond to it. That is why he is ambitious in setting goals for improvement and nurtures with prayer what he has sown with words. St. John Paul II affirmed that

> it would be a grave error to conclude [...] that the norm taught by the Church is in itself an "ideal" which must then be adapted, proportioned, graded to the—it is said—concrete possibilities of man: according to a "balance of the various goods in question." But what are the "concrete possibilities of man," and what man are we talking about? The man dominated by concupiscence, or the man redeemed by Christ? For this is what it is all about: the reality of Christ's redemption: Christ has redeemed us! This means that he has given us the chance to bring about the whole truth of our being; he has freed our freedom from the dominion of concupiscence. [...] The commandment of God is certainly proportioned to the possibilities of man: but to the possibilities of the man has been given the Holy Spirit; of the man who, though fallen in sin, can always obtain forgiveness and enjoy the presence of the Spirit."[10]

9   Francis, *Holy Mass and blessing of the Sacred Pallium for the new Metropolitan Archbishops on the solemnity of Saints Peter and Paul, apostles*, June 29, 2015.

10 St. John Paul II, *Address to the participants of a course on responsible procreation*, March 1, 1984.

b) Showing Oneself to Be Vulnerable

We earlier said that we don't need to be perfect. Not only because it is impossible, but also because it is not what the pupils expect. What they need is for their formator to be human, which means that he should be pleasant and empathetic, even if he has faults. Moral authority is not lost by having them, however obvious they may be—indeed, such authority is lost when one tries to hide or deny them.

Therefore, it is necessary to apologize when we have not done the right thing, and not excuse ourselves: "I was late for our appointment," "I was too insistent on what was only advice," "I was wrong to recommend you that you act in that way," etc. I will try to illustrate the point with the apology for being late. It is usually an excuse: "I've had a busy day," "The previous meeting ran long," etc., which may be true. It is probably not meant, but the implicit message—whether the person concerned interprets it that way or not—could be: "I had more important things than you on my plate," or "I have so many things to do and you are taking up my time." Conversely, a sentence such as "I'm sorry, I misjudged the time," or "I'm sorry, I stayed too long at the last meeting" (not "it took too long"), puts the responsibility on oneself (internal locus of control, even when we act in the wrong way) and facilitates the other person's response: "Don't worry, it's OK."

In other words, showing oneself to be vulnerable is another way of being a witness. The directees will not see their formator as a superior being or an unattainable model, but precisely as they are and want to be: someone who has limitations and tries to improve himself day by day.

Accepting one's own limitations and acknowledging them to others will allow formators to do something that is more important and more difficult: to show self-forgiveness. This will prevent many frustrations and discouragements.

c) The Formation of the Formator

Another way to make up for one's limitations is to take care of one's own formation. St. John of the Cross was a great master in the formation of formators, and in one of his works he states that the three conditions for directing souls well are knowledge, prudence and experience.[11]

11 Cf. St. John of the Cross, *The Living Flame of Love*, III, 30.

A good *knowledge* of what to transmit is necessary: scientific, spiritual, and theological contents, among others. But it is also necessary to present them in a manner appropriate to each type of audience and according to the internal dynamics of the recipients. This book is an attempt to shed light on this last point. I think that in Catholic circles the content to be conveyed is often vastly superior to the way it is conveyed, which ultimately makes formation less effective. Ongoing formation takes time and is a sign that the formator has a professional approach.

Throughout the book we have spoken implicitly about *prudence*, which we will return to in the remaining sections. I will mention just one aspect of this virtue. Sometimes it is necessary to question one's own competence and ask for advice. In a way, this gesture is related to knowledge: knowing enough to recognize that one's own knowledge is not enough and that it is better to turn to someone else who is better formed. As a comedian once said, "the important thing is not to know, but to have the phone number of someone who knows." Particularly when one first starts giving formation it is very useful to have a reference who can be consulted for more complex cases, obviously with professional discretion and without giving details about the identity of the person concerned.

We come to the third element, which for the great mystic and doctor of the Church is the most important: *experience*. It is not an absolute prerequisite, otherwise no one would be able to begin giving formation. It is a matter of going about it progressively, starting with people who do not have great difficulties or complex problems. Those who have more sensitive problems can be referred to a person with more experience. Sometimes this is not easy or possible, or the person concerned insists that we give them our advice. I do not think that accepting such request is necessarily a problem as long as we tell the person that we have little experience in the matter but that we will do our best to look after the individual in a competent manner. In these cases, one should be cautious. Because of their lack of experience, young formators will probably not be able to give more comprehensive advice or have ready solutions for a wide variety of problems.

Inexperience can be made up for by the prerequisites we have seen so far: a stable life of piety, the commitment to practicing the virtues, a solid intellectual preparation and the advice of more experienced people. In this way youth does not become an impediment to being a good formator, as we read in the Bible: "I understand more than the aged, for I keep your precepts" (Ps 119:100).

d) Concern for the Whole Person

The point of going to a formator is to gain specific skills: improving one's character, raising one's academic or professional performance, gaining social skills, growing in the spiritual life, etc. It is something of a "professional relationship," where a person turns to another requesting a particular service. In some cases, it may be a paid job (many forms of coaching, mentoring and tutoring, family counselling and teacher-student relationships), while in many others the service is free of charge by its very nature (e.g., spiritual direction).

A good formator will focus on the questions relevant to his competency. But he will not limit himself to giving cold advice from a technical point of view. On the contrary, he will take the person in all his fullness into account. That means that he will not seek to make a better student, professional, husband, etc., but a better person, which in a way encompasses all of the above. In this way he will avoid shaping deformed beings who, for example, have a brilliant career but compromised family lives.

The best way to achieve this is to be concerned with the person, and not just as one's relative, student, religious brother, spiritual directee, etc., but in his or her totality. This will help us set comprehensive goals without going beyond one's own competence or beyond the content for which the formative relationship has been established.

This will keep us from slipping into "behavioral training," an approach based on things to do or avoid but neglecting the real desires and difficulties of the person concerned. Often people need to talk more about what they feel than what they do, although they may not even realize it. As a case in point, I remember once giving spiritual direction to a young man who seemed a little on the formalistic side. I decided to start the conversation with a very open question: "Are you well, happy...?" He was a bit taken aback and answered evasively: "I don't know but maybe you do, that's why I tell you what I'm up to." It was a wonderful opportunity to help him to get to know himself, to delve into his inner dispositions, state of mind, motivations, etc. without limiting the conversations to the practices of piety he had carried out and the details of service he had done for others. In this way, many issues emerged that were connected to his spiritual life or things that simply helped (or hindered) him from living it out serenely and joyfully.

Obviously, this must be done in an affectionate way, so that *people feel loved and understood.* One way of doing this is to identify their concerns and take an interest in them: an anniversary, a health problem, the illness of a relative, pressure at work, financial difficulties, etc., even when we may be tempted to consider them insignificant or disproportionate ("My cat has fallen ill"). Objectively a given concern may be over the top, but subjectively it burdens the individual and we should show sympathy.

For this reason, it is a good idea to practice *empathic listening*, paying attention to what the directee says, what he wants to say and how he says it.[12] There are many telling signs and gestures that help us get to know him more than many words could: moments of silence, blank stares, looking down or to the clock, blushes when raising particular topics, yawns, arms tightly crossed in a closed attitude, relaxed attitude with eyes that look out with expectation and interest, etc.

The formator himself can also convey these unspoken messages and so he must be careful not to give his listener a false idea (or a real idea that would have been better to hide). The best thing to do in tricky cases is just to talk: simply say that we are tired, that we are in a hurry, etc. Being interested does not mean listening to everything someone wants to say without any time limits. It may be advisable, perhaps after one or two introductory conversations, to define the duration of the meetings, the topics to be discussed, etc. Sometimes it will be necessary to redirect the conversation in a gentle way: "I think we are getting off topic," "We are focusing on this issue but I think we should also deal with others," "We are running out of time and we haven't talked about this other topic yet," etc. Empathic listening is crowned with a final question that, in one way or another, should not be lacking in any conversation: "Do you have anything else to say?"

An honest attitude of affection and a professional approach are a great way to help others be open and sincere. It is often said that "trust is not

12 Cf. C.J. van-der Hofstadt Román, *El libro de las habilidades de la comunicación*, Diaz de Santos, Madrid 2005²; S.R. Covey, *The 7 Habits of Highly Effective People*, Simon & Schuster, New York (NY) 1989, pp. 235–260.

imposed, it is inspired," it is earned by the testimony of one's own way of life and by the interest and attention with which one listens to what the other person wants to say.

This opens the door to the gentle demands that are part and parcel of any formative relationship. Sometimes it is necessary to "press on" and set higher goals or point out behaviors and attitudes that are not compatible with the lifestyle that the directee claims he wants to follow. When a solid relationship has been established, when the directee feels understood and loved, then he is in a position to accept reprimands that, perhaps at first, he did not understand or was reluctant toward.

But there may be occasions where there is a discrepancy between what the directee thinks is best and what he is willing to accept, which brings us to the next section.

e) Respect for the Individual and Their Timing

People have their own value systems, hierarchies, and priorities, which may not entirely match those of the formator. It is necessary to draw a distinction between the core and the periphery. For example, in a teacher-student relationship, the aim is to improve academic performance, and in spiritual direction to progress in the Christian life. If in the first case the student did not want to study, or in the second case the individual rejected some basic points of doctrine or morality, it would be a matter of considering whether it is worthwhile to focus on other aspects or whether it is better to end the formative relationship.

However, there can be legitimate disagreement on many secondary issues, for example in relation to the time that should be devoted to various activities, the pace that the person concerned feels that he is able to follow, the relationships that help or hinder his progress, etc. How do we reconcile high goals with the actual dispositions of the directee? How do we discern between a task that is truly impossible—even if it is for subjective reasons—and excuses motivated by comfort-seeking or faint-heartedness? There are no straightforward answers, so I put forward some ideas that may open up new questions.

The task of formation requires a measure of mistrust in one's own judgment. Everyone has a richness and complexity that is impossible to grasp fully, and it would be naïve for the formator to assume that he has understood his directee entirely. It would be even more pretentious for the formator to believe that he knows the specific will of God for that person. We must not forget that the true formator is the Holy Spirit and the main character is the person concerned: it is he who must want to improve, and it is up to him to do so in an agile, magnanimous, and ambitious way. The task of the formator is to make him aware of his possibilities and obligations, to form his conscience, to help him reach a more sincere examination of his actions and his motives, to make him see his talents, to suggest how to develop them, and to open up horizons for improvement. St. Josemaría summed up these objectives with the concise expression, "to help the soul [the person's inner self] to want to accomplish God's will."[13]

It is true that sometimes the individual receiving formation could move faster, but all the resistances that are encountered are precisely part of what needs to be educated. It is not simply a matter of pointing out the path to follow, but also of removing internal obstacles, explaining the reasons in a meaningful and encouraging way, stimulating and strengthening their will, proposing alternative strategies, etc. The shortest way between two points is not always a straight line, and before tackling a goal it may be necessary to resolve other, more basic aspects of their life that are the real obstacle to progress.

It is wise to proceed slowly with those who are just starting out—regardless of one's age— and lead people gradually as if they were going up an inclined plane. If all the effects of the kind of life they want to take on are presented to them all at once, they may end up becoming discouraged when they compare the demand with their current strength, seeing those effects as a beautiful but unattainable ideal. This is why Pope Francis recalled that

> St. John Paul II proposed the so-called "law of gradualness" in the knowledge that the human being "knows, loves and accomplishes moral good by different stages of growth" (*Familiaris consortio*, n. 34). This is not a "gradualness of law" but rather a gradualness in the prudential exercise of free acts on the part of subjects who are not in a position to understand, appreciate, or

13 St. Josemaría Escrivá, *Letter, 8 August 1956*, n. 38.

fully carry out the objective demands of the law. For the law is itself a gift of God which points out the way, a gift for everyone without exception; it can be followed with the help of grace, even though each human being "advances gradually with the progressive integration of the gifts of God and the demands of God's definitive and absolute love in his or her entire personal and social life." (*Familiaris consortio*, n. 9)[14]

Finally, sincere affection for the learner will lead him to understand that he knows himself best, and that includes his talents and strengths. It is up to him to make decisions to improve his life freely. Only in this way will his actions result in virtues and make him better in the very core of his being.

f) Overcoming One's Own Demons

I remember speaking with a young man who told me how worried he was about his sister. She was deeply involved in the crisis of adolescence. There were many small problems, but fortunately none of them was serious. We took the time to talk about his family. His parents had a rather weak character, and for many years this individual had assumed the role of "head of the family" for his siblings, and sometimes also for his parents. Naturally, he had far too much responsibility. But he also had what we have called an obsessive-perfectionist personality, and the way he tried to manage his family's difficulties was by control. His sister's rebelliousness had plunged this fellow into a deep crisis. She was a bit "out of control." We looked further and deeper, and came to his core fear: that his sister would make the wrong decisions and that there would be irreversible consequences. His way of preventing this was to make all of the teenager's decisions subject to his approval, something she had peacefully lived by until a few months prior to the conversation. Now she refused.

It is useful to pray for the people you are trying to help, and sometimes you even obtain enlightenment that you recognize is not your own. It occurred to me to ask him if he had considered God's attitude toward us. He

14 Francis, Post-Synodal Apostolic Exhortation *Amoris laetitia*, March 19, 2016, n. 295.

watches over us providentially, but he created us free, and took the risk that we might do wrong and put our eternal salvation in danger. This fellow's answer surprised me: "Yes, I have thought about it many times and I have come to the conclusion that I would not have created man in this way. I would be very sorry if he were condemned." The conclusion we drew was that either he was mistaken in the way he dealt with his sister, or God had made a mistake in creating us free.

We all have our fears and insecurities, often stemming from a sincere affection for the people entrusted to our care. But sometimes this fear interferes with the help we want to give and causes us, with the best of intentions, to fall into an unhealthy educational style. That is why it is necessary for the formator to know himself well. Some of those "demons" that can interfere with the work of training will be outlined below.

The above case can be summarized as insecurity-control. Any task of formation is a big responsibility resting on the shoulders of the formator. He may be overwhelmed by the trust that superiors have placed in him or because of the possibility that the learner may not reach as high as he could or may even fail. One way to manage this fear is to anticipate and avoid all possible pitfalls even when the learner does not recognize them as such, or to urge him to consult all his plans with the formator so he can prevent those that fall outside a tight and safe routine.

These attitudes stifle the directee, prevent him from acting autonomously and bettering his judgment, and hinder the development of virtues and threaten to infect him with the formator's obsessive-perfectionist traits, so that in time he will become in turn another insecure and controlling formator.

It is not just a matter of faith. It is a psychological condition that hinders genuine formation work. Those who direct apostolates and institutions will have to be on their guard against such potential formators, because, even with the best of intentions, they can harm those who seek their help.

It is worth remembering that trial and error is one of the most effective ways for human beings to learn. Think of the way we learned to ride a bicycle. First, we started with training wheels, then with our father gripping the handle until he finally risked letting go, perhaps holding his breath as we zigzagged along. How many leg bruises are a token of affection from parents who knew how to trust their children despite their poor ability and went through the heartache of seeing them fall. As Guardini says, "Everyone has to do his own stupid things himself in order to learn not to do them anymore."[15] This is not to deny that it is very good to learn from the mistakes of others.

Pope Francis affirms that whoever is entrusted with the task of counseling others must be

> a witness: a very close witness, who does not speak but listens and then gives guidance. He does not solve [the problem] but he tells you: look at this, look at this, look at this, look at this, look at this … this does not seem a good inspiration for this reason, this one does …. But you go ahead and decide![16]

Another difficulty arises from the *fear of upsetting* when we correct or demand, which is different from respecting the times and rhythms of the person. A good formator must also go through a bit of a hard time when he makes the directee face up to his responsibilities. Otherwise, he would be betraying his own role and the trust that the person concerned placed in his hands by seeking him out.

The task of formation is a selfless giving of oneself. It has many rewards, but the good of the other must always be above the reward that he can give us in the form of affection, recognition, etc. It would be a disorder to try to solve one's own affective needs in the relationship of formation. I am not referring to formators who have great deficiencies but to normal people who feel loved by their directees or who see their desire for *generativity* fulfilled in them. This is all legitimate and in fact occurs naturally in any formational work, which makes it very satisfying. But if the good of the pupil requires correction—which must always be carried out sensitively and with charity—it would not be mature for the formator to sacrifice the good of the pupil for the sake of maintaining a peaceful and serene relationship. It would be to seek oneself above the good of the other, which would plant a seed of insincerity at the very core of the formative relationship.

15 R. Guardini, *Die Lebensalter. Ihre ethische und pädagogische Bedeutung*, Matthias-Grünewald, Mainz 1986, p. 37.
16 Francis, *Address to Students of the Pontifical Colleges and Ecclesiastical Boarding Schools in Rome*, March 16, 2018.

The formator must also be wary of attempts at encroachment on the part of the directee, in the event that he tries to find in the relationship what he should be looking for elsewhere: family, friends, etc. The formative relationship has its own objectives, it must take place in a climate of care and trust, but its aim is not simply that someone with whom one feels good listens and offers encouragement, but that offers help towards improvement. In this context, if we apply what we discussed in the chapter on relationships in adulthood, it is more akin to a parent-child relationship than to a friendship between equals. Just as the father has to act as a father, not as a friend, so too the formator must play his role, even if outside of the formative conversations there are ties of family, vocation or even friendship. Usually this distinction is reached intuitively, but sometimes—especially with young people or with immature or sick personalities—it may need to be made explicit.

Finally, the formator must know how to distance himself from the problems of others. He is not called to be an Atlas carrying the weight of the world on his shoulders. When we have real affection for the people we are helping, it is hard when they do not appear to be advancing at the pace they should or even are moving away from what is objectively best for them. But we cannot fall into pessimism, frustration, or the loss of our own inner peace. There is something wrong with the professor who comes home depressed after an unsatisfactory series of exams or the priest who after an evening in the confessional feels dejected by the weakness of human nature.

True affection for those who depend on us will lead us to respect their freedom by always being ready to give a hand, perhaps like fishermen who know how to release the reel so that the fish trying to escape does not end up breaking the line. And above all it will lead us to pray more insistently for them and to exercise our faith in the goodness of God and in the power of prayer, which he uses to move hearts.

4. It Is Worth It

It is worth it to be involved in tasks of formation, despite the hard work. It requires not only time, but more importantly the mind and heart. But when the years go by, we will feel the legitimate inner satisfaction of a father who sees that his children have gone far, even further than he has. "One of the greatest joys that any educator can have is to see a student turn into a strong, well-integrated person, a leader, someone prepared to give."[17] Then he feels his longing for generativity fulfilled, leading him to proclaim his thanksgiving with St. Paul: "For this reason I bow my knees before the Father, from whom every family in heaven and on earth takes its name" (Eph 3:14–15).

Some may not have gone as far as we would have liked, or perhaps they took a different path or reached a different place where they are happy. In any case, they followed their respective paths and reached their goals. "I planted, Apollos watered, but God gave the growth. [...] For we are God's servants, working together; you are God's field, God's building" (1 Cor 3:6–9).

17   Idem, Post-Synodal Apostolic Exhortation *Christus vivit*, March 25, 2019, n. 221.

BIBLIOGRAPHY

1. General Bibliography

Javier CABANYES, Miguel Ángel MONGE (coord.), *La salud mental y sus cuidados*, EUNSA, Pamplona 2017[4].

Stephen R. COVEY, *The 7 habits of Highly Effective People*, Simon & Schuster, New York (NY) 1989.

Francisco INSA, Dale PARKER (eds.), *Loving and Teaching Others to Love. The Formation of Affectivity in Priestly Life*, Independently Published, 2021.

Miguel Ángel MONGE SÁNCHEZ (coord.), *Medicina pastoral. Cuestiones de biología, antropología, medicina, sexología, psicología y psiquiatría*, EUNSA, Pamplona 2010[5].

Jordan PETERSON, *12 Rules for Life. An Antidote to Chaos*, Vintage Canada, Toronto 2020.

Ángel RODRÍGUEZ LUÑO, *Chosen in Christ to Be Saints: Fundamental Moral Theology*, Createspace Independent Pub, 2014.

Juan Bautista TORELLÓ, *Psicología y vida espiritual*, Rialp, Madrid 2008.

Wenceslao VIAL, *Madurez psicológica y espiritual*, Palabra, Madrid 2019[4].

— (ed.), *Ser quien eres. Cómo construir una personalidad feliz con el consejo de médicos, filósofos, sacerdotes y educadores*, Rialp, Madrid 2017.

Ricardo YEPES STORK, Javier ARANGUREN ECHEVARRÍA, *Fundamentos de Antropología. Un ideal de la excelencia humana*, EUNSA, Pamplona 1999[4].

2. Personality and Affectivity

Giuseppe ABBÀ, *Felicità, vita buona e virtù. Saggio di filosofia morale*, Libreria Ateneo Salesiano, Roma 1995.

Alfonso AGUILÓ, *Educar el carácter. Principios clave de la formación de la personalidad*, Palabra, Madrid 2019[12].

Gordon W. ALLPORT, *Pattern and Growth in Personality*, Holt, Rinehart and Winston, New York (NY) 1961.

ARISTOTLE, *Nichomachean Ethics*

Alexandre HAVARD, *From Temperament to Character. On Becoming A Virtuous Leader*, Scepter, New York 2018.From Temperament to Character: On Becoming A Virtuous Leader

Javier DE LAS HERAS, *Conoce tu personalidad. Por qué eres como eres*, La Esfera de los Libros, Madrid 2010.

Michel ESPARZA, *Amor y autoestima*, Rialp, Madrid 2009[7].

Leslie GREENBERG, *Emociones: una guía interna. Cuáles sigo y cuáles no*, Desclée de Brouwer, Bilbao 2000.

Romano GUARDINI, *Briefe über Selbsbildung*, Mathias-Grünewald, Mainz 1998.

Jacques PHILIPPE, *Interior Freedom*, Scepter, New York (NY) 2007.

Josef PIEPER, *Faith, Hope, Love*, Ignatius Press, San Francisco (CA) 1997.

—, *The four cardinal virtues*, University of Notre Dame Press, Notre Dame (IN) 1966.

Fernando SARRÁIS, *Personalidad*, EUNSA, Pamplona 2012.

—, *Madurez psicológica y felicidad*, EUNSA, Pamplona 2013.

—, *Temperamento, carácter y personalidad*, Teconté, Madrid 2016[2].

—, *Entender la afectividad*, Teconté, Madrid 2017.

Dietrich VON HILDEBRAND, *The Heart: An Analysis of Human and Divine Affectivity*, St. Augustine Press, South Bend (IN) 2012.

3. Inner Growth Throughout the Life Cycle

John BOWLBY, *A Secure Base. Parent-Child Attachment and Healthy Human Development*, Basic Books, New York (NY) 1988.

Blanca CASTILLA DE COTÁZAR, *Persona femenina, persona masculina*, Rialp Madrid 1996.

Mariolina CERIOTTI MIGLIARESE, *La coppia imperfetta. E se anche i difetti fossero un ingrediente dell'amore?* Ares, Milano 2012.

—, *Erotica & materna. Viaggio nell'universo femminile*, Ares, Milano 2015.

—, *La famiglia imperfetta. Come trasformare ansie & problemi in sfide appassionanti*, Milano, Ares 2016.

—, *Maschi. Forza, eros, tenerezza*, Ares, Milano 2017.

Alberto DELGADO CARDONA, *Aprender a envejecer*, Corporación CED, Medellín 2006.

Erik ERIKSON, *The Life Cycle Completed*, W.W. Norton, New York–London 1998.

Shaunti FELDHAHN, *For Women Only. What you Need to Know About the Inner Lives of Men*, Multnomah, Sisters (OR) 2013.

Shaunti FELDHAHN, Jeff FELDHAHN, *For Men Only. A Straightforward Guide to the Inner Lives of Women*, Multnomah, Sisters (OR) 2013.

FRANCIS, Post-Synodal Apostolic Exhortation *Amoris laetitia*, 19 March 2016.

—, Post-Synodal Apostolic Exhortation *Christus vivit*, 25 March 2019.

John GRAY, *Men Are from Mars, Women Are from Venus. A Practical Guide for Improving Communication and Getting What You Want in Your Relationships*, HarperCollins, New York (NY) 1993.

Romano GUARDINI, *Die Lebensalter. Ihre ethische und pädagogische Bedeutung*, Matthias-Grünewald, Mainz 1986.

Bärbel INHELDER, Jean PIAGET, *De la logique de l'enfant à la logique de l'adolescent. Essai sur la construction des structures opératoires formelles*, Presses Universitaires de France, Paris 1955.

Francisco Javier INSA GÓMEZ (coord.), *Cómo acompañar en el camino matrimonial. La pastoral familiar a la luz de* Amoris laetitia, Rialp, Madrid 2020.

Elisabeth KÜBLER-ROSS, *On Death and Dying. What the Dying Have to Teach Doctors, Nurses, Clergy and their Own Families*, Routledge, Abingdon (UK) 2009.

Clive Staples LEWIS, *The Four Loves*, G. Bles, London 1960.

Natalia LÓPEZ MORATALLA, *Cerebro de mujer y cerebro de varón*, Rialp, Madrid 2007.

Jean PIAGET, *Le jugement moral chez l'enfant*, Presses Universitaires de France, Paris 1932.

Lluís SEGARRA, *Cuidar y ser cuidado: aprender a envejecer*, EUNSA, Pamplona 2015.

4. The Christian Virtue of Chastity

Juan Luis CABALLERO (coord..), *El celibato cristiano. Una vida plena y fecunda*, Palabra, Madrid 2019.

Carlos CHICLANA ACTIS, *Atrapados en el sexo. Cómo liberarte del amargo placer de la hipersexualidad*, Almuzara, Córdoba 2013.

St. Josemaría ESCRIVÁ, *Friends of God*, Scepter, New York (NY) 2002², nn. 175-189 (homily *Because They Shall See God*).

—, *The Way*, Scepter, New York–London, 1979⁹, nn. 118-171 (chapters *Holy Purity* and *Heart*).

Miguel Ángel FUENTES, *La castidad. ¿Posible?*, Ediciones Verbo Encarnado, San Rafael (Mendoza, Argentina) 2006.

—, *La trampa rota*, Ediciones Verbo Encarnado, San Rafael (Mendoza, Argentina) 2008.

Francisco INSA, Dale PARKER, *Why Purity? Navigating the Confusing Culture Messages*, Scepter, New York 2020.

J. DE IRALA ESTÉVEZ, *Te quiero, por eso no quiero. El valor de la espera*, Independently published, 2020.

St. JOHN PAUL II, *Love and Responsibility*, Ignatius Press, San Francisco (CA) 1993.

—, *Man and Woman He created Them. A Theology of the Body*, Pauline Books and Media, Boston (MA) 2006.

André LEONARD, *Jésus et ton corps. La morale sexuelle expliquée aux jeunes*, Mame, Paris 1999².

Antonio PÉREZ VILLAHOZ, *¡Estás hecho para amar! Cómo vivir la pureza y no morir en el intento*, Cobel, Alicante 2014.

Fernando SARRÁIS, *Afectividad y sexualidad*, EUNSA, Pamplona 2015.

Jesús María SILVA, *Sexo: cuándo y por qué*, Palabra, Madrid 2018.

James R. STONER, Donna M. HUGHES (eds.), *The social costs of pornography. A collection of papers*, Witherspoon Institute, Princeton (NJ) 2010.

Christopher WEST, *Theology of the body for beginners*, Recording for the Blind & Dyslexic, Princeton (NJ) 2008.

Gary WILSON, *Your Brain on Porn. Internet Pornography and the Emerging Science of Addiction*, Commonwealth Publishing, United Kingdom 2017.

5. When Affectivity is Disturbed

Manuel ÁLVAREZ ROMERO, Domingo GARCÍA-VILLAMISAR, *El síndrome del perfeccionista. El anancástico*, Almuzara, Córdoba 2017[4].

AMERICAN PSYCHIATRIC ASSOCIATION, *Diagnostic and Statistical Manual of Mental Disorders (DSM-5)*, American Psychiatric Association, Arlington (VA) 2013.

Martin M. ANTONY, Richard P. SWINSON, *When perfect isn't good enough. Strategies for coping with perfectionism*, New Harbinger Publications, Oakland (CA) 2009.

Aaron KHERIATY, John CIHAK, *The Catholic Guide to Depression: How the Saints, the Sacraments, and Psychiatry Can Help You Break Its Grip and Find Happiness Again*, Sophia Institute Press, Manchester (NH) 2012.

Allan E. MALLINGER, Jeannette DE WYZE, *Too Perfect: When Being in Control Gets Out of Control*, The Random House Publishing Group, New York (NY) 2011.

Javier SCHLATTER NAVARRO, *Ser felices sin ser perfectos*, EUNSA, Pamplona 2016.

Fernando SARRÁIS, *Aprendiendo a vivir: el descanso*, EUNSA, Pamplona 2011.

—, *El miedo*, EUNSA, Pamplona 2014.

6. A Healthy Formative Style

Julio DIÉGUEZ, *He Knows Not How: Growing in Freedom*, Independently published 2020.

Fulgencio ESPÁ, *Cuenta conmigo. El acompañamiento espiritual*, Palabra, Madrid 2017.

Francisco FERNANDEZ-CARVAJAL, *Through Wind and Waves: On Being a Spiritual Guide*, Scepter, New York (NY) 2012.

Antonio PÉREZ VILLAHOZ, *Formar bien es posible. 10 claves en la formación de un adolescente*, Corbel, Murcia 2014².